Reading a Daniel Bu...
Discovering God When...

This book is incredibly refreshing and profound—and so practical. Here, you will find real-life "hard places" and the good news that Jesus shows. It's the kind of book one reads often to be reminded that one doesn't need any defense but Jesus because, in his love, grace, and acceptance, there is nothing to defend. In his presence (and thus the presence of others) one is free to laugh and dance with great joy and freedom. This is a book that could change your life.

—STEVE BROWN, radio broadcaster and founder,
Key Life Network; professor emeritus of preaching and
pastoral ministry, Reformed Theological Seminary;
author of *Hidden Agendas* and *Three Free Sins*

Are we willing to let ourselves need God? In *Undefended* we are let in behind the scenes of one man's wrestling with this question and invited to ask it ourselves. As we do we may just find it's what we've wanted all along.

—MANDY SMITH, author of *The Vulnerable Pastor*

Undefended: Discovering God When Your Guard Is Down is not a book that you will want to read cover to cover in one sitting. Instead, this is a book that you will want to walk through chapter by chapter, and let God speak to you in the depths of your heart, mind, and soul. By weaving together scriptural truths with relevant stories and illustrations that open us to see how we are not *Undefended*, Daniel Bush has provided us a guide to facilitate a release from the barriers in our lives that keep us from experiencing the full depth and breadth of God's grace.

—JAMES F. KIRKLEY, associate professor,
religion and ethics, Shaw University

Forged in the fires of dryness, discouragement, and pain, Daniel Bush writes from experience: his defenses burned down, his soul exposed to his own weakness and vulnerability. He writes broken by an acute awareness of unfulfilled needs and the struggle to surrender to his heavenly Father. Although intellectual and astute, *Undefended* is no academic perusal. It's a story of spiritual awakening, the journey from personal competency and self-determination to broken dependency we all must make.

If you're looking for a book of principles for spiritual maturity or steps to Christian joy, look elsewhere. *Undefended* stubbornly refuses to reduce the Christian life to a set of disciplines or propagate the notion that faith means denying the pains of this life and donning a veneer of niceness and joy. Again and again we're shown that Jesus came to save the sick, broken, and needy, that he meets us in our pain, our fear, our need, our loneliness— and even in our doubt.

Christian growth isn't a byproduct of discipline or striving, but surrender to the inevitable reality of our own sinfulness and dependence upon the love and grace of the Father. For those wounded and wearied by life, here is hope that God is present in our life and may be discovered even now if we will only seek Him. An opportunity for a deeper acquaintance with His love is near.

—DR. JEFFREY PIPE, licensed psychologist,
Tapestry Associates, Marietta, Georgia

Undefended strikes truth after beautiful truth at the bull's-eye of what it means to be human. In an age when vulnerability has arguably become glib, author Daniel Bush provides a refreshing reminder that when we guard our hearts in the love of Christ first, we are then freed to let down our guard to love others more fully. Informed yet accessible, with humor and humility, Bush offers poignant wisdom relevant to any life season, but especially to those times in which we are laid most bare. To me, this book will always be a timely, needed, and reorienting read. In other words, Bush indeed gives a blood transfusion to the anemic advice: "Just trust in God."

—DR. CAROLYN WEBER, professor, speaker,
and author of *Surprised by Oxford*
and *Holy Is the Day*

Weary of defending a false self that proves over and over again to be indefensible? Ready to entertain the notion that the real you is on offer in the person of the only "True Self" ever to have lived, who lives even now to live in you, freeing you more and more from "pretense, people-pleasing, playacting, pomposity, self-protection, and phony, pharisaical righteousness"? If so, you are ready for this beguiling read from Daniel Bush.

—The Very Rev'd. Dr. Reggie M. Kidd, dean,
Cathedral Church of Saint Luke, Orlando, Florida,
and professor of New Testament emeritus,
Reformed Theological Seminary Orlando

undefended

discovering God
when your
guard is down

Renee Shea
8/2 3

undefended

discovering God
when your
guard is down

DANIEL BUSH

KIRKDALE PRESS

Print ISBN 9781577997467
Digital ISBN 9781577997474

Kirkdale Editorial: Allisyn Ma, Lynnea Smoyer, Abigail Stocker,
    Danielle Thevenaz
Cover Design: Brittany Schrock
Back Cover Design: Liz Donovan
Typesetting: ProjectLuz.com

To my mother,
Marlene Patricia Strang
—a caring & tireless giver

contents

foreword by Gerrit Dawson   xiii

prologue: let them see you   xxi

1: crossing all points   1

2: leaving eden   21

3: taming the mississippi   45

4: shadow boxing   69

5: drowning the victim   91

6: peering beyond the depths   113

7: surrendering at appomattox   135

8: bedazzling embrace   159

9: dancing in the desert   183

10: digging for potatoes   205

11: living at tether's end   227

epilogue: simply undefended   249

afterword by Michael Card   255

acknowledgments   259

notes   261

scripture index   277

foreword

DANIEL BUSH HAS STORIES FOR US. LOTS OF STORIES. SOME from his own life, some from the people he encounters and others from the great authors he reads. They are all stories which resonate authentically with the way our own lives are unfolding. Daniel makes us aware of how God is up to something significant precisely in the life-narratives where he seems to have gone quiet. Reading the wisdom of the stories in *Undefended* led me to rethink the meaning in the stories running through my daily life. He made me want to open up to what God has been saying all along.

For instance: My wife and I had a bit of a "discussion." A little while later, we took the dogs for a walk. For the first few minutes we just chatted about anything and nothing. Then she brought up what was between us. "You know, I don't really think it was fair when you said... ." Before she finished, I had six counterarguments at the ready. My verbal dukes yearned to be put up in fighting mode. I had been silently planning my defense. This spat could escalate to war. Of course I wouldn't win, but I could make the cost of engagement very pricey.

But I also had been reading some early chapters of the book you hold in your hands. In a grace-filled moment, it occurred to me: Actually, she *is* right. What if I just admit it and apologize? So I let my guard down. I dropped my verbal fists to my side and stuck out my metaphorical chin for her to smack if she wished. "I'm sorry. I wasn't fair. I wish I hadn't been that way." In that moment, she could have levelled me with more truth about myself. After all, no one knows me better. But she didn't want to condemn me, just to set things right. When I declined to defend my actions, she dropped her accusation. Within a minute we were laughing and enjoying a day I had nearly ruined. I let in the truth, and surprise! Love, not judgment, returned to me.

Don't you love the title of this book? *Undefended.* The word beckons to us with an intriguing paradox, "What if self-protection is actually the worst strategy for a flourishing life, both with God and other people? What if fortification against admitting uncomfortable truth is the more certain way to be defeated by those truths? What if we actually get embraced by what we most long for when we let down our spiritual guard?" Sounds like risky business. But then the old ways of stonewalling, hiding, and denying haven't worked for quite some time. This strategy of non-defense not only frightens, it beckons with possibility.

Recently I spoke with a father concerned about his relationship with his grown daughter. A divide seemed to growing between them. She accused him of meddling in her family's life. She claimed he created tension for her when he was around. These charges pierced him. He loves her. She's been through some hard years. His deep desire is to help, to undergird her family and shine favor on her life. But her accusatory words made him want to put up his defenses and explain himself. He didn't want to give credence to her claims because he couldn't bear being inadequate in his love. He had details of his every word and action to prove that he was indeed the kind of supportive father he meant to be. He wanted so badly to punch back with these facts.

I counseled against it. Proving you're right doesn't necessarily mean you can bring someone near to you. In fact, counterattacking could just widen the rift. I thought of the pages I'd read in *Undefended* and asked him what could happen if he laid himself wide open to her. I asked him to imagine saying, "It breaks my heart to think I have hurt you. I grieve when we don't feel connected. I'm sorry for any mistakes I've made. My heart's desire is to bless you and care for you as a dad who loves his daughter."

This strategy frightened him. His daughter could crush him with his own words. He replied, "If she rejected me after I said that, I don't think I could carry on." I felt scared too. I didn't want to lead him into driving a deeper wedge between them. I steeled myself to trust the truth. "She won't reject you. I can't imagine this daughter turning against her father's open heart." She didn't. They reconciled. This undefended path of Jesus actually leads to more life and more love.

I remember a year of crisis in my family relationships. I wondered often if everything I thought I knew about my life as a husband and a father was wrong. The world spun around with a sense of unreality as the safe ground of my assumptions dropped out beneath me. I no longer knew anything with certainty. In those days, I stumbled upon Psalm 25. For weeks, I prayed verse 5 every desperate morning, "Lead me in your truth and teach me, for you are the God of my salvation; for you I wait all the day long." No more pride. No more certainty. Just my raw, confused heart crying out for God to show a way when all expected roads had closed. I opened all the borders between my Father in heaven and my prideful independence. He came to me then. Every day. Steadily guiding each and all of us with his swift, sure, invisible hand. When I was helpless, he did not destroy me. He helped me. He became, in a deeper way than I had ever known, my salvation. The more I cried my need for the God of grace, the more he supplied.

How can it be that this undefended posture actually works? In our relationships with God and with one another, leaving self-protection strangely leads to healing. Burning up the list of my self-justification leads to a sense of acceptance. Laying down arms leads to peace. What reality undergirds this paradoxical way to abundance? On the threshold of Daniel's wonderful book, let's think about the story that underlies all the stories.

Jesus, as the incarnate Son of God, took the undefended path and became the savior of the world. This way has been opened for us because Jesus walked it first. An old prayer declares, "Most gracious God, we give you thanks for your tender love in sending Jesus Christ to come among us ... and to make the way of the cross to be the way of life." Jesus lived the contradiction that the way up goes by the way down; in losing our lives for God we find them; in spiritually dying we rise to renewed lives of love and joy. He blazed the trail in his days of healing, loving, redeeming ministry, which culminated in the ultimate undefended event of the cross. In that supreme sacrifice we will see why this way of life works now for us as well.

Jesus knew what was coming. Like any other Jew in occupied Israel, he had seen the method of execution the Romans used to control the people. They nailed people up to die on crosses in very public places. It was a shameful, horrifying death that took all the fight and rebellion out of those who witnessed it. Yet, the symbolism of disgracefully hanging on the cross became an emblem of the glorious love Jesus, the Son of God, had for the world he came to save. How did Jesus pull off this great switch, turning shame to glory?

On the cross, Jesus' arms were stretched wide open. The Romans forced his body into a position that Jesus had already willingly offered: the opened-arm welcome of love. Jesus was God himself coming to us with open arms. He stretched out his embrace of sinful, outcast, diseased, broken, compromised, oppressed, and lost humanity. On the cross, they pinned him in the position he had already freely assumed. God himself stretched out his arms to us.

Once nailed and tied to a Roman cross, no one could get off. There was no running away. And there was no leaping down to try to fight for freedom. You were just there, arms stretched out, enduring until you could take no more. Again, the symbolism is so strong. The open-armed Jesus on the cross took the position of love in which he could not go forward or backward. He just endured in love until it killed him. Scripture tells us he could have called legions of angels to save him. He could have run away to save himself. But then we would have been lost. We would have been left in our sin, under sentence of condemnation and death. But he chose to stay on the beams, loving us to the end even as he prayed, "Father, forgive them, for they know not what they do."

Suspended on the wood of the cross, Jesus willingly entered the condition of not being able to fight or flee, to run away or to disappear. He simply remained with arms open in undefended, forgiving love. He would not force himself on us. He would not make us accept him. Instead, he allowed himself to be rejected by us. He took it. Loving us the whole way, he endured the agony of love that will neither demand acceptance from someone nor withdraw into self-protection. He took our rejection. He offered acceptance in return. Until it killed him.

The history of Christian art includes many moving representations of Jesus on the cross, from the mystic to the graphic. I find it particularly moving when the artist has rendered a spiritual reality of the crucifixion that remains unseen to our eyes. Jesus hangs on the wooden cross bar. But hands are underneath the ends of the cross. We look more closely and see that the vertical beam of the cross is planted before the Father seated on his throne. His arms are outstretched, too. The Father holds the cross. His mighty countenance, saddened with sacrifice but yet infinite in power, bends compassionately over his Son's agony. He supports Jesus in his dying. This horror is not falling outside his providential care or sovereign love. The most despicable act of humanity against God is embraced by the Father so that even this may be atoned for as the Son gives his life.

The theological backdrop to *Undefended* is this eternal, utterly giving love of the Father and the Son. Following the way of Jesus, Daniel Bush takes us again and again to the places where we, too, are suspended on the beams of love, unable to move forward or backward. He knows that precisely in these places of pain, we discover the glorious backdrop behind the very cross. We are held in the Father's loving arms. He turns this suffering into redemption.

This is not a quick book. Nor would we want it to be. It's not a simple thought for the day to prop you up continuing in your usual life. It's a journey book, and Daniel intends that in following this undefended path, we will be transformed along the way. So Daniel invites us to go with him into hard places. These are the situations where we get stripped of our defenses. I found that the book routinely unmasked me in my self-protection strategies. You might think that would prove an intolerable read. But Daniel makes us feel that we are not alone. He has been there. And he stays with us, in vulnerability and compassion, while we journey deeper into the truth about the meaning in life's tough spots. Daniel let me as the reader admit my own helplessness and weakness before him, and he, following our Master, does not condemn. He shows us where to find grace.

Daniel also brings along some wonderful and reliable guides in the many great authors he quotes. There is actually a great company of wise witnesses who have discovered the truth in the cross. In the undefended life, we discover the bedrock strength of the God who is love. Enjoy! You won't be the same when you're finished.

Gerrit Dawson
pastor, First Presbyterian Church of Baton Rouge
author of *Jesus Ascended* and *The Blessing Life*

Humanity is not divinity. Humanity is inherently being in need—the creaturely need of continual connection to the Creator.

prologue

let them see you

AN HOUR BEFORE A SPECIAL DINNER ON THE LAST NIGHT of an intense, seven-day seminar at a training center in the mountains near Asheville, North Carolina, we were busy in our rooms spiffing up. I popped my head into the hallway and, to my surprise, saw a few ladies in beautiful summer dresses. Back in my room, my roommate donned a dress shirt and slacks. "Drat! I missed the memo," I thought. I hadn't packed anything remotely appropriate.

A week earlier I had thought my roommate was nuts when he moved in, accompanied by a full rack of ironed clothes and a couple of suitcases on a trolley. This was one time, however, where not being a minimalist paid off. He had slacks to spare and fortuitously offered me a pair. Thankful, I quickly changed out of my blue jeans and we headed off to dinner. I still sported my leather fisherman sandals; it was Asheville, after all.

We stood outside the small banquet room, laughing and taking pictures—would we ever see each other again? Then the doors opened, and inside stood beautifully adorned tables and a window framing a breathtaking view of the Blue Ridge Mountains. Conversation ensued and music filled the air while we dined on food that was to die for.

Yet I still felt a bit self-conscious wearing someone else's pants. In recalling that feeling, I'm led to wonder why we care so much about what everyone wears. Why are we so uneasy about being caught out of place? Why do we struggle to take off our masks and be seen as we are—people in need of the divine Tailor? "The imposter must be called out of hiding and presented to Jesus, or feelings of hopelessness, confusion, shame, and failure will stalk us from dawn to dusk," says Brennan Manning.[1]

After dinner we took a break, mingling a bit before the evening's events continued. I took the chance to chat briefly with the seminar speaker. With a certain solemnity he charged me, "Let them see you." Did he somehow know about my wardrobe problem? Certainly he wasn't suggesting I come to dinner without pants.

For the better part of a year, I struggled to figure out what he meant. I had never shied away from personal anecdotes in my preaching and teaching, but I knew he was driving at something more profound. The friends I spoke to about it since each have had a slightly different take. But one thing became clear: "being seen" requires neither playing hide-and-seek nor putting on an act.

In the summer of 1984, the Gillette Company launched a series of television commercials advertising its Dry Idea antiperspirants, which led to one of the wittiest and most memorable slogans in the English language: "Never let them see you sweat." There's deep truth in that tagline, at least with regard to antiperspirants. I'll even go as far as to apply it to business negotiations, trade deals, and global politics—but apply it to personal relationships, especially your relationship with God, at your peril.

Being seen as you truly are, in all of your mess and undignified glory—the jam-packed fears, feelings, and experiences of far too many emotional and spiritual famines—is at the heart of personal connection. Connecting is about you being present. It's about *you* being present—not a caricature, or a dolled-up version, or an angel masquerading as you, just you. It's about you *being* present—your existence, life, the spiritual actuality of your very self. It's about you being *present*—being in this immediate time and space with your body, mind, and soul, not mentally a million miles away, distracted or preoccupied. It's never fearing being human. Humanity is not divinity. Humanity is inherently *being in need*—the creaturely need of continual connection to the Creator.

So much goes awry in the Christian community and in the lives of Christians when spiritual growth and maturity is equated with perfection. Perfection is the furthest thing from maturity—first of all, because it's an attribute of God alone, and second, since perfection implies the absence of need, a perfect being wouldn't need God. Neediness is an essential attribute of being truly human—and without it, you would be separated from connection with God. Spiritual maturity is, therefore, not perfection, but the unique amalgamation of authenticity and need. It's seeing yourself and God rightly, as well as seeing and living out of that connection in every area, attitude, and action. This is becoming truly human: Finding your true self in Christ, who is Immanuel ("God with us")—divine love in its outward expression.

By contrast, the "false self" (a term that will appear from time to time in the forthcoming pages) is when you exist without conscious mindfulness of and trust in Christ. It's looking at your own mechanisms, accomplishments, abilities, and prowess—what you can produce—or looking at what others can provide and produce for you, as the basis and substance of your existence. You put on a mask and play a part in order to obtain what you think you need from others.

Current literature often discusses the true versus the false self. We are told time and again to "just be your self"—after all, this is no longer the Age of Aquarius, but the Age of Authenticity, is it not?

Authenticity means eliminating the gap between your inner belief and what you reveal to the outside world—in other words, letting your true self be seen. According to one *New York Times* op-ed writer:

> We want to live authentic lives, marry authentic partners, work for an authentic boss, vote for an authentic president. ... But for most people, "be your self" is actually terrible advice.
>
> If I can be authentic for a moment: nobody wants to see your true self. We all have thoughts and feelings that we believe are fundamental to our lives, but that are better left unspoken. A decade ago, the author A. J. Jacobs spent a few weeks trying to be totally authen-

tic. He announced to an editor that he would try to sleep with her if he were single and informed his nanny that he would like to go on a date with her if his wife left him. He informed a friend's five-year-old daughter that the beetle in her hands was not napping but dead. He told his in-laws that their conversation was boring. You can imagine how his experiment worked out.[2]

Utter and complete neglect of self-monitoring is the furthest thing from what I mean by authenticity and becoming your true self, especially since a lot of what gets passed off as one's true self is defensiveness or neediness. For those who are naturally high self-monitors it could even be an exorbitant concern with reputation and how others perceive them, which still entrenches them in garnering existence from what others provide or produce. In this book, the true self is the person you are when your identity and dignity derive exclusively from who Jesus is. Your false self is how you think about and present yourself to the world (or hide from it through debilitating self-monitoring or downright seclusion) when you function apart from the one crucial connection of human existence: the conscious actualization of God in real time.

As I've said, being authentically human, living out of your true self, isn't wholesale subtraction of self-monitoring, but it does lead to a surprising degree of undefended living, trusting God himself to be the only security blanket you'll ever need. Life undefended is life without pretense, people-pleasing, playacting, pomposity, self-protection, and phony, pharisaical righteousness. Think about that for a moment.

Life without such might just leave you in a precarious position—like recklessly attempting backflips on the high wire without a net. Yet being truly human, wholly animated by the Spirit, abiding in the cross of the Son, is what this book will unpack as we move from chapter to chapter.

Would you like to get a glimpse of heaven on earth? Begin living in continual prayer and offering others a glimpse of your true self. "Prayer is not asking. Prayer is putting oneself in the hands of God, at His disposition, and listening to His voice in the depth of our hearts" (Mother Teresa).[3]

When your heart is undefended, awakened to the fact that it is secured in nothing other than the love of the Lord Jesus, a relational space opens where another can emerge from his or her hiding to join you—authentic connection occurs. When I no longer live for myself, I can be open to God and my neighbor.

At a concert I recently attended, Michael Card (who you'll hear from at the end of the book) illustrated in vivid color this undefended life. That night he performed a solo recital of more than a dozen pieces from his many years of songwriting. During his marvelous performance, the Spirit touched me, and I silently rotated through the stations of repentance, prayer, and praise on a spiritual Ferris wheel. At one point, Mike attempted a difficult piece he hadn't played for years. He stopped and started a few times, then sang just the chorus, before moving on to another piece altogether. He wasn't embarrassed. He simply told those gathered that it just wasn't flowing—no excuses, no humiliation—a man at peace, revealing how he'd fallen from the high wire but safely rested in the net of love. Mike was undefended, authentic, and his true self shone forth. This opened up a relational space, filled by the Spirit, into which friends were invited to come and connect as family—a powerful moment.

I don't suppose it's easy to stand before a couple hundred folks and have things go south, but "faith develops out of the most difficult aspects of our existence, not the easiest" (Eugene Peterson).[4] In other words, the aspects and circumstances of life that we would rather play hooky from— the toils and tribulations and conflicts and doubts—are all channels by which, if we attend to Christ in them, we shall become truly human, proving in our own experience who God is. When financial crisis comes, when a spouse or child dies, when natural disaster threatens your world, when you find yourself lonely in a difficult marriage, or when the story of your life is anything but smooth sailing, the impulse is to batten down the hatches and minimize the pain and hardship. It's not natural to press into the storm, to see it as an invitation to deeper spiritual awakening and thereby communion with God that will lead from the false self into the true self. Yet deep transformation of our existence is possible, as is a greater knowing of God, when we "move beyond simply trying to get back to how things were before the crisis" (David Benner).[5]

This isn't a prescription for what you can do so you'll feel better or achieve the life you long for. Authentic spirituality doesn't work that way. It's much less about what you do than about who you are.

On April 25, 1518, at the lecture hall of the Augustinian order in Heidelberg, Germany, Martin Luther, as a delegate of his order, presented 28 theses; the 26th read, "The law says, 'do this,' and it is never done. Grace says, 'believe in this,' and everything is already done."[6] The spiritual are those who believe, who relentlessly trust the God who has shown himself in the gospel of Jesus Christ; they are those who are finding their existence, as well as their character, in their workaday worlds (Luke 6:45)—through God's very outward extension. Trust develops through awareness— of God, and of yourself in relationship with him. Undefended living, then, flows out of dependence and reliance; it's living in an ever-deepening relationship, one that is— and I wish it weren't this way—forged not on mountaintops, but in the refiner's fire and strengthened in the valleys of the shadow of death.

Because this is so, this book will traverse those channels of awakening that we'd just as soon avoid and pass through them by seeking the Spirit of the Lord, who beckons: "Taste and see that the LORD is good. Oh, the joys of those who take refuge in him!" (Ps 34:8 NLT).

The undefended life is not discovered in the notion that God helps those who help themselves.

It's not discovered by committing to act out the top ten techniques of refined religion.

It's not discovered in being doubt-free, fearless, and befriended.

It's not discovered in holding an excellent test result, a sober spouse, a stable job, a reduced attraction to a hated perversion, or with the mentality that a vacation at the beach is all you really need.

It's not discovered by being fit and trim and ready for another round in the ring.

The undefended life is of an altogether different order. It is discovered through the sneaking suspicion that the thorn in your flesh may just possibly be God's greatest gift to you, even though you hate the thought that it might be so.

It's discovered in admitting you're a slave to coping and realizing that you may have given up hoping.

It's discovered in continuing to walk in the dry, dark valley, longing for a flashlight.

It's discovered when you're burnt out, exhausted with trying to reignite your life.

It's discovered when you find yourself banking on the desire that there really is something to the anemic advice, "Just trust in God."

Even the triune life of God suggests that the spiritual life is not simply disciplines—at its heart is relationality.

1

crossing all points

A YOUNG MINISTER, CONDUCTING HIS FIRST WEDDING service, becomes exceedingly nervous. It's a story I'm sure you've heard. He gets his tongue tied in knots, and perspiring profusely, his spoonerisms go from bad to worse. Not only does he welcome those present as the "beerly deloved," he invites the groom to place the "fing on the bride's ringer," but, of course, not before asking if anyone can give a good reason why the two shouldn't be joyfully loined. Which, in one sense, is what a wedding is about. Surprising as it may seem, being "joyfully loined" isn't unspiritual. Or has your Bible omitted the Song of Solomon?

The skittishness present when acknowledging the joy of marital sex points to a bigger problem: isolation of the spiritual from the material. Such dualism dominated the mindset of the ancient Greeks. Food and drink, art and literature, music and entertainment, humor and playfulness, sports and sex—none of these made the list of spiritual activities or were understood as touching the spirit. Anything went in the Greek world because of such bifurcation.

That same line of thinking sneaks into the Christian life when spirituality is sequestered to the classic disciplines of prayer, Scripture reading, fasting, corporate worship, silence, solitude, and the like. The spiritual life becomes smothered when these are placed in one hemisphere while the other 90 percent of our lives' activities fall squarely in the other. It forces us to shuttle back and forth between spirituality and earthly considerations. But as Nicodemus learned under the moonlight, neither ethnicity nor liturgy, piety nor intellectualism, integrity nor respectability, consistency nor decency constitutes the spiritual life (John 3:1–8).

The classic disciplines feed and water the spiritual life; they aren't the spiritual life itself. Spirituality is the tone and tenor, mood and flavor, atmosphere and character of a person's life—or, even better, the *relational space between people*. Recall Jesus' words that when two or more are gathered in his name—not merely assembled in one space, but when their hearts, minds, attitudes, and actions are truly oriented toward him and, in turn, toward loving one another well—then he's in their midst. His Holy Spirit inhabits that relational space (Matt 18:20).

In his work *On the Trinity*, Saint Augustine speaks about love in terms of the one who loves, the one who is loved, and the love itself. He asserts that the Holy Spirit personifies love—the bond of love that exists between the Father and the Son:

> The Holy Spirit, whatever it is, is something common both to the Father and the Son.

> But that communion itself is consubstantial
> and co-eternal; and if it may fitly be called
> friendship, let it be so called; but it is more
> aptly called love. And this is also a substance,
> since God is a substance, and "God is love," as
> it is written.[1]

He's talking about nothing less than the relational space between persons.

This isn't the place to get into a full treatment of the Trinity. It's enough to notice that even the triune life of God suggests that the spiritual life is not simply disciplines—at its heart is relationality. As one writer says:

> The conviction about the centrality of rela-
> tionship in the spiritual life is rooted in the
> unique Christian understanding of God. Since
> the God of the Christian people, the Trinity, is
> a communion of persons in loving relation-
> ship, it is important to see human relational-
> ity as a privileged locus for the encounter with
> God. Because that uniquely Christian way of
> speaking of God affirms that God is a commu-
> nion of divine persons in a loving relationship,
> it is our capacity for relationship which is the
> very image of God in us. Relationality is the
> matrix wherein we are to be conformed to the
> person of Christ by the presence and power of
> the Spirit.[2]

The relationality of Christian spirituality undercuts the bifurcation—the dualism of the secular and sacred as well as the body and the soul. The material realm is not walled off from the spiritual; it has an acute connection to, and participates in, it.

In fact, the material is instrumental in cultivating the relational-spiritual reality of our lives. When we ignore this, we might be in for a rude awakening. Playwright David Lodge tells a story about a day—November 22, 1963, to be exact—when he was watching one of his own creations being performed.[3] On this day, the theater was full. The actors were caught up in the drama of their performance—the scripted lines and choreographed movements and prescribed emotions. The audience was spellbound, pulled into the world powerfully conjured up before them. A scene came where a character took a radio, flicked it on: a crackle and hiss of static. He dialed the tuner: a jumble of noise, voices surged and faded, music blared and then sputtered. Then, stark and urgent, a voice broke through: "Today in Dallas, Texas, President John F. Kennedy was shot and killed ..."

The actor quickly switched off the radio, but it was too late. With just a few words, the real world had burst in upon the closeted, self-created world of the drama being staged, and the play ended.

What spiritual reality inhabited the theater in that moment? The dramatically intensified moment carried attention to the radio, which captured, converted, and broadcast a most tragic message. The material world participated in conducting the relational space, relating confusion, pain, fear, and loss—changing the reality of everyone present. From that moment, life was different.

Words matter. On one level, they're just mechanical waves of pressure and displacement of air, yet their effect on thoughts and emotions—and, in turn, our physiology—is monumental.

The Greeks borrowed nearly all of their gods from the ancient Egyptians, but the Greeks changed the gods' form. The Egyptians had animal-headed gods; the Greeks didn't—why? Because animals can't speak. Humans alone speak and, thus, have reason. The act of speaking was of critical importance to the Greeks; it connected them to their gods. In the ancient world, the words that came out of one's mouth carried a heavy sense of purpose—make promises at your peril. Relationships and society would unravel without this ability to connect through words.

Long ago the Desert Fathers understood the spiritual to be what the Word proclaimed and, hence, its effect was cognitive, affective, and behavioral. The Word changed things. In fact, everything created was made through the Word:

> In the beginning was the Word, and the Word
> was with God, and the Word was God. He was
> in the beginning with God. ... And the Word
> became flesh and dwelt among us, and we have
> seen his glory, glory as of the only Son from the
> Father, full of grace and truth (John 1:1–2, 14).

A little girl once said, "Some people couldn't hear God's inside whisper and so he sent Jesus to tell them out loud." In Jesus, the incarnate Word, we meet God, who is Spirit, in bodily form (Heb 1:1–3; Col 1:15). God himself can be met through Jesus. Words are supremely relational—their personal quality is what reaches out and touches us.

A man once went to his dentist complaining of a toothache. She examined him and said, "It's your molar."

Looking puzzled, the man asked, "What's a molar?"

"It's your six-year molar," she replied.

"You'll have to excuse me," said the patient, "but I don't really remember which tooth came through when I was six years old."

The dentist's assistant was more in tune. She reached out and put her finger on the man's cheek near the back of his mouth. "Thanks, that I understood," said the man.

Communication experts say that 48 percent of our message is communicated through tone of voice, 45 percent through body language, and only 7 percent through the words that are actually spoken. As my father continually reminded me growing up, actions speak louder than words. It's not that words aren't meaningful—they're immensely meaningful!—but their meaning is found in relationships. Theoretical physicist J. Robert Oppenheimer put it this way a generation ago when encouraging the exchange student program: "The best way to send an idea is to wrap it up in a person."

That's "incarnation." Just so, Jesus' experience of the Father—his obedience and faith learned through crises and trials (Heb 5:8)—is wrapped up in his human self, leading us into authentic humanity by demonstrating what it means to be creatures dependent upon our Creator and to find our true selves within his continual presence, restoring the relationship between God and us. Like Jesus' journey, and as Eugene Peterson noted, "Faith develops out of the most difficult aspects of our existence, not the easiest."[4] Awakening to the notion that God is often nearest in the places we don't dare to look—those which we, honestly, would rather avoid—is what this book is about.

HAS IT EVER OCCURRED TO YOU THAT THE DISCIPLES DID ALL the same miracles as Jesus? They walked on water, healed the sick, exorcised demons, prayed for their enemies, raised the dead, and loved to the last drop of blood. They didn't enter the right formula or utter the right incantation; rather, miracles occurred because the Holy Spirit filled them, just as he had filled Jesus. The limitation of our nature isn't because we're human, but because we're turned in on ourselves. William Wand, former Anglican Bishop of London, said:

> If we say that human nature as we know it is not capable of doing all the things that are ascribed to Jesus Christ in the New Testament the answer is that we do not know what perfect humanity is capable of. Still less do we know what perfect humanity can do when used as the means of self-expression of the eternal Word of God. ... As perfect man he was in complete contact with every element of human nature apart from sin. ... Jesus was so in touch with God that he knew from moment to moment what was the will of God for him. ... Here was no split personality ... but a perpetual and simultaneous collaboration between the human and divine. As a note struck on a piano may evoke a corresponding vibration in a glass tumbler, so the motion of the divine produces an immediate but voluntary response in the human consciousness of Jesus.[5]

My point is simply that Jesus isn't separated from us by some astronomical gap; he isn't Superman to our Jimmy Olsen. He is Jimmy Olsen, Superman's beloved photojournalist, or Jimmy as he should be. His demonstration of humanity is our goal; his nearness to the Father, his love, and his other-centeredness is humanity restored.

Jesus wasn't playing dress-up; he knew hunger and thirst, weariness and pain, isolation and loneliness, misunderstanding and misrepresentation; he was tempted in all things (Heb 4:15), which includes the essence of temptation—namely, to go it alone, to turn from Love to loving oneself—yet he learned to entrust himself to the Father instead. Jesus entered the hell of the crucifixion, turning to trust, believing the promise of God (e.g., Ps 16:10). He was a true man, finding his identity in God. His faith thereby proclaims the Father's presence and faithfulness. Jesus' experience of God's fatherhood awakens our own.

When Corrie ten Boom was a little girl, her father tucked her into bed at night. He talked and prayed with her, then laid his big hand on her little face. Later, when she was imprisoned in a brutal Nazi concentration camp, she would ask God to tuck her in, praying, "My heavenly Father, will you lay your hand on my face?" Reflecting on those hard nights, she said, "That would bring me peace, and I would be able to sleep."[6] Her thoughts held to the promises of the Word in dark times. Affectual and behavioral states effected by the world the Word affects. This awareness of the Word allowed her to experience God and find peace in him.

This is not a psychological sleight of hand, but the mind and heart united. Believing in God and his promises is the very means by which we're declared righteous, all guilt banished, and fellowship with God gained (Gen 15:6). Sensations in the body follow suit with what has been laid down by the mind, which finds ground for faith in the fulfilled history of the mighty acts of God, especially the cross. We're not talking pie-in-the-sky wishful thinking here, but simply down-to-earth spirituality, driving the pilings deep into the Rock (Matt 7:24–27). Here the true self emerges. Even fear of a concentration camp evaporates into restful sleep under the Spirit's understanding, ubiquitous hand.

TOWNS IN THE ANCIENT WORLD EACH HAD THEIR OWN DEIties. Some gods were revered by certain castes in certain places. Although Yahweh met with Moses on Mount Sinai, the God of the Israelites wasn't confined to that locale. He was no less present with Abraham in Ur of the Chaldees than at Shechem; no less present to the Israelites in Egypt than at the foot of Sinai; and he's no less present to Christians in the Holy Land than he is to those who have broken the bonds of earth in the Lunar Module (Acts 17:28; Deut 30:14). God is with us in Jesus Christ across all points of the compass.

As our days roll on they run over a variety of terrain, into and around innumerable obstacles. Sometimes the turbulence is extreme, the current of the river carrying us seems to turn back on itself and run upstream, the white water is immense, and we lose track of where we've come from and where we're going. Yet Jesus is there in the disorienting rapids as much as in the river's lull, when all is calm and peaceful. And we shall awaken to his presence if we will only surrender to the current.

It's somewhat like how, on the Day of Atonement, Israel's high priest would enter the temple's most holy place, and he would make a sacrifice for his own sins and then for the sins of the people, wearing a breastplate of precious stones representing the tribes of Israel. In essence, what he did, the people did. He took the people on his heart, quite literally, into the presence of God. We're present with Christ in the same way, but it's a spiritual condition: We're on his heart—this is our true position, secured in the Father's presence. And remembering this makes all the difference when facing our neediness, fears, and vulnerability, even as we wrestle through the discomfort they bring.

The late Bible teacher Harry Ironside was on a trolley car in Los Angeles when a rather peculiar-looking lady got on board and sat down beside him. She wore a pieced-together outfit of red handkerchiefs, with a shawl over her hair and a lot of spangles on her forehead. As soon as she sat down, she asked Ironside if he would like to have his fortune told. She charged a quarter.

Ironside asked her if she could do it. He explained that he was Scotch, and he hated to part with a quarter if she couldn't deliver the goods. She looked a bit bewildered, but then assured him that she could reveal his past, his present, and his future. For just a quarter, she would tell all.

Ironside replied, "It's really not necessary because I have had my fortune told already. I have a little book in my pocket that tells my past, present, and future."

"You have it in a book?" she asked.

"Yes," he answered, "and it's absolutely infallible. Let me read it to you." He got out his New Testament, and the fortuneteller looked startled. He opened to Ephesians 2 and said, "Here is my past." He read verses 1–3, about being dead in his trespasses and sins and living in the lusts of his flesh.

The nervous fortuneteller said, "I don't care to hear more."

But Ironside held her gently by the arm and said:

> But God, being rich in mercy, because of the great love with which he loved us, even when we were dead in our trespasses, made us alive together with Christ—by grace you have been saved—and raised us up with him and seated us with him in the heavenly places in Christ Jesus (Eph 2:4–6).

"That's plenty," the woman said. "I don't wish to hear any more."

But Ironside said, "There's more yet, and I won't charge you a quarter to hear it. Here's my future." And he read verse 7, "So that in the coming ages he might show the immeasurable riches of his grace in kindness toward us in Christ Jesus."

By now, the woman was on her feet, and Ironside couldn't hold onto her arm any tighter without being charged with assault. She fled down the aisle, saying, "I took the wrong man! I took the wrong man!"[7]

Our past, present, and future are sorted. Yet it's supremely difficult to remember that we're seated in the heavenly places with Jesus (Eph 2:6) when we run headlong into the reality of inner needs that demand immediate fulfillment. Our fears make us weak and feeble, controlling our choices and actions more effectively than the air traffic controllers manage the skies over Atlanta International, and shame holds us back from the vulnerability and uncertainty we need to truly connect and experience love.

Years ago my wife and I were going through a difficult time. We were living in Europe, and she took a scheduled trip to visit her parents in Hong Kong. A few weeks into the trip, she sent me a letter explaining that she had canceled her return flight. The news was devastating; I was sure our marriage was over.

I experienced nearly every emotion imaginable, drank every label of scotch under the sun, and prayed every prayer conceivable. And somehow, even in my drunken stupor, hiding beneath an overgrown beard and behind drawn curtains, God was present. He confronted me with a thought too disturbing to ignore: Surrender all, including your future dreams, and move to China.

For two weeks I wrestled violently with this thought. During the last few days of that period, the intensity grew until I found myself one night on the sofa, confronted by the question: Do you trust me?

The question slammed into my consciousness several times. I yelled back into the silence, "I've been to China. I don't want to spend the rest of my life there!"

"Do you trust me?" the silence said.

The pressure was agonizing, the fight intense, and then like a twig, I broke. "I'll go," I said to the dark empty room. "If you really exist, this is it—you better not drop me." At that very moment I physically experienced the words of Jesus, "Come to me, all who labor and are heavy laden, and I will give you rest" (Matt 11:28).

For Jesus is also present with us through his authority. If we're honest, we struggle to comprehend how having "all authority on heaven and earth" is of any value—what kind of influence can Jesus hope to have in absentia, in a world that grants and strips power so easily?

But as Matthew records, Jesus' final words to his disciples were: "Behold, I am with you always, to the end of the age" (Matt 28:18–20). Jesus' authority is mysterious, known only through revelation. His followers are simply left, trusting his promises—believing. Yet in leaving us with that, Jesus leads us deeper still into his presence in spite of his absence. In fact, by leading us into his presence, he empowers us to join him spiritually "outside the camp" (Heb 13:13), to join him in his suffering, to be released through relentless trust into spiritual and physical martyrdom. The river of blood that flows from the winepress in Revelation 14 is that of the faithful and has the same effect as the great river of pure water that flows eastward from the temple in Ezekiel 47, namely to make the dead sea fresh—that is, to bring life.[8] We participate in Jesus' life-giving as we cleave to him, even when following him leads us to die to ourselves, to endure suffering or even physical death; he invites us to enter into conflict with a curiosity about the soul transformation that may occur rather than desiring mere resolution. Faith flows forth in witness as our own experience proves the truth of Jesus' words: "I am with you always, to the end of the age" (Matt 28:20).

Where is the current of the Spirit running? To which point on the compass is the Spirit of Christ bidding you to come and know him this day? During the months before my move east to China, I clung to the promise the Lord had confirmed on that dark night—"I'll not drop you." At the end of myself and the start of his power, I awoke to his presence active in the recollection of and reliance upon his promise, which strengthened and empowered both my thoughts and actions.

When we cry, "Abba! Father!" it's the Spirit of Christ teaching us this song, for not one of us seeks after God on our own (Rom 3:11). When the soul sings of God, Jesus is near; his Spirit inhabits the relational space, communing with our spirits. By drawing us into this space and deepening our awareness of it, the Spirit is our Helper, Comforter, and Advocate (*parakletos*)—or, as expressed in one of the Central African languages: "the one who falls down beside us." In other words, the one who finds us collapsed on the road and kneels down to care for our needs.[9]

Few folks imagine their life filled with acute pain moment after moment, month after month. Christina Levasheff and her husband Drake experienced such piercing pain when their bright, sweet-spirited, and articulate two-year-old son unexpectedly began to lose his sight and the ability to walk. After emergency tests, a misdiagnosis, and more tests, the doctors finally gave the Levasheffs the heartbreaking news: Their son was afflicted with Krabbe Leukodystrophy, a rare, genetic, and terminal disease. Within five months, their son's body became paralyzed; he went completely blind, lost the ability to speak, experienced painful spasms in his limbs, and then he could neither swallow, nor breathe. He died just shy of his third birthday.

"Affliction makes God appear to be absent for a time, more absent than a dead man, more absent than light in the outer darkness of a cell. A kind of horror submerges the whole soul" (Simone Weil).[10] This anguish leaves you wondering, *where's God?*

Christina found the faith to peer through her pain, writing:

> Our Father never promised us lives without hardship. In fact, I am beginning to see that even though suffering is a result of evil and sin, it is also one of God's greatest tools for drawing people unto himself. He may not promise to remove our pain, but he does promise to be with us through the valleys.
>
> "How do you know he is present?" one might wonder.
>
> I am reminded of an evening when Jud had been crying out in pain during the night. I went and kissed him, then laid my head next to his—face to face, just inches away. No words were exchanged.
>
> Suddenly Jud got a very fearful look on his face and began to cry. Though his eyes were staring directly at me, he had no idea I was still with him. Judson was fully blind. He felt alone, scared and vulnerable. I placed my hand on Jud's back and gently patted him; he immediately calmed and smiled. It did not diminish his pain, but he knew he was being cared for.[11]

Encouraging words or letters, prayers, gifts of meals or finances, and many other unexpected blessings are a few of the many ways we know that Jesus is directly in front of us, just "inches" away. Perhaps one of the greatest ways the Levasheffs witnessed God's presence was through watching how Jud lived with incomprehensible joy during his final months—God stayed near. "Certainly I never imagined my life would include this kind of pain, but I also never anticipated knowing the grace and love of my Shepherd in such fresh and profound ways because of it," said Christina.

The Greek poet Aeschylus rooted his philosophy of learning in the hard ground of suffering. Robert Kennedy quoted him on April 4, 1968, as he announced the assassination of Dr. Martin Luther King, Jr., in Indiana:

> Even in our sleep, pain which cannot forget
> falls drop by drop upon the heart
> until, in our own despair, against our will,
> comes wisdom through the awful grace of God.[12]

God frees us not by removing difficulties and trials—the suffering that pushes us into doubt and sorrow—but by sharing in it with us. Jesus is "God-who-suffers-with-us." This reality prompted John Stott to say, "I could never myself believe in God, if it were not for the cross. The only God I believe in is the one Nietzsche ridiculed as 'God on the cross.' In the real world of pain, how could one worship a God who was immune to it?"[13] God uses the suffering and sorrow in the world to awaken and drive his people from doubting his presence to knowing his nearness.

TRIALS SHOW FAITH'S AUTHENTICITY (I PET I:7), ESPECIALLY those trials intense enough to dredge up doubt from the seabed of the soul or send it into a sunless despair—akin to David's valley of the shadow of death (Ps 23:4). C. S. Lewis was reportedly to have been once asked, "Why do the righteous suffer?" "Why not?" he replied. "They're the only ones who can take it." For they are the ones who attend to Christ in that valley, they recollect the Word and are changed for "the life of the people of God is life under the Word of God," his communicative presence.[14]

The doctrine of Christ's presence in the preached word (and his presence in the sacraments stems from this same principle) was written of by Martin Luther:

> I preach the gospel of Christ, and with my bodily voice I bring Christ into your heart, so that you may form him with in your self. If now you truly believe, so that your heart lays hold of the word and hold fast within it that voice, tell me, what have you in your heart? You must answer that you have the true Christ, not that he sits in there, as one sits in a chair, but as he is at the right hand of the Father. How that comes about you cannot know, but your heart truly feels his presence, and through the experience of faith you know for a certainty that he is there.[15]

Luther speaks about being touched by the Spirit-empowered Word—the story becomes a cognitive, affective, and behavioral reality. What a great encouragement to the lonely and heavy laden! Christ is present with us. As the psalmist asks, "Where shall I go from your Spirit? Or where shall I flee from your presence?" (Ps 139:7).

To live in the presence of God (or, as it's commonly expressed, "to practice the presence of God") does not occur by merely reading about God. "For God is spirit, so those who worship him must worship in spirit and in truth"

(John 4:24 NLT). "The Truth who is Christ is not something purely rational," says Brennan Manning.[16] The truth of God's presence is experienced through spiritual union, through the warmth of relational connection. The Lord is in the room; he inhabits his Word, which is in our very mouths and hearts (Rom 10:8). Receiving grace through the message preached in Word and sacrament as him speaking into our lives, especially when our soul is crushed by loneliness and heavy burdens, fills us with solace and stamina. God comes to us and makes his home in us. To live in such grace is to live without focusing on yourself and therefore to dwell in deeper relationship and better health—who do we need but God?

In John's Gospel, Jesus spoke to his disciples, saying:

> I will ask the Father, and he will give you another Helper, to be with you forever, even the Spirit of truth, whom the world cannot receive, because it neither sees him nor knows him. You know him, for he dwells with you and will be in you (John 14:16–17).

Just as every point on the compass brings different hardships with it, so Jesus also is with you in every direction—in your anxiety, loneliness, weariness and in your freedom, fulfillment, and fortune. We aren't waiting for God to come; he's already here. Experiencing his presence, like the full manifestation of the kingdom, is a function of letting down our guard before him and living in his Word.

To be free from need is
to cease breathing.

2

leaving eden

"THERE'S A UNIQUE NEEDINESS IN AMERICAN DOGS— I've seen it in their eyes and felt it in their energies on the first day I crossed over the border into the United States," writes the world's most prominent dog behaviorist, Cesar Millan. "America's pet dogs long to have what most dogs in the wild have naturally: the ability simply to *be dogs*, to live in a stable, balanced *pack*. American dogs struggle with an issue unknown to most of the world's dogs—the need to 'unlearn' their owner's lovingly motivated but ultimately destructive efforts to transform them into four-legged people with fur."[1] Millan has observed that dog owners usually attribute the behavioral problem to the dog, but more often than not the issue is with the owner. His observation about dogs is also true for people: we have deep yearnings to be truly human. A prominent characteristic of being human is neediness, and influencing our chronic neediness is the fact that we've been fathered by lies disguised as light (John 8:44; 2 Cor 11:14).

Our needs never end: We need food and clothing and shelter; we need a job and a vacation; we need companionship and solitude; we need encouragement and conviction; we need a freezer, and a fireplace, and a futon, and on and on. To be free from need is to cease breathing. Still it's only those who are acutely aware of their neediness who are truly human.

"Neediness" is typically talked about in a jaundiced fashion. The needy are either down-and-outers whose needs are impossible to miss, or those who, overstepping healthy boundaries because they've not learned to self-soothe, depend on the object of their love for their essential well-being.

Relationships are often the playground of such neediness. Take falling in love, for example. According to Carl Jung, two people bump into each other and their "infinitely intelligent" psyches unconsciously run the numbers and compute that the other is the definitive image and perfect instrument to fulfill their *own* needs and bring about their *own* growth (although the latter is scarcely desired).[2] In other words, they've determined that their "happiness quotient" depends, in some measure, on the other. It all goes sideways when eventually they discover they don't equally depend on each other for happiness. One longs for emotional connection, while the other is less emotionally available and instead seeks a sense of well-being from beer, bratwurst, and ball games—but both people are deeply needy. It's an unbalanced dependence that hangs onto trivialities, and yet we stake our well-being and happiness on it.

In so doing, seeds of disappointment are sown and fear and anxiety are reaped through manipulation, power plays, or resentment.

Becoming truly human involves awakening to our neediness, realizing how our stories propel us to particular mollifiers in an attempt to satiate our needs and quell our greatest fears of abandonment and rejection. Becoming truly human is coupled to another awakening: awakening to the Spirit of Christ, who communicates the love of God. Only when we satisfy our internal, spiritual needs does the tyranny of external neediness end.

Mohandas Gandhi wisely said:

> The greatest of man's spiritual needs is a need to be delivered from the evil and falsity that are in himself and his society. Tyranny, which makes a sagacious use of every human need and indeed artificially creates more of them in order to exploit them all to the limit, recognizes the importance of guilt. And modern tyrannies have all explicitly or implicitly in one way or another emphasized the *irreversibility of evil* in order to build their power upon it.[3]

ALIENATION FROM EDEN HAS ENGULFED THE HUMAN RACE IN a false life philosophy that confines knowledge to absolutely objective experience. The result: we're thrown into the chaos of a collective neurosis. We were made to know ourselves in light of one who is bigger than ourselves. In leaving Eden, then, a void has opened within us, into which we

thrust one unhealthy substitute after another—the societal definitions of "good" or "useful"; prejudices that cut us
off from "considering what is really distinctive, the orien-
tation to self-transcendence, the fullness of human existence," and leave us in a one-dimensional existence.[4] We're
woefully lost and unhinged.

In not knowing ourselves as divinely determined, we've
lost our true purpose and fallen into the pain of an existential vacuum, where our despair dominates personality
and pendulates between emptiness and boredom, filling
our thoughts, paralyzing our actions, and reducing us to
be forever maladjusted in our search for substitute meaning. In Eden we enjoyed our heavenly Father's fathering; we
knew the wholeness and sanity of inner peace; our hun-
gers were unsoiled and satisfied—even work was satisfying.
But beyond its borders to the east we live as orphaned street
children, endlessly warring and wheedling; our sweeping
freedom displaced by our self-imposed self-sufficiency,
which is anything but safe or satisfying. A profound neediness underlies the collective neurosis and begins every
story of spiritual awakening.

But until awakening comes, we're addicted to our neediness, left grasping for the next fix that didn't stop with that
first apple tree:

> Addiction exists whenever persons are inter-
> nally compelled to give energy to things that
> are not their true desires. To define it directly,
> addiction is a *state* of compulsion, obsession,
> or preoccupation that enslaves a person's will
> and desire. Addiction sidetracks and eclipses
> the energy of our deepest, truest desire for love

and goodness. We succumb because the energy of our desire becomes attached, nailed, to specific behaviors, objects, or people. *Attachment*, then, is the process that enslaves desire and creates the state of addiction.[5]

Need can hijack and redirect anything—from structure and routine, to hobbies and exercise, to music and morning muffins; from benevolence to bona fide employment, to relationships and relaxation; from a fine wine to just plain whining.

How do you know when need is tyrannizing you? When the thought of turning from the behavior or object of love would so tear at the root of who you know yourself to be that it would feel like suicide—you could likely will yourself to go without it for a week, but the obsessive and neurotic craving for the forbidden fruit screams addiction.

A woman, literally on her way to file for divorce, made a detour and popped into my study to talk. Her stated reason for the divorce was that her well-educated husband was an unemployed drunk.

I counseled the husband and wife individually and together. After one session the woman apologetically pulled her electric bill from her purse and requested financial assistance. A little while later, working with the man, I serendipitously discovered that they owned a cottage, a boat, and operated a summer business at the marina.

What do we really need?

Slowly it became evident that the woman was using material status to pacify her need for meaning and self-worth. The husband also lived out of his false self, grasping the bottle to soothe his feelings of rejection from employers and his wife—she'd applied for a divorce multiple times and, wrapped so tightly in her own needs, was oblivious to how her berating wounded him.

One day, the wife called to let me know she no longer wanted counseling. It seems I'd delayed her getting what she needed—namely, a divorce. Both parties were equally addicted to satisfying their own insecurities and needs, and I never heard from either of them again.

Leaving Eden has made us desperate for life. Somehow we believe we can catch it by rearranging behaviors, objects, and people like deck chairs on the Titanic. Yet inner peace and contentment always slip away, because personhood, well-being, and happiness aren't bound to what we've set our love upon. Second homes and happy spouses are, fundamentally, amenities, not necessities. Our deepest need is spiritual and that is what our multifarious undertakings are unknowingly trying to fill.

Nearly two million people stave off hunger in Haiti each year. To quiet rumbling tummies and reduce the pain of starvation, some Haitians make cookies out of dirt. But these treats neither remedy malnutrition nor stop starvation; they simply keep the stomach distracted.

Empty calories can't satiate our cravings. We need sustenance.

Neediness has played us for fools, cutting us off from Eden, where all of our human needs were satisfied and meaning was realized in the transcendence of our human selves. Yet—and this is amazing—the Savior appeals to our need as the very thing to call us back.

WHEN TURNED UNCONSCIOUSLY TOWARD THE WORLD, NEED-
iness refuses to receive what grace longs to give. What hin-
ders us from receiving such help isn't ultimately the *experience* of need, but the *awareness* of need. Consciousness has
the uncanny ability of heightening the force of need, dis-
rupting the outward grasping for fulfillment and turning
neediness inward. In other words, when we will not receive
from God, we're not, so to speak, "needy enough." Our need
isn't clearly known within us. Like a ball player breaks in a
new glove, it has yet to break in the soul (i.e., to tear the
seams of rebellious and self-righteous posture). Only when
"broken enough" to squarely face the truth of need can the
joy of grace be discovered.

Many who claim the Christian faith suffer from blindness and unbrokenness. Filled with the calories of their
many works, they're distracted from the hunger of personal
neediness, and they're too secure to risk repentance of anything other than surface faults. "Our deepest spiritual need
is for whatever thing God wills for us. To will something
else is to deprive ourselves of life itself. So, when we sin, our
spirit dies of starvation" (Thomas Merton).[6] In other words:

> Self-righteousness is not the bastion only of the
> religious; it is the fortress of all who don't want
> to involve themselves in the roller-coaster ride
> of ambivalence that comes when they care for
> people who will fail them. "I am all I need; I am
> enough," is the presumption of self-righteous-
> ness. If I need someone or something, it is only
> temporary and need not obligate me to anyone.[7]

Self-righteousness is not merely the perception that I am good and right, it's also the notion that I'm not in need. The false self dresses in unbreakable pride, shirttails tucked in and secured against gale-force winds.

Nebuchadnezzar II was such a man. A powerful and capable leader of Babylon in the conquest of Judea in 597 BC, he struggled to rely on any power higher than himself. The pompous ruler was brought low when Daniel interpreted his dream of a strange, enormous figure with a head of gold, chest of silver, belly and thighs of bronze, legs of iron, and feet made from a mixture of iron and baked clay (Dan 2:31–38). According to Daniel's interpretation, the king was the head of gold, possessing dominion, power, might, and glory. But rather than this bringing him in humble thanksgiving before God, Nebuchadnezzar concluded that God was the lucky one, and he ran out to erect a forty-five-foot golden image of himself, decreeing all to bow and worship it:

> You are commanded, O peoples, nations, and languages, that when you hear the sound of the horn, pipe, lyre, trigon, harp, bagpipe, and every kind of music, you are to fall down and worship the golden image that King Nebuchadnezzar has set up. And whoever does not fall down and worship shall immediately be cast into a burning fiery furnace (Dan 3:4–6).

Nebuchadnezzar was absorbed by the dream, and his response to it exposed his need for significance and adoration. Yet he missed the dream's point; he was only listening for what he wanted to hear. It's like the story of a farmer who conversed with his friend in Midtown Manhattan. As they walked along, the farmer suddenly blurted out, "I hear a cricket."

"Oh, you're crazy," his friend replied.

But the farmer insisted, walked over to a planter on a corner, then looked beneath a shrub and found the cricket. His friend was shocked. "You have an incredible sense of hearing," he said.

"No," replied the farmer, "my ears are no different from yours. It simply depends on what you're listening for." At that moment the farmer reached into his pocket and pulled out a handful of coins and dropped them on the concrete. Nearly everyone on the corner turned to look. "You see what I mean? It all depends on what you're listening for."

Nebuchadnezzar's expectations and needs influenced his comprehension such that only an acute personal crisis could disrupt his percipience. As Richard Rohr has noted, "Humility and honesty are really the same thing. The humble person is simply a brutally honest person about the whole truth."[8] The truth is that the false self lives in fear— fears of abandonment or rejection—and is consumed with its need for approval, acceptance, achievement, and worth; it's out of touch with its own innermost feelings; it's reliant upon others for its identity; it lives a life teeter-tottering between sadness and euphoria; it finds it nearly impossible to distinguish between itself and what it does; and it demands to be noticed (in overt or subtle ways).[9] If you hear yourself in this description, you're not alone—I do too.

Seeing ourselves against the backdrop of the false self shows us something far greater than surface needs, namely the soul's need—that is, the need to become truly human, to recover what we lost upon leaving Eden so we can stop eating dirt in an attempt to feel full.

In his second dream, Nebuchadnezzar awoke to a reality he never could have fathomed. The dream foretold his impending sojourn into madness—how he'd be driven from society like an ox—until, broken, he acknowledged the Most High's rule of human kingdoms and that his place in it was a gift (Dan 4:24–25). The confessions of the broken are accompanied with pain. The conscience cringes when the defensive shutters fall and sunlight surges in. Such realness and rigorous honesty, rather than barring God, hears the sound of sandaled feet (Luke 15:20). "To be alive is to be broken; to be broken is to stand in need of grace."[10]

I CANNOT RECEIVE SAVING GRACE APART FROM ACKNOWLedging my abject neediness. And unless I receive grace there's no union with God (John 13:8). My fear of exposure is the greatest hindrance to brokenness, and yet if I drop my mask and shield, be vulnerable and undefended, cling to nothing but humanness, then I gain, in real time, conscious awareness that to be loved is my greatest need. Without such self-surrender, God can't use me. The sixteenth-century theologian Richard Sibbes said: "[God] empties people of themselves, and makes them nothing, before He will use them in any great services."[11] In the experiences of breaking and emptying, in becoming nothing before God, we move beyond the surface needs and arrive at the soul's essential existential need: to become what it was always meant to be.

Once upon a time, in the heart of an ancient kingdom, there flourished a beautiful garden. And there, in the cool of the day, the master of the garden walked. Of all the plants in the garden, the most beautiful and most beloved was the gracious and noble Bamboo. Year after year, Bamboo grew yet more noble, conscious of his master's love and watchful delight, but modest and gentle nevertheless. Often when the wind reveled in the garden, Bamboo would play, tossing and swaying and leaping and bowing in joyous abandonment, leading the great dance of the garden, which most delighted the master's heart.

Now, one day, the master himself drew near to contemplate Bamboo with eyes of curious expectancy. And Bamboo, in passionate adoration, bowed his great head to the ground in a loving greeting.

The master spoke: "Bamboo, Bamboo, I will use you."

Bamboo flung his head to the sky in utter delight. The day of days had come, the day for which he had been made, the day in which he would find his fulfillment and destiny.

His voice came low: "Master, I'm ready. Use me as you wish."

"Bamboo," the master's voice was grave, "I will have to take you and cut you down!"

A trembling of great horror shook Bamboo. "Cut ... me ... down? Me ... whom you, master, have made the most beautiful in all your garden? Cut me down?! No, not that. Not that. Use me for your joy, use me for your glory, but do not cut me down, master!"

"Beloved Bamboo," the master's voice grew graver still, "if I do not cut you down, I cannot use you."

The garden grew still. Wind held his breath. Bamboo slowly bent his proud and glorious head. He whispered: "Master, if you cannot use me other than to cut me down, then do your will and cut."

"Bamboo, beloved Bamboo, I will cut your leaves and branches from you too."

"Master, spare me. Cut me down and lay my beauty in the dust; but will you have to take from me my leaves and branches too?"

"Bamboo, if I do not cut them away, I cannot use you."

The Sun hid her face. A listening butterfly glided fearfully away. Bamboo shivered in terrible expectancy and said in a muted tone: "Master, cut away."

"Bamboo, Bamboo, I will yet split you in two and cut out your heart, for if I cut not so, I cannot use you."

Then Bamboo bowed to the ground. "Master, master, then cut and split."

So the master of the garden took Bamboo...

and cut him down...

and hacked off his branches...

and stripped off his leaves...

and split him in two...

and cut out his heart.

Lifting him gently, the master carried Bamboo to a spring of fresh sparkling water in the midst of his dry fields. Then, putting one end of broken Bamboo in the spring and the other end into the water channel in the field, the master gently laid down his beloved Bamboo. The spring sang a welcome, and the clear sparkling waters raced joyously down the channel of Bamboo's torn body into the waiting fields. Then the rice was planted, and the days went by; the shoots grew, and the harvest came.

In that day Bamboo, once so glorious in his stately beauty, held yet more glory in his brokenness and humility. For in his beauty he had life abundant, but in his brokenness—in his place of accepting his need of a greater purpose—he became a channel of abundant life to his master's world.

FOR JESUS, HUMILITY WAS NOT LOW SELF-ESTEEM, FEELINGS of unworthiness, or flagellating himself over sins. It was refusing to shield himself against his deepest need: to be connected to his Abba's love and acceptance by surrendering his will to Love (John 6:38; Luke 22:42).

Jesus led a terrifying life. It reads like an episode of *America's Most Wanted*, broadcasting that radical security is paradoxically gained by throwing off worldly authorities—the Occupational Safety and Health Administration wouldn't be impressed.

Our understanding of our identity has been so interwoven with coping strategies that it's impossible to distinguish self from sin. Pulling on a loose thread wouldn't simply unravel the security blanket, it would unravel our identity. But hear Merton on this:

> We are warmed by the fire, not the smoke of
> the fire. We are carried over the sea by a ship,
> not by the wake of a ship. So too, what we are

is to be sought in the invisible depths of our own being, not in outward reflection in our own acts. We must find our real selves not in the froth stirred up by the impact of our being upon the beings around us, but in our own soul which is the principle of all our acts.[12]

What may betide when we're not trying to become ourselves by the force of our acts but rather by embracing ourselves in our Abba, as Jesus did? The constricting grip of anxiety and fear loosens, and others experience our inner freedom, too, as peace pours into our relational space.

Thirty years ago, Donnie Ray Moore pitched in the American League Championship Series for the California Angels against the Boston Red Sox. He was the relief pitcher and didn't come to the mound until the fifth game, a point at which the Angels were winning both the game and the series—one more strike and they would clinch their first ever pennant.

Rather than a strike, however, Moore gave up a home run, and the Red Sox came back to eventually win the game and series. Unable to move beyond the loss, Moore fell into depression. He was traded to the Kansas City Royals and cut within two seasons—his baseball career finished.

One night a heated argument with his wife ensued, and he shot her three times—she lived. Then he turned the gun on himself—he didn't. Moore had robed himself with baseball. So when guilt and failure unrobed him, he couldn't bear the shameful exposure.

Safety is our most basic human need—and it's what love provides. It's also the greatest fault line in fractured relationships and the primary emotional condition that God's work in the world satisfies. After all, the safety of Eden was the safety of God's loving presence and determination, which fulfilled all human needs. The loss of safety planted seeds of distrust in our attitude toward the divine Lover: *Do I really have all I need?* Ever since leaving Eden, humanity has struggled to recapture safety, and with every hesitant step into the future, our past guilt has driven us to justify and thereby seize our own selfhood.

As Genesis 3 tells us, Adam transferred culpability from himself to God, for wasn't God after all responsible for placing Eve with him? The blame then shifted from Eve to the serpent, for it had beguiled her. Then—if you'll indulge the creative license and imagine the serpent's retort—it completed the circle and went from the serpent to God: "Did you not put me in the garden too? Am I not also your creature with all my functions?" And so it regresses until God himself is blamed as the first cause.

Do you see the neediness behind this game of hot potato? The attempt to reconstitute guilt into fate is actually a plea for acquittal. Every twist and turn to name the source of evil screams, "Make me free! I wanted autonomy ... just not like this." The blame game blew up in Adam's hands. He's left holding mashed potatoes, as is Eve; they're irrefutably identified with their deed—the serpent no more than an accessory to evil. In other words, they didn't simply grasp the forbidden fruit; it's the manifestation of their fallen identity. Eden is lost.[13] Yet they could have grasped for God and found their identity in self-surrender, living undefended. How we grapple with fear and feelings of insecurity is what either causes us to leave or lay hold of Eden.

Edmund Spencer's 16th-century Arthurian poem *The Faerie Queene* tells of the Redcrosse knight, who accompanies a fair lady across a plain. On their journey a storm arises and they're forced to take shelter in a beautiful forest; unfortunately, this particular forest is the Wandering Wood, where an evil enchantress has her lair.

The enchantress deceives the Redcrosse knight into thinking that the fair lady has been unfaithful. So at dawn he leaves her and strikes out on his own. Eventually his path crosses that of another fair beauty with whom he soon falls into a quiet, secluded repose under a foreboding tree. As they rest, from somewhere comes a cry of warning, entreating him to stand firm and flee lest he buy pleasures from this lurking lady and lose his life. Initially the warning frightens him, but he's caught in the spell of the lady's beauty.

It's then that the tree speaks to the knight, explaining that it was once a man. When he discovered the lady's true identity as that of the filthy, old enchantress and recoiled in horror, she transformed him into a tree. Even as a tree, he still must endure pain from the heat and cold.

Sin promises to keep us safe and warm in this hostile, cold world. We're convinced that life is unfaithful, and it whispers, "Walk with me. I'll help you gather resources and recruit minstrels. I'll take you across the plain." Sin is a coping strategy, but it never delivers us to our desired destination or quiets our fears. Holding us beneath its spell, it roots us, stealing our freedom, amplifying our fears, and quieting our attempts to subdue it.

Some of us hang out backstage in life, exposing little of ourselves, never risking fears, feelings, or thoughts; some project an air of confidence and dominance; some retreat in furious, uncompromising silence; some amass as many allies as possible; some are chameleons, matching the mood and energy of the crowd; some push back with belligerence, reassuring themselves of their individuality; some join a caravan of complaint, pelting with contempt those who withhold what they want; some collect symbols and artifacts, feeding on the adulation and power they provide; and some of us maintain such rigid ordering of our lives so as to circumvent vulnerability completely. The myriad of possible constructions that fear erects to shore up insecurities and satisfy needs is staggering.

When we emphasize guilt over fear, following Jesus becomes primarily about moral reform, but, in fact, it's about risk, risking the release of one strategy or another that we have sought security in. Guilt is a serious matter; as the heat of a fire consumes the wood it burns, such is guilt to the fear in our hearts. As one writer has said:

> The fear narrative suggests that guilt, objectively, is a social recognition that social relationships have been disrupted. Someone has been hurt in some way, and therefore seeks retribution, revenge, or reparation. Guilt alerts us to threat—there is now danger and hostility in play. We are afraid. The emotion of fear leads to all kinds of acts of hostility in return. ... However, the one of whom we are most afraid is God himself—hence the response in the

garden of Eden to hide and reveal selectively. God is now no longer reliably for us.[14]

If we look a little deeper beneath Christ's substitutionary atonement, we find that it works to reinstate safety. The Father is, in fact, not mad at us—he never was. With compassion he sent his Son into the world that he might present God "to our heart as being a kind Father who has received us into his favor," as Luther put it.[15]

Peter's walk of faith illustrates the greater point: As the disciples rowed vigorously against the wind—getting nowhere, I might add—Jesus was making his way across the Sea of Galilee toward them. But as Mark's account tells, he had no intention of climbing into the boat, lending a hand, or even of calling cadence (Mark 6:48). When the disciples saw him walking on the water they were terrified, and thought it was a ghost. Nevertheless, Peter's impetuousness, as usual, got the better of him, and he risked asking Jesus for an invitation, then stepped from the boat (Matt 14:28–29).

This scene is much more than comic relief before diving into something more substantive, like the healing in Gennesaret. Jesus' reply, "Come," to Peter's request was a call to leave behind all harnesses, tethers, and flotation devices that previously had provided him peace of mind. Peter was encouraged to risk all, even his life, on the idea that Jesus would entirely meet his need.

WHEN I CONSCIOUSLY FACE THE FACT THAT ALL MY NEEDS are connected and met by God's immeasurable power and grace, my fears fade, enabling the risk of faith. I can even dare to look squarely at my neediness, for grace already knows me beyond my comprehension—the Spirit has been hovering over my chaotic waters from the very beginning.

Faith risks receiving without control; it ceases grasping outward; it relinquishes life in order to have life in true depth. "Whoever loses his life for my sake will find it," promised Jesus (Matt 10:39). It's a counterintuitive and paradoxical movement, which Richard Rohr fittingly has called "falling upward." He writes:

> You will not know for sure that this message is true until you are on the "up" side. You will never imagine it to be true until you have gone through the "down" yourself and come out on the other side in larger form. You must be pressured "from on high" ... because nothing in you wants to believe, or wants to go through it. Falling upward is a "secret" of the soul, known not by thinking about it or proving it but only by risking it.[16]

When my daughter was very young I would take her to experience the magnificent music of the Scottish Chamber Orchestra. We would arrive sufficiently early to take our seats before the orchestra began tuning. In the fullness of time, a cacophony of sound would fill the Aberdeen Music Hall—oboes and bassoons, French horns and flutes, cellos and violas, timpani and marimbas each contributed to the chaos. But then, over all the noise would sound a long high-C. Within moments a migration commenced: one instrument after another joined in—the great disorder aligned—and ran on together, readied for the evening's performance. In a similar fashion, the turmoil of need fills life with discord until it alights upon Christ. "Thou hast formed us for Thyself, and our hearts are restless till they find rest in Thee," wrote St. Augustine.[17] "God wants to provide our ultimate security, but we seek our safety in power and possessions and then we find we must continually worry about them. We seek satisfaction of our spiritual longing in a host of ways that may have very little to do with God. And, sooner or later, we are disappointed" (Gerald May).[18]

Jesus' words, "I did not come to judge the world but to save the world" (John 12:47) could be paraphrased: "If you insist on running from the light of [my] word into the darkness of your own guilt ... I cannot help you. Or, better said, you cannot receive the help I have already delivered to you because you choose not to trust my assurance that you already have it. ... I have put a billion-dollar deal in your left hip pocket and you won't even move your hand to check it out."[19]

The parable of the importunate friend at midnight in Luke 11 deepens the point. In teaching his disciples about prayer, Jesus spoke of a man who received a mob of visitors who conveniently timed their arrival to occur after the shops closed, and instead of going straight to bed they wished to stay up—which meant food. (For the parable to make any sense we have to imagine that they've already eaten their host out of house and home.)

In telling this parable, Jesus is asking his disciples to imagine themselves as the annoying friend, breaking down God the Father's door with their needs. In the parable, the sleeper is persuaded to rise but not before first giving his friend the cold shoulder: "Do not bother me," he says, "the door is now shut, and my children are with me in bed. I cannot get up and give you anything" (Luke 11:7). The street walker feels his need so greatly, however, that he *will not* take a hike—the sleeper is his only hope.

This parable isn't teaching that the way to get things from God is to keep nagging until his arm is well and twisted. Jesus' point is that God doesn't give the cold shoulder. Out of death, not life—don't miss the allusion to the resurrection—he rises to fill all our needs, even the petty, annoying ones. But neither the reasonableness nor uniqueness of the need moves him. The sleeper rises because his friend isn't playing "prim and proper" but is shameless; he's died to any instinct to retain self-respect (Luke 11:8)— he's dead to himself, possessing nothing but the confession that he's an atrocious host. Because he's consciously aware of his neediness, radically ready to receive, he will be raised from his death by the sleeper.[20]

Lest you think I've taken too many liberties in my interpretation, Jesus makes the same point with the needy Canaanite woman who nagged him to do something, anything, about her demon-possessed daughter (Matt 15:21–28). Again, the cold shoulder routine is executed with style— the disciples try to get rid of the nag, and Jesus doesn't answer her a word. She refuses to take a hike, nonetheless.

Finally, Jesus turns abruptly to her and pops off: "It is not right to take the children's bread and throw it to the dogs"(Matt 15:26). Now the woman doesn't bat an eyelash, doesn't defend herself; instead, she absorbs the blow and, still in dogged pursuit, replies, "Yes, Lord, yet even

the dogs eat the crumbs that fall from their master's table"
(Matt 15:27). Such is her readiness to receive Jesus' provision.

He will come to us in no other way than as savior, and
only those who've awoken to their need of him shall find
him. "His love seeks out the needy, not in order to give
them a little but in order to give them all."[21]

God would fill our needs, first, by tearing us from the
objects of love that we've tethered ourselves to for security
and satisfaction but that leave us in fear and chronic neediness. Second, his Spirit would turn our gaze to the work of
the Son; so, third, we might come fearlessly to him empty
of everything, undefended, and ready to receive anew the
gift of his presence. It's by this gift that Eden is rediscovered
and we become truly human.

*Our flight into fear is a flight
away from all that God is.*

3

taming the mississippi

A SMALL RIVER MEANDERS SOUTHWARD FROM LAKE ITASCA, Minnesota, and grows slowly into the mighty Mississippi. Running 2,300 miles to the Gulf of Mexico, the Mississippi River is considered one of the world's most powerful and dangerous rivers. When it floods, whole cities are in jeopardy.

The same is true of fear. Fear gives rise to flood waters of frustration, anger, and hate. We fear for our physical and emotional safety; we fear we don't measure up to expectations; we fear what lies ahead, as well as what lies behind; we fear we're not loved or accepted, or we'll lose what little love and acceptance we have. When we don't fully know and experience love, our insecurities rise like a destructive Mississippi flood.

THE APOSTLE JOHN SAW THE CONNECTION BETWEEN LOVE and fear clearly when he wrote: "There is no fear in love, but perfect love casts out fear. For fear has to do with punishment, and whoever fears has not been perfected in love" (1 John 4:18). Therefore, beneath our multiplied insecurities lies fear—fear of "punishment" (i.e., that something will be taken from us as retribution for our sins or foolishness).

I recently read about the death of Russian general Mikhail Kalashnikov. Until he died, he served as an ambassador for the Russian arms industry, and although publicly cheerful, he lamented that criminals and terrorists had made use of the weapon he designed for defensive purposes: the AK-47, or Automatic Kalashnikov, 1947 (its production year). Few knew of the psychological guilt that plagued him and how he would've rather invented a lawnmower.

Shortly before his death in 2013 he wrote an emotional letter to the Patriarch of the Russian Orthodox Church unveiling the unbearable guilt that privately tormented him. "My spiritual pain is unbearable," he said. "I keep having the same unresolved question: if my rifle claimed peoples lives, then can it be that I ... a Christian and an Orthodox believer, was to blame for their deaths?" Then he added, "The longer I live, the more this question drills itself into my brain and the more I wonder why the Lord allowed man to have the devilish desires of envy, greed, and aggression."[1] The reply he received—expressing appreciation for his defense of the country—was a loving gesture meant to assuage his guilt.

But Kalashnikov's conscience was never freed. "After all," we tell ourselves, "penance *must* be performed; amends *must* be made; love is entirely conditioned on my performance." But it's always too little, too late.

Our thoughts prevent us from seeing how we might be freed, but the Apostle John reminds us: "God sent his only Son into the world, so that we might live through him. In this is love, not that we have loved God but that he loved us and sent his Son to be the propitiation for our sins" (1 John 4:9–10). Perfect love has perfectly atoned! As Martin Luther so aptly put it, "He who does not know that he has a propitious Father does not know God."[2] When this truth is buried, our consciences remain tethered to the stake of religious effort.

The truth: Divine love *finished* all such justifying work. "On judgment day the Lord Jesus is going to ask each of us one question, and only one question: Did you believe that I loved you; that I desired you; that I waited for you day after day; that I longed to hear the sound of your voice?"[3]

As Brennan Manning has said, "If you're afraid of God, you don't know him." Our flight into fear is a flight away from all that God is.

FEAR WEARS MANY MASKS. CLOAKED IN APATHY OR ANGER; inquietude or insouciance; pride or pessimism, self-hatred or self-righteousness—any one of these can enter shaved, well-dressed, and deeply persuasive. Fear provokes us. We cling to people, possessions, and power like a shipwrecked sailor to flotsam. Fear pushes us toward perceived safety—the elimination of all uncertainties. Scarcely wetted by the wellspring from which true security flows, we fear its loss—not just the loss of life and limb, but status, reputation, acceptance, and love, too.

Incessantly comparing our gifts and abilities renders us incapable of encouraging others who may eclipse us. Freedom from ruminating on how others perceive and respond to us is hard to achieve. Perhaps the greatest ill in this area is the tendency to lug around what Dr. Brené Brown calls the "20-ton shield of perfectionism" to keep ourselves from being hurt. In truth, perfectionism keeps us from actually being seen or vulnerably exposed. Perfectionism isn't the pursuit of excellence or holding high standards, it's an addictive belief system fueled by the thought, "If I look perfect, live perfectly, and do everything perfectly, I can avoid or minimize the painful feelings of shame, judgment, and blame."[4] When perfectionism is at the wheel, shame is always sitting shotgun, and fear is the annoying backseat driver yelling, "Criticism, blame, ridicule at twelve o'clock—turn left!"

A friend of mine, who is one of the nicest people you'd ever meet, has a certain innocence and naïveté about her that would remind you of *The Andy Griffith Show*, but she lives behind a self-imposed shield to control her life and alleviate her fear. Over the years we've spent quite a few hours together talking and looking into her fears.

On one occasion, she was following me in her car. I took a turn, got on the freeway, and thought, "Drat, I've lost her." For nearly a half hour I waited for her to arrive at the destination. When she finally did, she explained that she hadn't taken the freeway but went through town—a more congested, slower route—to evade her fear of driving on the freeway.

Some would say that's a small egg, a small fear, so what's the big deal? Well, when one egg after another is added to a wicker basket, the weight and stress can become too much. Andrew Carnegie once said, "The wise man puts all his eggs in one basket and watches the basket." That might be good for business, but it's a bad policy for life. Obsessing over the basket turns you into a basket case.

My friend is brilliant with children. She's creative and engaging; kids love her. For nearly a decade she has worked as a teacher's assistant at a private preschool. On numerous occasions the administration has sought to promote her to lead teacher; it pays more, and she's more qualified and better equipped than her colleagues in that position. Yet time after time, she's declined the offer, fearful of the possibility that one day she would have to tell a parent the unwanted truth about sweet little Jill or Jack.

For a gentle woman who loves children, you might be surprised to learn that she has none of her own. Her empty home isn't due to a medical condition, but fear of not meeting her own expectations. This fear held so much power over her that she took the extreme measure of undergoing surgery to silence it.

These examples suggest perfectionism on overdrive, and her default gear has been to repeatedly opt out of engaging her fears. Kenny Rogers once sang about looking for love in all the wrong places; the song sums up my friend's personal search for assurance.

Assurance is a wonderful adjunct to salvation, but lifting our eyes only as high as ourselves, our abilities, and our experiences won't bring it. Seeking assurance in our activities or decisions, in our participation or non-participation, in new blessings or deeper mystical experiences, is why we keep coming up short, bobbling between sadness and euphoria. The assurance that muzzles our fears is found only when we lift our eyes higher than ourselves.

Paul knew this well. In an exposition on suffering, morality, judgment, and a crossed response to the gospel, he included the words: "We are always of good courage ... for we walk by faith, not by sight" (2 Cor 5:6, 7). This isn't an over-spiritualization of the difficulties he or the Corinthians faced. Walking by faith isn't *running from* reality; it's *awakening to* reality. Rather than pretending everything was peaches and cream and avoiding the fact that the Corinthians spilled the bowl in their laps, Paul called attention to where their confidences must be placed.

Sometimes it seems like the Lord is wearing noise-canceling headphones; it's true. Instead of waiting patiently, we turn inward: "If I take matters into my own hands ... if I were just more committed, more religious, prayed more ... if I live more vigorously, it will result in a more fulfilled me."

Such thinking ignores the cross, turning God into a passive passenger on our journey, as surprised as we are at the dips and bends in the road. If he's just along for the ride, there's hardly a reason to have confidence and courage. "The tendency in legalistic religion is to mistrust God, to mistrust others, and consequently to mistrust ourselves" (Manning).[5]

Look again at the cross. Clueless priests, a mercenary betrayal, and a fearful governor nailed a carpenter of Nazareth to a tree. Why? Because they were profoundly afraid of the weakness inherent in the kingdom he was building. How ironic! Even as he was crucified, Jesus was building a foundation beneath their feet sufficient to carry the weight of them all. Their "power" couldn't demolish his; divine weakness trumps human strength (1 Cor 1:25).

Now catch this: The power structures Jesus targets for demolition are primarily internal. Coups d'état and revolutionary uprisings exchange one power for another, but the direct, intervening power of such revolutions, while it treads on our team colors, doesn't torpedo our ego and arrogant self-reliance. What Jesus preached, however, wasn't the overthrow of the other team, but the overthrow of *me*—that is, my desire to make the world work for me and to escape criticism, blame, and ridicule. Such a desire, incidentally, turns fear into a firearm and blows holes in one relationship after another. Robert Capon contrasts the weak, left-handed power of Jesus' kingdom with the right-handed strength of the Jewish and Roman framing crews:

> If you take the view that one of the chief objects in life is to remain in loving relationships with other people, straight-line power becomes useless. Oh, admittedly, you can snatch your baby boy away from the edge of a cliff and not have a broken relationship on your hands. But just try interfering with his plans for the season when he is twenty, and see what happens, especially if his chosen plans play havoc with your own. Suppose he makes unauthorized use of your car, and you use a little straight-line verbal power to scare him out of doing it again. Well and good. But suppose further that he does it again anyway—and again and again and again.

What do you do next if you are committed to straight-line power? You raise your voice a little more nastily each time till you can't shout any louder. And then you beat him (if you are stronger than he is) until you can't beat any harder. Then you chain him to the radiator till ... But you see the point. At some very early crux in that difficult, personal relationship, the whole thing will be destroyed unless you—who, on any reasonable view, should be allowed to use straight-line power—simply refuse to use it; unless, in other words, you decide that instead of dishing out justifiable pain and punishment, you are willing, quite foolishly, to take a beating your self.

But such a paradoxical exercise of power, please note, is a hundred and eighty degrees away from the straight-line variety. ... [It] looks for all the world like weakness, intervention that seems indistinguishable from nonintervention. More than that, it is guaranteed to stop no determined evildoers whatsoever. It might, of course, touch and soften their hearts. But then again, it might not. ... The only thing it does ensure is that you will not—even after your chin has been bashed in—have made the mistake of closing any interpersonal doors from your side.[6]

Standing up to take it on the chin deliberately, or better yet, dying to the urge to bash someone else's, is a supremely terrifying overthrow of personal power, not to mention security. How can God's will be done like this? For surely the motley crew that gathers isn't about to show such weakness. So we're left wondering: Is the cross just the outcome of some yahoos with crowbars and hammers, or really the predetermined plan of God?

The answer is: Both!

In the cross, God flipped humanity's hyper-fear of death on its head. God's power lies in weakness to the point that he let us do our worst—namely, kill the Son of God himself, an act that, ironically, opened safe passage to the Father. So consider this: If this is the case for the most momentous event in history, dare we think God's care is any less creative, charitable, and commendable when it comes to every other detail of our lives? Hear Paul: "For you did not receive the spirit of slavery to fall back into fear, but you have received the Spirit of adoption as sons, by whom we cry, 'Abba! Father!'" (Rom 8:15).

In sum, our best actions have mixed motives. We stray after ever-greener grass; get lost or beset by predators; or on the flip side, stubbornly refuse to leave our pens at all. Depending on our personality and temperament, our straying or staying is motivated by the fear that doing the exact opposite will kill us.

But the way to life—paradoxically—just happens to be death. The Bible tells but one story: death and resurrection. God calls us to look away from ourselves and our fears and focus our eyes on him alone—which also means looking away from our accomplishments, perfections, multitudinous failures, and the possibility of such. In his love and faithfulness we find confidence, and our true selves are freed.

TWO MEN, BOTH SERIOUSLY ILL, OCCUPIED THE SAME HOSPI-tal room. One man was allowed to sit up in his bed for an hour each afternoon to help drain the fluid from his lungs. His bed sat next to the room's only window. The other man had to spend all his time flat on his back.

The men talked for hours on end. They spoke of their wives and families, their homes, their jobs, their involvement in military service, where they had taken vacations. Every afternoon when the man in the bed by the window could sit up, he would pass the time by describing to his roommate all the things he could see outside the window.

The man in the other bed lived vicariously during those one-hour periods when his world was broadened and enlivened by the activity and color of the outside world.

The window overlooked a park with a lovely lake, the man said. Ducks and swans played on the water while children sailed their model boats. Lovers walked arm in arm amid flowers of every color of the rainbow. Grand oak trees bordered the landscape, and a fine view of the city skyline could be seen in the distance. As the man by the window described all this in exquisite detail, the man on the other side of the room closed his eyes and imagined the picturesque scene.

One warm afternoon the man by the window described a parade passing by. Although the other man couldn't hear the band, he could see it in his mind's eye as the gentleman by the window depicted it with descriptive words. Unexpectedly, an alien thought entered his head: *Why should he have all the pleasure of seeing everything while I never get to see anything?*

It didn't seem fair. As the thought fermented the man felt ashamed, but as the days passed and he missed seeing more sights, his envy eroded into resentment and soon turned him sour. He began to brood and found himself unable to sleep. He should be the one by the window—the thought now controlled him.

Late one night as he lay staring at the ceiling, the man by the window began to cough. He was choking on the fluid in his lungs. The other man watched in the dimly lit room as the struggling man by the window groped for the button to call for help. Listening from across the room he never moved, never pushed his own button, which would have brought the nurse running. In less than five minutes, the coughing and choking stopped, along with the sound of breathing—now only silence, deathly silence.

The following morning the nurse arrived to bring water for their baths. When she found the lifeless body of the man by the window, she was saddened and called the hospital attendants to take it away. As soon as it seemed appropriate, the other man asked if he could be moved next to the window. The nurse happily made the switch, and after making sure he was comfortable, she left him alone.

Slowly, painfully, he propped himself up on one elbow to take his first look. Finally, he would have the joy of seeing it all himself. He strained to slowly turn to look out the window beside the bed. It faced a blank wall.

Avarice and resentment arise when we turn from God and attempt to procure life for ourselves. We cling to what we

we cling to

hope will eliminate fear, especially the fear of being unful-filled, unhappy, and undefended. Such fear itself is death.

But this fear is also a fear of life. True life flows; it's flexible and free, but we've become rigid and frozen, stagnant. Some people can't bear the thought of losing anything—a relative, a friend, a pet, a belief, a view—and they dread trials because they might lose the person or thing that they're convinced they can't live without. But life, like a river, carries away the old and ferries in the new.

Yet we crave permanence. Anthony De Mello asked a revealing question: "Do you want to measure the degree of your rigidity and your deadness? Observe the amount of pain you experience when you lose a cherished idea or person or thing, the pain and the grief betray your clinging, do they not?"[7] All things change and pass by. Rivers flow perpetually, and yet we're taken by sheer surprise and laid low at times when we've locked ourselves in a cabin, filled with our illusions, thinking that nothing—at least nothing significant—will ever change or be allowed to change. That we can, with just a few more sandbags, hold the river back, stabilize life, and tame the mighty Mississippi.

If you're like me, you know the feeling: I'm insecure. In my scramble to pile sandbags, my defenses rise, and feelings of hatred, envy, resentment, cynicism, and severity spill out—fear lurking behind them all. I want very much to be somebody—or at least to avoid criticism, blame, and ridicule—and thereby belie my fear of being a nobody. At times, I, too, have chosen not to enter into life, keeping my boat on land, remaining in death, and fearing change.

In a very different way, a young businessman, who spent much time working in another city far away from home, found himself dealing with the same fear. When work stress and isolation got to him, he fell into a malaise and mild depression, and he feared his new marriage had stolen the freedom he was convinced he couldn't live without. So one night, he went to a pub, got drunk, and went home with a few cavalier ladies. About four o'clock in the morning, he woke, left their apartment, and walked the streets, utterly appalled with himself.

Over the next year his secret gnawed away at his soul, till one night he found himself on the bathroom floor having a panic attack and crying. The Lord finally broke his levee. With great sorrow and remorse he went to his wife, confessed, and asked for forgiveness. About a year later she came to see me, unable to move beyond the devastation. Understandably she felt betrayed, hurt, angry, insecure, and hateful.

We talked. She vented, cried, and asked, "Why?" Yet after all of this, her peace would still not return; bitterness gnawed on her soul.

Divorce might have set her free from facing her husband. It wouldn't, however, have set her soul free from hostile feelings, nor would it have done a thing to bring about reconciliation and peace. Her unforgiveness stemmed from not only hurt and hatred, but also fear—fear of appearing weak and stupid; fear of not being the primary person in her husband's heart; fear that it could happen again.

"Resentment is like drinking poison and then hoping it will kill your enemies" (Nelson Mandela). Complete forgiveness requires moving beyond envy and resentment, hurt and bitterness, anger and self-pity. God has ordained a spiritual cycle: When we allow the spirit of complete forgiveness to reign in our hearts, our peace returns, but where we dwell with resentment on a matter, our peace departs. "When we are bitter, we delude ourselves into thinking that those who hurt us are more likely to be punished as long as we are set on revenge," writes R. T. Kendall. "We are afraid to let go of those feelings. After all, if we don't make plans to see that justice is done, how will justice be done? We make ourselves believe that it is up to us to keep the offense alive."[8] Faith moves us beyond fear to forgiveness when we lay down our shields of envy and bitterness and anger. Faith emboldens us to take God at his word: "Vengeance is mine, I will repay, says the Lord" (Rom 12:19). Faith strengthens us to take a bashing on the chin just to keep the relational door open.

PAUL KNEW POWER, BOTH STRAIGHT-LINE AND WEAK. His natural intellect and tenacity drove all before him, terminating in bloodshed. Yet encountering Christ on the Damascus Road did for him what wrestling with the angel did for Jacob: It broke him. Never again would he boast of *his* strength, only Christ's. A deepening awareness of Christ transformed him from a natural inferno that burned down relationships into a spiritual one, igniting them with love through the death of his ambition and self-erected identity that had been constructed upon his self-righteousness.

Peter was also a strong character. Undoubtedly he was the most assertive and natural leader of the Twelve, yet he was also the most hotheaded. When Jesus was arrested, Peter jumped violently to his defense. On one level we can certainly understand the degree of Peter's love—

no doubt it wasn't lost on Jesus either—but notice the contrast between Jesus and Peter: Jesus gave himself over to the guard, full of trust in the Father, while Peter gave himself over to the fight, full of trust in Peter. His three denials stemmed from the same root—self-reliance: Preserve Peter at all costs.

Thankfully grace meets us where we are, but doesn't leave us where it found us.[9] Peter was thoroughly crushed by his abandonment of Jesus and his dissembling denials. His impetuousness left him broken and publicly humiliated. He died, yet there was also resurrection. The words of the angel, who met the women at the tomb, call out Peter specifically: "Go, tell his disciples *and Peter* that [Jesus] is going before you to Galilee" (Mark 16:7, emphasis added). When Jesus met them on the shore, he had a special appointment with his leading disciple—not to rub his nose in his failure, but to reassure him of his life. Peter's failure awoke him to grace. Forgiven and restored, he was also commissioned: "Feed my sheep" (John 21:17). The truth is simple: The one who will not die cannot live!

In the Lord's Prayer, Jesus teaches us to pray "deliver us from evil" and, in his high priestly prayer, Jesus himself prays that his disciples would be kept from the evil one (John 17:15). One of the devil's chief aims is to dupe us into believing that direct, straight-line power is the fastest and most efficient way to dispel our fear and to achieve our greatest aspirations and noblest goals—that is, to reject our saving death and to proceed on our own. Yet that swift river leads us further away from faith, not deeper into it.

The death Paul and Peter experienced—death to their exercise of natural power (to save and secure themselves and eliminate fear), their being made weak—was their salvation. Jesus' faithfulness defined them, not their failure.

Every confidence in ourselves must be shattered. "In [Christ] we possess all things. But in order to possess Him Who is all, we must renounce possession of anything that is less than God" (Saint John of the Cross).[10] The Lord must bring us to the place where we flee the temptation to resist our own death, a resistance wholly motivated by fear.

If Jesus' power is made perfect in our weakness (2 Cor 12:9), why do we fight it? The late Scottish theologian T. F. Torrance reflects:

> Then Jesus was betrayed and crucified, and the disciples found themselves utterly overwhelmed and bewildered at what had taken place, standing in the crowd of those who mocked and jeered at the helplessness of Jesus on the Cross. Jesus was now utterly alone, and they his disciples were separated from him by an unbridgeable chasm of shame and horror for they had all forsaken him and betrayed the very love with which he had bound them to himself. Then the disciples remembered the Holy Supper and Jesus' solemn enactment of the new covenant for the remission of sins in his body and blood. Jesus had meant them to remember, for in that act he had taken their very sins, even their denial of him, as he explicitly showed Peter, and used them as the very means by which to bind them to him. Then the disciples understood the passion of Christ, not as something for the holy but precisely for

the sinner. It was their sin, their betrayal, their shame, their unworthiness, which became in the inexplicable love of God the material he had laid hold of and turned into the bond that bound them to the crucified Messiah, to the salvation and love of God forever.[11]

Peter and Paul were grateful and humbled, loving as they had been loved. Their failures shifted their focus to his face—which is all God really wanted. Jesus' perfect love cast out their fear of failure and death.

ALL THE POSITIVE AND WISHFUL THINKING IN THE WORLD and a library of self-help books cannot free you from the burden of fear. Only an outside force has such power.

When John says: "There is no fear in love, but perfect love casts out fear" (1 John 4:18), he's pointing us outside of ourselves to a prior love, asking only that we believe that it is so. The aim of the gospel is love, and the aim of love is freedom: "For freedom Christ has set us free," says Paul (Gal 5:1). Freedom is life!

The journey from fear to freedom is the journey of living in a reality where the primary center of who you are and where you are is in the Father's love, undefended. This truth made all the difference to a woman who found herself one evening at dinner with a few friends and the late author and professor Robert Mulholland. When her friends asked her to share her spiritual journey she began by stating that she was a job-related accident—she was the daughter of a prostitute. Since her mother continued to ply her trade, her upbringing was largely conducted by family members, as she was shuffled between the homes of her relatives. As an early teen, she'd been drawn into a church youth group where, through friends, she began to discover and respond to the love of God in Christ. After high school, she attended a Christian college, met a young man, fell in love, and got married. Her husband provided well for them, and they had a wonderful home and two lovely children. From the outside, it seemed like a fairytale "rags to riches" story.

But her home, marriage, and family were being torn to pieces by her compulsive need to know and find her father. She spent every ounce of energy and all of the resources she could muster to discover who her father was. She badgered her mother about who her clients had been nine months before her birth, but of course her mother didn't have the foggiest idea. Finding her father seemed impossible.

Then one day while home alone, standing in front of her kitchen sink washing dishes, the anguish of her heart swelled and tears streamed down her face, dropping into the dishwater. She cried out, "Oh God, who is my father?"

She heard a voice say, "I am your Father."

The voice was so real that she spun around to see who had snuck into the kitchen. No one stood behind her.

Then she heard the voice a second time: "I am your Father, and I have always been your Father."

In that moment she was released from the obsessive need to know who her biological father had been. In that moment, she discovered the truth of Paul's words, "[God] chose us in [Christ] before the foundation of the world" (Eph 1:4). In that moment she learned that in spite of the strange dynamic surrounding her conception and birth, she was a person spoken forth out of the heart of God's love.[12]

That's who we are, too. We also can journey from fear to freedom by awakening to the reality of our identities in the Father's love. As we perceive ourselves in God, our longing for him increases. David Benner noted, "Awakening involves a brush with the Divine. And each encounter with the Divine increases our appetite for more. Rather than satiation, we experience increased longing for a deeper taste and a fuller knowing of God."[13] As we awaken to the reality of God's fatherhood, a reciprocal desire for God himself begins to unseat self-centeredness, self-promotion, and self-protection as our means of shielding ourselves from and overcoming our fears. Such change is transformational and exhibits growth toward the Spirit of peace.

The first words Jesus spoke when he appeared to the disciples in the upper room after the resurrection were words of peace. "Peace to you!" he said, showing them his hands and feet. It was as if he was showing them the true source of their peace and freedom from fear.

The Father's love through his Son changes everything, beginning with freeing us from fear. He travels the raging Mississippi with us, using every bank and bend as well as the very cover of night to work his life into ours—this is God's objective. Perhaps it should be no surprise that Paul can write with such certainty:

> Neither death nor life, nor angels nor rulers, nor things present nor things to come, nor powers, nor height nor depth, nor anything else in all creation, will be able to separate us from the love of God in Christ Jesus our Lord (Rom 8:38–39).

Living with our defenses down means trusting that God's loving-presence will guide us along the river of our lives. Mark Twain writes in his memoir, *Life on the Mississippi*, of the calming presence of a father-figure under whose wing he, as a fledgling boy, learned to pilot a steamboat:

> During the afternoon watch the next day, Mr. Bixby asked me if I knew how to run the next few miles. I said—
>
> "Go inside the first snag above the point, outside the next one, start out from the lower end of Higgins's wood-yard, make a square crossing and—"
>
> "That's all right. I'll be back before you close up on the next point."
>
> But he wasn't. He was still below when I rounded it and entered upon a piece of river which I had some misgivings about. I did not know that he was hiding behind a chimney to see how I would perform. I went gaily along, getting prouder and prouder, for he had never left the boat in my sole charge such a length of time before. ... Once I inspected rather long, and when I faced to the front again my heart flew into my mouth so suddenly that if I hadn't clapped my teeth together I should have lost it. One of those frightful bluff reefs was stretching its deadly length right across our bows! My head was gone in a moment; I did not know which end I stood on; I gasped and could not get my breath; I spun the wheel down with such rapidity that it wove itself together like a spi-

der's web; the boat answered and turned square away from the reef, but the reef followed her! ... The awful crash was imminent—why didn't that villain come! If I committed the crime of ringing a bell, I might get thrown overboard. But better that than kill the boat. So in blind desperation I started such a rattling "shivaree" down below as never had astounded an engineer in this world before, I fancy. Amidst the frenzy of the bells the engines began to back and fill in a furious way, and my reason forsook its throne—we were about to crash into the woods on the other side of the river. Just then Mr. Bixby stepped calmly into view on the hurricane deck. My soul went out to him in gratitude. My distress vanished; I would have felt safe on the brink of Niagara, with Mr. Bixby on the hurricane deck. He blandly and sweetly took his tooth-pick out of his mouth between his fingers, as if it were a cigar ... and lifted up these commands to me ever so gently—

"Now get ready. Wait till I give the word. She won't want to mount the reef; a boat hates shoal water. Stand by—wait—WAIT—keep her well in hand. NOW cramp her down! Snatch her! snatch her!"

He seized the other side of the wheel and helped to spin it around until it was hard down, and then we held it so. The boat resisted, and refused to answer for a while, and next she came surging to starboard, mounted the reef,

and sent a long, angry ridge of water foaming
away from her bows.[14]

Taming the Mississippi isn't about fighting to control
the waters but riding them with confidence in the Father's
presence. Our security rests in his perfect love.

The heart of Christian spirituality
lives in a place of vulnerability,
not a fool's paradise.

4

shadow boxing

Mizaru, Kikazaru, and Iwazaru will attest: *Hear no evil, see no evil, speak no evil*, is the way to live in the world. The Japanese proverb intends to encourage the heart to focus on doing good and not evil—to be of good mind, speech, and action, to rein yourself in, exercise self-control, and maintain propriety in all things.

The meaning has been lost in translation. In the West the mystic monkeys are understood as communicating that we can be good by ignoring the bad. "It is the nature of the false self to save us from knowing the truth about our real selves, from penetrating the deeper causes of unhappiness, from seeing ourselves as we really are—vulnerable, afraid, terrified, and unable to let our real selves emerge" (James F. Masterson).[1] True virtue demands sight, but it's a struggle with and against ourselves to become self-aware. We don't realize that, in the moment, we don't want to truly see.

We're boxing with our own shadows; we're fighting to keep our eyes closed.

On an evening in early summer I gathered with six others in a cozy family room to examine the connection of God's story with our own. The Bible study had barely begun before I had a powerful urge to contact mission control: "Houston, we have a problem." My invitation to turn to the first chapter of Genesis and read about "God's story" had launched exasperation—a *humph*, followed by a contentious remark from a woman I'll call Dolores: "How can you call the Bible *a story*?"

I asked a substantive question: "Ancient Israel often repeated the failings of Adam and Eve. Can you share a time when this repetition of failure has appeared in your life—when you've spoken, acted, or felt like Adam and Eve? Why do you think you responded the way you did?" The answers were guarded and superficial. Then Dolores brazenly said what everyone seemed too congenial to say: "*No!* I've never felt or acted in a way that suggests I've lacked self-control or forgotten God!"

Our craft's wicked shimmy continued the following week. After examining Job's story I asked those gathered to share stories of how they'd suffered and their responses to it. Again, Dolores spoke sharply: "I've never suffered!" Which wasn't true. She had steeled herself against the hard, debilitating reality of a bitter divorce, which had also left her estranged from her adult children. Sadly, like too many, Dolores only let people see her outer shell. She obstinately insisted that her life was trouble-free.

Many of us relate to God no differently than to the highway patrol: Follow the rules, and you can go. Disobey, and get a ticket.

Life isn't that simple.

When we deny our deep struggles, cling to stories of triumph, avoid fellowship with those who pry beyond what our simple answers account for, those who dig into longings, relationships, and motives, and when we use obedience to both sidestep and inflict pain, we're imprisoning ourselves on Fantasy Island. Feigning ignorance and hiding from what we fear about ourselves separates us from God, making us susceptible to evil. The heart of Christian spirituality, however, lives in a place of vulnerability, not a fool's paradise.

The patriarch Jacob is a case in point (see Gen 27:1–35; 32:3–32). As the younger twin, born grasping his brother's heel, Jacob also laid hold of his brother's birthright and blessing before fleeing north. Fourteen years after the fact, he made his way home, a wealthy man with a large family and flocks. As he neared the land of his brother Esau, he grew increasingly fearful. Defenseless before his brother's might, and no doubt his memory, Jacob conducted a campaign of appeasement, sending animals and gifts across the Jabbok River as tribute in hopes of gaining Esau's forgiveness and his family's survival. On the night before he met Esau, he found himself at the ford of the Jabbok, where he left his family to spend the night in solitary prayer. That night he wrestled with a mysterious figure who had been sent to ensure this habitual runner didn't flee again. Jacob was left with a dislocated hip in the struggle, which essentially made him vulnerable before Esau—a precarious position indeed. Yet such weakness transformed Jacob, not to mention his relationship with Esau.

Emotional pain can tear you asunder—which is why the anticipation of such pain can incite a flatfooted sprint.

Running gives instant relief. Brené Brown has researched vulnerability extensively and observed several common defenses deployed against it. Some of these include *foreboding joy*: when we think, "I'm going to shut down this feeling of joy, because it won't last"; *perfectionism*: when we think, "If I do everything just right, I can escape shame and rejection and arouse approval and acceptance instead"; and *numbing*: when we think, "I'll find something to embrace me, to take the edge off the pain and disappointment"—including alcohol, drugs, food, sex, relationships, money, work, caretaking, gambling, staying busy, exercising, shopping, planning, continual change, the Internet, and much much more.[2] "Far from being an effective shield, the illusion of invulnerability undermines the very response that would have supplied genuine protection," namely, undefended identity, which engenders not merely an embrace, but authentic connection with others.[3] Christian psychologist Larry Crabb has said that when we make protecting ourselves from risk our priority, especially by whitewashing our lives, our freedom to connect is restricted.[4]

We harden our hearts to those who hurt us; after all, they might do it again. We crave the ability to eliminate the risk of trusting someone else. We don masks to keep from being seen. We make ourselves sick through obsession—so much so that no one expects any commitment from us. We raise a shield of willfulness by argumentation, complaint, accusation, and judgment, clothing ourselves in the chainmail of pride and rigidity to maintain control. We bow before those who manipulate us, cemented in deeply painful patterns of living because we fear what change may bring.

We run through relationships like revolving doors, seeking others who feel obliged to remove our emptiness and supply our security. All of our neurotic tendencies promise us power and invincibility, but as Simone Weil said: "Power ... is essentially vulnerable; and therefore it is bound to defend itself."[5]

Pursuing invulnerability ultimately imprisons us. A jail cell can be a safe place, I'll grant you that. But it's anything but freedom. Unless we're honest and admit we can't meet our own needs, that making another do it for us is not only neurotic but wicked, unless we take off the mask and allow ourselves to be seen and loved, the free and abundant life Jesus promised will remain a fairy tale.

God is known only in the vulnerability of faith (Heb 11:6). Our prevailing tendency, on the other hand, to see clearly in the here and now and eliminate the fuzzy vision we think that standing close entails, to decamp the promised land, to need reassurance and protection from ruination is a flight from faith, a flight that binds the soul to achievements, rule-keeping, and the approval of others, rather than risking life in union with the God of Jacob.

Fourteenth-century mystic Julian of Norwich said, "Some of us believe that God is almighty and may do everything; and that he is all wise, and can do everything; but that he is all love, and will do everything—there we draw back. As I see it, this ignorance is the greatest of all hindrances to God's lovers."[6] A dear friend of mine is fond of saying, "If you can never take a risk because you are afraid of what will happen to you, you are living in a prison ... the prison of fear."[7] Yet the serenade sounds: "There is no fear in love, but perfect love casts out fear" (1 John 4:18).

I've heard it said, "So risk your life on Christ, that if he has not told you the truth, you will have lost everything." Without risking love, you'll never be free.

What does it take to be pliable, to trust that the chapters of your days are being written as part of a larger story and that it is a good story? It takes trust, risking nakedness, allowing God to see us and love us precisely as we are.[8]

MERRIAM-WEBSTER DESCRIBES VULNERABILITY SIMPLY AS the capacity to be physically or emotionally wounded. (The Latin root, *vulnerare*, means "to wound.") Therefore, at the most basic level, to be vulnerable is to be open to attack or danger.

This is quite different from weakness, which, by the way, is the inability to withstand wounding. Vulnerability, on the other hand, is the willingness to risk being in a situation where we're not in control, where, frankly, we are susceptible to getting our chins bashed in (metaphorically as well as literally). The courage to be totally exposed comes from getting in touch with our creatureliness: we are "creatures who are situated in particular times and places with particular bodies, desires, capacities, needs, and life spans, and who come to know something of [our] situatedness and interdependence in relation to vaster contexts and purposes."[9]

Vulnerability "is not winning or losing; it's having the courage to show up and be seen when we have no control over the outcome. Vulnerability is not weakness; it's our greatest measure of courage."[10] Conversely, invulnerability leaves you hard and disconnected. As Simon and Garfunkel attest: "I touch no one and no one touches me. I am a rock, I am an island. And a rock feels no pain; and an island never cries."[11]

When we have no control over the opinions, mistakes, feelings, attitudes, words, or actions of others, the risk of being wounded is enormous. Yet without risk there is no commitment, and without commitment there is no relationship—vulnerability is critical for connection.

I've been a Detroit Lions fan since birth. DeAndre Levy is a leading defensive star for the Detroit Lions and one of the most complete linebackers in the National Football League. His job is to line up in the middle behind the line of scrimmage and tackle the offensive player with the ball. In a split-second he must commit to blocking a run or a pass by putting his weight forward and rushing in. If he commits to the run, he's vulnerable to the pass and vice versa. Not committing to either would leave him dead on the field—the opposing offense would gain yards. Relationships are similar: without commitment you lose. Yet commitment always entails vulnerability. And how we hate that! The only way to connect with others and the bounty and beauty of life is being open to the possibility of being wounded. "The vulnerability of precious things is beautiful because vulnerability is a mark of existence" (Simone Weil).[12]

Since vulnerability reveals character, it's through our vulnerability that we can take ownership of those things blocking us from deepening our connection to God. Faith counteracts and overcomes the constant pull toward invulnerability and disconnection.

JOSEPH STALIN'S MOSCOW RESIDENCE HAD EIGHT BEDROOMS.
Fearful for his safety, each night he chose a bedroom at random to ensure none knew exactly where he slept. Fear—
which we gave attention to earlier—has us on the move,
inciting more than night sweats.

What do we fear? We fear being found out as a fraud,
more incapable and sinful than we care to admit. We fear
being abandoned or rejected. We fear being misunderstood
and judged, defenseless against the powers in our lives—
the economy, the government, bosses, parents, you name
it. We fear tragedy may befall us and alter the course of our
life. We fear tripping over death—"It's a poor thing to fear
that which is inevitable" (Tertullian, second-century theologian). Jewish spiritualist Marianne Williamson flipped
our fear in a most unique direction:

> Our deepest fear is not that we are inadequate. Our deepest fear is that we are powerful beyond measure. ... We ask ourselves, who
> am I to be brilliant, gorgeous, talented and fabulous? Actually, who are you not to be? You
> are a child of God. Your playing small does not
> serve the world. There is nothing enlightening
> about shrinking so that people won't feel insecure around you. We were born to manifest the
> glory of God that is within us.[13]

All of our fears can be boiled down into the rich reduction: *We fear not being loved.*

The freedom to risk, to stop playing dress-up and to be
bare, honest, truthful, to face what you've avoided, is possible when you know you're deeply loved, and love itself

is not vulnerable (Rom 8:35–39). According to Gerald May, "Honesty before God requires the most fundamental risk of faith we can take: the risk that God is good, that God does love us unconditionally. It is in taking this risk that we discover our dignity. To bring the truth of ourselves, just as we are, to God, just as God is, is the most dignified thing we can do in this life."[14]

The need for reassurance is the drive to eliminate risk by exerting control over the uncontrollable: our children, our relationships, our careers, our checking accounts, whatever essentially involves a person or situation outside of ourselves. Giving up control is terrifying but also liberating—much easier than trying to be comfortable in a straitjacket. However, to tame these wild horses, you have to trust someone stronger than yourself. Demanding reassurances amounts to fleeing from faith. But in trusting ourselves to Christ, we receive not only intimate communion but also freedom.

In the 2014 film *Freedom*, a group of runaway slaves are escorted along the Underground Railroad to freedom in Canada. In one scene, the party is in peril of being discovered by bounty hunters. Samuel, one of the slaves, confronts his fear of capture with Thomas Garrett, his Quaker escort:

> "How many men he got with him?" asks Samuel.
>
> "He's got two."
>
> "That's it? We got more than that."
>
> "The Railroad doesn't go out of its way to confront these people, Samuel. Our fate is in God's hands. And we'll protect you, with his guidance."[15]

Risking openness with God, which necessitates openness with ourselves, lays responsibility for the outcome in
his hands, trusting him not to squander a drop of our docil-
ity. By doing so, we actually invite God to bestow his grace
on us. His grace replaces our needy, sinful, bedraggled, and
broken pieces. We behold the truth of our true selves in
him: "Yes, Lord. This is what I'm really like. And, in fact,
I'm even less dignified than this." Such is a readiness to be
filled with divine love. Such openness is the vulnerability of
spiritual brokenness. It is coming to the end of ourselves
and finding God. "It is here our stubbornness is melted, our
rights are renounced, and we stand stripped of our glory
and foolish pride."[16] Here is where we become the glory of
God as recipients of his love and mercy (2 Cor 3:18).

Late Benedictine monk Sebastian Moore wrote:

> The gospel confession of sin is the most gen-
> erous, secure, adventurous expression of the
> human heart. It is the risk that is only taken in
> the certainty of being acceptable and accepted.
> It is the full and final expression of that confi-
> dence. Only to your lover do you expose your
> worst. To an amazed world Jesus presents a
> God who calls for this confession only so that
> he may reveal himself in a person's depths as
> his lover. This confession in a context of divine
> acceptance releases the deepest energies of the
> human spirit and constitutes the gospel revo-
> lution in its essence.[17]

Awakening to my worst is awakening to God's best.
The self who is a mess is the self who Jesus loves. Yet we do

not know or experience the depth of his love until we know and experience the extent to which we can be loved. This is why spiritual brokenness is necessary—it implies vulnerability (which we hate when we imagine it without love present). The crux: Unconditional love is not experienced because we dare not accept our horrifying helplessness.

The apostle Paul sounds like a loony to most when he writes, "I will boast all the more gladly of my weaknesses" (2 Cor 12:9). His speaking, however, is coming out of a neediness that has been met in Christ. His boast in weakness is so the power of Christ may rest on him. Through vulnerability he's been wrapped in God's love, and that just so happens to be the same place in which love, belonging, joy, courage, empathy, creativity, hope, and authenticity are also born. Without risk there's no connection, no relationship.

Luke 14 tells of Jesus' parable of the great banquet, in which the kingdom of God is compared to a feast. This wasn't the first time Jesus made such a comparison, and it wouldn't be the last (Luke 14:12–24). As the parable goes, the people on the guest list all had regrets, and regardless of their legitimacy the householder is miffed by their refusals. Yet he was going to have a party anyway, because he liked parties! So people who wouldn't normally attend a proper party— those who couldn't have found it with both eyes open and those who were sitting in doorways having a solo party of their own, drinking port out of a paper bag—were invited, and they came in droves. There's an interpretation of this parable that delves beyond the surface invitation to the less fortunate and reveals that in all of these dysfunctional folk are aspects of our own inner selves. Jesus' invitation is not a request to bring merely our holy and spiritual parts to the party, but also the untouchable, unpardonable, and unacceptable parts. Why? Because grace doesn't give two figs about rights and fairness and appropriate responses; it's not about revitalizing the living, but raising the dead. "Our fearful, angry and wounded parts of self can never be healed unless they are exposed to divine love. This is why we must meet God's love in our vulnerability and brokenness, not simply in our strength and togetherness" (David Benner).[18]

I HATE VALENTINE'S DAY. I CAN TRACE MY AVERSION TO THE holiday to as early as fourth grade. As I recall, our class spent a few hours decorating brown paper bags and then standing them along the windowsill. Everyone needed to write valentines and drop them into the corresponding person's bag the following day. That night I stayed up late to fill out the little store-bought valentines for each classmate. With care I wrote a note on each, decorated them, and taped on a Dum Dum sucker. With expectant joy I took my cards to school, distributing them into the parade of paper bags. Sometime during the day we went to collect our bags with their hidden treasures. When I turned over my bag, only four valentines fell out. Two were generic; nothing more than a signature. The other two sent me reeling; they were anti-valentines, which read something to the effect: "We don't like you. We wish you weren't in our class!"

For years I struck that episode from my memory. Then, one evening in the hills of West Virginia, on a mercy ministry trip as a high school student, the work teams gathered to worship and share about the day's events. As a team building exercise the staff worker passed out brown paper bags and slips of small paper, explaining that we were to write "hope notes" to each other. The situation suddenly felt familiar, and at once I was uneasy. This wasn't, however, fourth grade; it was a church mission trip. So I dismissed my apprehension and joined in, spending a good hour writing notes of encouragement to my teammates. When the activity was over, the leader handed out the bags and encouraged us to find a quiet place alone to read the notes and ponder God's love for us expressed through our teammates. One of the first notes I pulled from my bag was a hateful, nasty message. I was devastated. The emotions from years earlier slammed into me like a semi-truck barreling down the freeway. I struggle to this day with vulnerability, opening myself up to the opinions and comments of others. I'm just not certain if they will love me well. Trusting anyone is risky business, no ifs, ands, or buts about it.

Our greatest difficulty, however, isn't grief over hazardous exposure, but distrust of God's heart. Is he really present in every situation and relationship? Awakening to his presence in every situation is a challenge, but it is also a channel of soul-transformation. Transformation doesn't occur by chance or osmosis. It comes by consenting in the moment to where God's Spirit is leading, and staying sufficiently open—trusting in his heart when all that can be seen is darkness and disorder so his light may illuminate your soul.[19] Latent unconditional love isn't transformative; authentically showing up and allowing myself to be loved unconditionally is. In God's love we hear: I love *you*—but we neglect that final word. In that word we're given the gift of ourselves—personal histories, temperament, flaws, and foibles, all included. We're freed to release control—a knockout blow to the false self, the shadow-self, that pretends, evades, and hides.

Such vulnerability was exhibited by James Braddock, famed boxer of the Great Depression era. In *Cinderella Man*,[20] the cinematic portrayal of his life, there's a period in the film where he's down on his luck. With fractured hands and the loss of several bouts, he's slipped from a successful run in the ring to slinging sacks on the Jersey docks. One scene reveals how thoroughly difficult his state has become. His pride, however, has been overpowered by the stressful reality of starvation and brought him to a place of brokenness, enabling a hat-in-hand visit to the club where his manager and others relax in luxury. Braddock says:

> "The thing is I can't afford to pay the heat. I had to farm out my kids. You know, they keep cutting shifts down at the docks—you just don't get picked every day.
>
> "I sold everything I got that anybody would buy.
>
> "I went on public assistance. I signed on at the relief office. They gave me $19.00. I need another $18.38 so I can pay the bill and get the kids back.
>
> "You know me well enough to know that if I had anywhere else to go I wouldn't be here. If you could help me through this time, I sure would be grateful."

There's a brimming silence in response. Then, one man stands and reaches into his wallet. "Sure, Jim, sure." He puts a couple of dollars in Jim's flat cap. "Good luck." Jim waits.

A voice here and there calls to him. Most, however, look at the floor; a few look with disgust on the has-been. From across the room Jim's manager, Joe, looks on, anguish marring his face as Jim's eyes meet his own. Joe, nearly in tears, is obviously shocked by the extent of Jim's plight. The room seems to expand by a mile as Jim makes his way past censuring stares toward Joe. In a faint whisper Jim begs his pardon: "Joe, I'm sorry."

"What do you have to be sorry about?" replies Joe. "Jim, how short are ya?"
"About a dollar fifty."
"Okay." Joe reaches for his wallet.

In the next scene the Braddock kids burst through the door: "We're home! We're home!"

Now and again we must yield control to others, accepting our own vulnerability, so healing may come. Shutting down and avoiding vulnerability slams the door on connection and communion with God. "There can be no vulnerability without risk; there can be no commitment without vulnerability; there can be no peace, and ultimately no life, without community," writes M. Scott Peck.[21]

Need places us where we're ready to receive; our hands are empty. Knowing God well requires personal acquaintance with that which he's ready to give—namely, mercy, grace, and love. Simply hearing about divine love without a personal encounter with it fosters no connection. That's why spiritual intimacy is often forged and fortified in valleys; they're deeply personal and unavoidably real.

Community does not exist without risking vulnerability—community with God or anyone else. An abundant life is life in love and, thus, life in community. A friend of mine discovered this when he was invited to spend a week speaking to a group of missionaries.[22] While eating lunch with several of them one afternoon he listened as they spoke about those who had found Christ and those they had lost. They talked about their doubts and their faith, about their successes and failures. They rejoiced at how God healed their pain and they consoled one another over the pain that hadn't been healed. There were tears that day, but there was laughter and joy too. For a whole week my friend was fed by their transparency, vulnerability, and authenticity, but it also made him sad. For most Christian life isn't like that. It should be, but it's not.

The freedom of authenticity comes only with an honest assessment of a world full of loss and pain and uncertainty, realizing its intensity in one's own life and yet experiencing the calm of being borne by the Father's love. That's *abundant life*: spiritual connectedness cultivated by love— trust, respect, kindness, affection risked and offered often and freely.

The eighteenth-century German poet and philosopher Friedrich von Schiller noted that for plants and animals, nature not only sets the goal, but through instinct leads to it. Humans are different. The goal is given, but we are left to individually actualize it. We're faced with the possibility of failing to reach our individual destiny, of failing to become truly human and experience abundant life.[23] This is why we're summoned to self-awareness: the discovery of our true selves, our identity in the freedom of God's freely given love. "Paradoxically, the abundant life promised us in Christ comes not from grasping but from releasing.

It comes not from striving but from relinquishing. It comes not so much from taking as from giving," writes David Benner. "Surrender is the foundational dynamic of Christian freedom—surrender of my efforts to live my life outside of the grasp of God's love and surrender to God's will and gracious Spirit."[24] The price paid for authenticity, vulnerability, and humility, the risk of openness, clarity, and renunciation, is more than offset by the community gained with others, and even more so, by awakening to the One who alone gives security in poverty.

JOHN HALL WHEELOCK WROTE, "THE JOB OF AN EDITOR IN A publishing house is the dullest, hardest, most exciting, exasperating and rewarding of perhaps any job in the world. Most writers are in a state of gloom a good deal of the time; they need perpetual reassurance."[25] He's right; writing for others unrobes the real me.

I often write for hours trying to figure out what to write. When I pause to read over what I've just written, I very nearly burn it. But instead I drop my pen, don my workout clothes, and go for a run to clear my mind—no luck. I'll probably resort to my old ways, although I shouldn't: sending samples to a few select friends I'm sure will lie and say something reassuring. I'm an approval addict. If you don't give it to me, I'll find another who will.

I have a friend who is also a writer. He hides his manuscripts in a safety deposit box until his publisher releases the finished book. But it's not because he's less of an approval addict; his need for reassurance is equally elevated. It's just that he fears rejection more.

"I used to try to write better than certain dead writers of whose value I was certain," Ernest Hemingway reportedly said. "For a long time now I have tried simply to write the best I can. Sometimes I have good luck and write better than I can." Maybe he grew comfortable with turning it over to his editor, Maxwell Perkins, and hoped for the best—that's my tack. But maybe he didn't; after all, Hemingway committed suicide.

What is it like to simply be filled with the certainty that the All-Knowing, All-Powerful, and All-Loving has neither forgotten you, nor rejected you? Courageous living becomes a possibility when faith trusts that everything—even tears, throes, and losses—has purpose (Rom 8:28–30). Such vulnerability isn't foolishness; it's worship—an indispensable aspect of spiritual vitality.

The boxing ring is ours; we're alone. Yet we need community—not to reassure us, but to keep us connected to the promise that enables risk-taking. Dietrich Bonhoeffer has written well:

> The Christian needs another Christian who speaks God's Word to him. He needs him again and again when he becomes uncertain and discouraged, for by himself he cannot help himself without belying the truth. He needs his brother man as a barrier and proclaimer of the divine word of salvation. He needs his brother solely because of Jesus Christ. The Christ in his own heart is weaker than the Christ in the word of his brother; his own heart is uncertain, his brother's is sure.[26]

Faith neither controls results nor removes the possibility of pain. It simply trusts that the divine presence will make itself knowable. It seeks the movement of the Spirit, following willingly, relinquishing all claims and expectations. The writer to the Hebrews explains: "Faith is the assurance of things hoped for, the conviction of things not seen," namely, that he who loves will not forsake (Heb 11:1; 13:5).

In James Cameron's romantic epic *Titanic,* as the ship sinks, a desperate crowd gathers around a minister, who consoles them from the 23rd psalm. Does the crowd expect a miraculous rescue that will save them from the inevitable icy sea? If so, the majority of those who went into the water that night were disillusioned. The faithful are not disheartened by outcomes; they're secure in the hope that God forgets not his own, and even death cannot cut off the relationship he has begun with them.

It is natural to call out to God in distress; the psalmists even give voice to our deepest groaning. But take note, it is vulnerability that shows us the presence of the one to whom our call is directed. By awakening to his presence our fears are banished and openness, authenticity, affection, and affability freed. Shutting down emotionally or contending for control censors the Spirit's work in us for liberation from the false self.

Identifying my damaging impact on others and theirs on me is vulnerability; identifying my attitude toward and distrust of God is vulnerability; identifying my neediness is vulnerability. Yet until I risk resting my head on Jesus' chest and hearing his heartbeat, there's no peace with vulnerability, no connection, no deepening community.

He invites me to come as a little child (Matt 18:30). He doesn't command, but invites with his own vulnerable love, tenderness, and unimaginable kindness. When he stands at my door knocking—far too often after I've climbed into bed—he does so with nail-pierced hands promising a feast for my emaciated soul if I'll only risk coming to the door. Doing so, however, means I must crawl out from under my warm blankets and allow my true self to be released. I am loved, accepted, forgiven, and redeemed the way I am; that is security, and that enables me to risk freedom. An ephemeral eyeing of God's back under radiant moonlight, obscure as it may be, is nonetheless sufficiently real, transforming, and glorious.

Even in drowning we're already safe in his embrace.

5

drowning the victim

A MINISTER—A VETERAN IN THE MILITARY AND MISSION- ary fields with a doctoral degree in theology—received a call from a congregation he'd never visited and which had been declining in membership nearly since its inception twenty years before. With heartfelt sympathy he accepted the call, hoping that unabashed gospel preaching would revitalize the church.

His hope was romantic idealism.

Barely out of the blocks, he careened into the uncomfortable reality that the church is marked by the same frailties and failures as the world. Infighting and politicking ruled the tiny congregation, religiosity trumped spiritual reliance and prayer, and by the time he'd been there six months, half of the folks weren't.

That pastor was me.

Disenchanted with politics, disgusted with "religion," dispirited by spiritual deadness, my sunny hope of a genuine spiritual community had rounded a corner and slammed into a brick wall of facts. And without realizing it, I'd fallen into spiritual depression and become a Pharisee, confident everyone but me needed change.

Eventually God sent an elder brother into my life. After months of correspondence I felt free enough to unload not only my complaints but also my most concealed sins. My friend understood my disillusionment, sympathized with my desire to run, and yet found it neither fascinating nor unusual—the prophet Jeremiah had felt the same. "Remember what Augustine said," my friend asked me, "'the Church is a whore, but she's my mother.' Your problem is you've had an illusion of the church."

Many of our problems have their roots in the delusions we've nourished, obsessing over "ought-to-be" instead of "what-actually-is." It's easy to fall in love with an idealized caricature of the church, all the while hating the true bride upon whom Christ lavishes love and grace. Such romanticism may just lead to a messianic complex sure to get neighbors rising up with hammer and nail—yet few of us are ready to stand and confess that we're the problem.

More often, we see ourselves as the victim. When people are drowning, they often panic, even when a rescue swimmer is trying to save them. They thrash in a furious and frightened terror, seizing anything that will float. Sometimes they even climb onto the rescue swimmer with adrenaline-charged strength and drown him. So rescue swimmers are taught to break free by partially drowning the victim in order, ultimately, to save the person.

But as the victim, it's hard to see when we're preventing our own rescue—when we're the one that needs to be drowned.

A FRIEND OF MINE GREW UP IN A FERTILE VALLEY IN SOUTH Australia. Today that region produces some of the world's finest wine. A little way to the north, however, barely over the Mount Lofty Ranges, an endless sunbaked plain emerges. Sandy soil blankets hard limestone, making farming difficult. Farmers scratch clumps of limestone from the surface, heaping it into mounds to permit some semblance of agriculture. But each season the plows need to overturn more limestone.

Like those farmers, we may clear off as much sin from the surface of our lives as possible, but our inherent condition continues to unearth itself. It's been said, "'We are not sinners because we sin. We sin because we are sinners.' We are not theoretical sinners or honorary sinners or vicarious sinners. We are sinners indeed and in deed."[1] While Christians commonly confess this truth, many see their sin as a superficial blemish and everyone else's as a bottomless sinkhole. What produces such blindness?

Frederick Buechner sees the incongruity in how we live and traces it to our self-securing struggle:

> Starting with the rather too pretty young woman and the charming but rather unstable young man, who together know no more about being parents than they do the far side of the moon, the world sets in to making us what the world would like us to be, and because we have to survive after all, we try to make ourselves into something that we hope the world will like better than it apparently did the selves we originally were. ... Instead, we live out all the other selves which we are constantly putting

on and taking off like coats and hats against the world's weather.[2]

IN ANCIENT ISRAEL, MINISTERS USED POWER JUST AS SELF-ishly and abusively as the surrounding heathen nations, and the people were just as greedy, self-interested, and immoral. Speaking through Jeremiah, God said as much: "An appalling and a horrible thing has happened in the land: the prophets prophesy falsely, and the priests rule at their direction; my people love to have it so" (Jer 5:30–31).

Christians need the Holy Spirit not because they're pure and need protection from the polluted world, but because, like Israel, they're profane and need protection from the lies they perpetuate that keep them from being inconveniently unsettled. But why keep up with those lies? Professor John Webster suggests an answer:

> We lie because the truth is too painful or too shameful for us to face, or because the truth is simply inconvenient and has to be suppressed before it's allowed to disturb us. We invent lies because, for whatever reason, we want to invent reality. And the false reality which we invent, the world we make up by our lying, has one great advantage for us: It makes no claims on us. It demands nothing. It doesn't shape us in the way that truth shapes us; it faces us with no obligations; it has no hard, resistant surfaces which we can't get through. A lie is a made-up reality, and so never unsettles, never criticizes, never resists, never overthrows

us. It's the world, not as it is, but as we wish it to be: a world organized around us and our desires, the perfect environment in which we can be left at peace to be ourselves and to follow our own good or evil purposes.[3]

Left on our own we would remain entrenched in fantasy—constantly putting on and taking off coats and hats—for the aim of our hearts is "deceitful above all things, and desperately sick; who can understand it?" (Jer 17:9). Augustine knew the sickness of his own heart, and said:

> Do I then love in a man that which I, who am a man, hate to be? Man himself is a great deep, whose very hairs Thou numberest, O Lord, and they fall not to the ground without Thee. And yet are the hairs of his head more readily numbered than are his affections and the movements of his heart.[4]

In other words, we're enigmas to ourselves, blind to our own blindness, unconsciously incompetent. We play the victim.

California gangster Mickey Cohen's relationship with Christianity illustrates such blindness.[5] He quietly lived out his last years at his suburban Los Angeles home, dying of cancer on July 29, 1976. Mickey was alone when he stepped from this world. His wife had divorced him years earlier; there were no clamoring crowds of reporters, no dancing girls, no bodyguards. The over-publicized accounts of Mickey's exploits had faded from memory; even his public flirtation with Christianity became a minor story, buried in an old newspaper microfilm.

Why Mickey was first drawn to Christianity we will probably never know. Maybe he saw it as a way to gain respectability he could never earn on his own. Maybe he saw a glint of hope—and real power. Whatever it was, the image of Jesus knocking at the door compelled him as it has millions throughout the centuries. He began to open that door, only to discover that doing so involved a choice: he must surrender himself or close the door. When he finally understood what was demanded of him, what repentance meant, he closed the door. Mickey Cohen could not repent.

Granted, he was flamboyant and neurotic, a gangland figure guilty of every crime in the book; his guilt splashed across the headlines, and his sins were public knowledge (some of us have experienced that too).

But in voicing his comical, outrageous, poignant question—"What's the matter with being a Christian gangster?"—Cohen echoed millions of professing Christians who, though unwilling to admit it, pose the same question through their very lives—not about being Christian gangsters, but about being Christianized versions of whatever they already are and are determined to remain. People whose identity is determined by something other than Jesus alone, other commitments or traditions, are "hyphenated" Christians. Mickey was pinned to the earth unable to escape his contextual identity, and like him we also can neither love nor obey God and remain what we are. Repentance is necessary, and the God who calls us to himself in grace is neither blind nor shocked; he knows what we're really like.

Resistance to repentance, as well as the desire for a custom-made, "hyphenated" Christianity, is so unyielding because repentance not only involves regret and sorrow, but involves—and this is more fundamental—a change in reality; that is, a change in mind, which, any way you slice it, is royally humiliating. The biblical word for repentance is *metanoia* (from *meta* [change], and *noia* [mind])—resulting in "a change of mind." This is, however, no superficial change of thought: "I think I'll have Boston Cream Pie, instead of Chubby Hubby." Rather, it's a transformation or transmutation of consciousness, the whole inner nature—intellectual, affectional, and moral.[6] Archbishop Richard Trench noted that from its initial Greek usage, *metanoia* increased in depth until, in the New Testament, it came "to express that mighty change in mind, heart, and life wrought by the Spirit of God."[7]

That kind of change is nothing less than being capsized. Since, unsurprisingly, few embrace drowning, it's precisely here that iniquity is so insidious, whispering, "I'll keep you afloat. Swim from me, however, and you'll drown."

And it's absolutely right! Drowning will come. Such death, however, isn't death to life. It's death to death. Jesus said, "For whoever would save his life will lose it, but whoever loses his life for my sake will find it" (Matt 16:25). In other words, death is the only way to life, and without dying to ourselves we are—as strange as it sounds—dead to our true selves, enslaved to unreality.

Alternately, this could be expressed, "The way to win is to lose." Like drowning, folks typically don't volunteer to be on the losing team. That's why sin, which is insistent on living in unreality, remains so attractive—it's disguised as winning. Mickey Cohen had such a hard time with repentance because he was a winner; he won at all costs. But the flip side is that Jesus "saves losers and only losers. He raises the dead and only the dead. And he rejoices more over the last, the least, and the little than over all the winners in the world."[8]

THE BABYLONIANS WERE THE ANCIENT WORLD'S SUPER-power; they swept mighty Assyria off the board like plastic chess pieces and rendered Judah's alliances meaningless. Ezekiel and Jeremiah preached repentance with heartache, wept at the judgment to come, then pointed at life beyond brokenness. As Lamentations, authored probably by Jeremiah, reads:

> But this I call to mind,
>   and therefore I have hope:
> The steadfast love of the LORD never ceases;
>   his mercies never come to an end;
> they are new every morning;
>   great is your faithfulness.
> "The LORD is my portion," says my soul,
>   "therefore I will hope in him."
> The LORD is good to those who wait for him,
>   to the soul who seeks him.
> It is good that one should wait quietly
>   for the salvation of the LORD (Lam 3:21–26).

These encouraging words hold even more power when understood in context. Jeremiah witnessed the death of Jerusalem: Babylon laid siege to the city, and then, with Jerusalem on the edge of starvation, destruction rushed in. Thousands were killed and those who survived were deported. Jerusalem became a dusty ghost town. Yet through the cloud that was stirred up as they marched from the city, Jeremiah saw hope—not hope in spite of suffering, but because of it.

Centuries of misplaced "love" had made the Hebrews spiritually blind, deaf, and dumb. False prophets were honored while genuine prophets were persecuted; evil kings reigned, and lost priests led the people in debased worship. But the Lord was faithful to his covenant and became the deliverer who removed his people's blindness. Jeremiah and Ezekiel saw God's ultimate faithfulness beyond judgment—it's no coincidence that some of the most magnificent new covenant promises are contained in their writings (e.g., Jer 31:31–34; 33; Ezek 36–37).

The covenant God made with Abraham (and ratified in subsequent covenants) was unilateral: God alone bore responsibility for both sides. In Genesis 15, when animals were halved and placed in juxtaposing rows (forming an alley for the covenanters to pass between, signifying liability to the same fate if they broke the covenant) God alone passed between them. Abraham slept. The upshot of this scene is that if God failed to uphold his promises, he would fall under the covenant curse, but if Abraham (or his progeny) failed to uphold the promises, the onus would also be on God.

That's a crazy covenant!

In the death of Jerusalem, God's son, Israel (Exod 4:22) fell under a curse for having broken the Mosaic covenant, a covenant in which they pledged to personally perform the law as the terms for "living in the land." Yet the Lord didn't make an utter end of the nation (Jer 4:27). Rather, it was resurrected through a remnant, foreshadowing the scene in which his only begotten Son, who will not in the least be spared, would make a radical resurrection from the depths of death. God would unilaterally bring about the salvation of his people through Abraham's seed, namely, Jesus (Gen 22:18).

We can't afford to miss the fact that only God could uphold the covenant obligations (Abrahamic or Mosaic); that is why he alone ratified the Abrahamic covenant under which the subsequent ones fit. In other words, at the beginning God made a way to life beyond the broken covenant. The new covenant, in which he would write his law on his people's hearts (Jer 31:33), is erected on Abrahamic grace.

But how is the law written on hearts? God simply writes the words of his love song there, the same song the prophets sang in exile. It's what propelled their hope and endeared them to their God. "We love because he first loved us," says John (1 John 4:19)—love is the heart of the law (Matt 22:37; Rom 13:10). We too must remember this promise of life beyond brokenness.

SOMETIMES CHRISTIANS ARE STUPID AND SPOIL IT. SOMEtimes Christians are stinkers and know it. Sometimes Christians muster all the wisdom and prayer possible and blow it. It's times like these when either you throw in the towel, or you surrender to the reality that you are not in control and need grace.

Regardless of our response, the pain experienced through an incident is unclouded; what's cloudy is how God is building faith with it. How ripping us from the stranglehold our illusions and idols have on us, extinguishing our self-produced light and plunging us into darkness, actually enables true sight. John was getting at this when he wrote of Christ: "In him was life, and the life was the light of men. The light shines in the darkness, and the darkness has not overcome it" (John 1:4–5).

So why hang on to our illusions, idols, and light? Without a doubt, it's because of what they promise. Above I said that they promise life; they also promise reward.

Sometimes I desire a reward after a hard day's work. Sometimes I want one for just having gotten out of bed in the morning. But the desire for a reward isn't "darkness"— darkness is the willingness to settle for a weak and lifeless reward. In Jeremiah's language, it's not the desire for water that is misguided, but digging cisterns that are broken and can hold no water (Jer 2:13). This is where the Spirit of God enters, leading us toward living water and true light.

Too often, though, we mistake the direction of the Spirit's leading. The Spirit is guiding us to freedom and abundance, but all we see is burdensome rules obliging us to die to all desires, leading us, we suspect, to somewhere horrible. But C. S. Lewis refutes such a thought:

> The New Testament has lots to say about self-denial, but not about self-denial as an end in itself. We are told to deny ourselves and to take up our crosses in order that we may follow Christ; and nearly every description of what we shall ultimately find if we do so contains an appeal to desire. If there lurks in most modern minds the notion that to desire our own good and earnestly to hope for the enjoyment of it is

a bad thing, I submit that this notion has crept in from Kant and the Stoics and is no part of the Christian faith. Indeed, if we consider the unblushing promises of reward and the staggering nature of the rewards promised in the Gospels, it would seem that Our Lord finds our desires, not too strong, but too weak. We are half-hearted creatures, fooling about with drink and sex and ambition when infinite joy is offered us, like an ignorant child who wants to go on making mud pies in a slum because he cannot imagine what is meant by the offer of a holiday at the sea.[9]

Even though we're promised so much more than a dingy back alley, we scream bloody murder at the suggestion of leaving the mud. That's because we naturally assign all pain to the "bad" bucket. At the very thought of pain, our head and heart make a pact against us—"You shall not pass!" they scream.

Yet not all pain is bad. Consider the pain experienced during physical training. Thirty intense minutes on a treadmill leaves you sweaty and your muscles sore, including your diaphragm, which works overtime to keep you from passing out. That's good pain. It's leading to something positive: the building of muscle, the cutting of fat, and the provision of a well-deserved lunch for your neurons. If you don't wrench your knee, the result is improved health. Indeed, such pain is very different from when your knee does blow out. So, Jane Fonda rightfully ripped off Ben Hei, a second-century rabbi who said, "According to the pain is the gain."[10]

Legitimate pain is necessary to move into spiritual maturity, to become fully conscious. Detouring around legitimate pain only leads to more, unnecessary pain—neurotic pain. "Neurosis is always a substitute for legitimate suffering," said Carl Jung.[11] Therefore, in trying to avoid legitimate pain, neuroses pile up like bricks, until we're stuck behind a barricade of our own making. Without help dismantling the wall, our spirits starve and shrivel. This tendency of ours to avoid problems, and certainly emotional suffering, means all of us are, to one degree or another, malnourished mentally and spiritually.[12] We're all victims of our own unrealities.

The pain of repentance, of giving up our self-made reality, is like other pain insofar as they share the instinctual sense that our well-being is in jeopardy or our connection to ourselves and others is being diminished. This triggers a shift in our emotions, which we typically counter with resistance: denying something said or done; dodging interactions that may lead to truly being known; avoiding opportunities to peer deep inside ourselves (by keeping busy or defensively blocking others); or even finding consolation in crying, resolving to remain alone at sea. In such moments, the lower temporal cortex (responsible for activity we're not immediately conscious of) fires on all cylinders, and electrical waves oscillate across our brains like a tsunami, integrating our functions and emotions, which bleed out through our body language.[13] These physical reactions actually boost our emotional state like a feedback loop reinforcing the barricade against collapse.

Undefended living comes not from fortifying the barricade, but from its collapse. Awareness of true life is experienced in brokenness on the far side of emotional discomfort. The torment sustained, which the soul experiences by pressing into such pain instead of running, is the legitimate pain that crucifies us in one reality in order to be resurrected in another.

Years ago, Dr. Larry Crabb successfully battled cancer, and for many long years his cancer was in remission. However, the cancer returned; malignant nodules reappeared on his liver, and there wasn't enough liver remaining after previous surgeries to permit further dissection. Crabb's prayer letter contained a vulnerable openness to push into his soul's pain accompanying the difficult news and fear. He wrote:

> I value prayers for my health, of course; but I even more value prayers that God's Spirit would do His work that will allow me to welcome whatever comes as an opportunity to reveal Christ's sustaining grace in my inner being, and to display Christ's never compromised love no matter the circumstances.[14]

There is purpose in his pain: To know and reveal the grace and love of Christ in whatever the circumstances. A longing to be further awakened to God's grace through his ordeal fills his consciousness, so he has surrendered to the pain rather than fight it.

Because the epicenter of spiritual awakening is in our thought life (our consciousness), Jesus' instruction to love God with our minds and Paul's words—to be transformed by the renewal of our minds—are not surprising (Luke 10:27; Rom 12:2). Thoughts are even at the heart of the unconscious fear of losing our present reality in repentance. If, however, the epicenter is the mind, then our mind is where life begins anew. A change of thought effects our emotions, opening a relational space with God in which the fight against his Spirit is overcome by a greater passion—namely, to know and reveal God.

Being ripped from unreality is a necessary part of awakening. Without it, there is neither growth in self-knowledge nor God-knowledge. Pain is a paradox of grace.

My cousin Mike is a dozen years older than me. He was hockey skating and checking before I could walk, so it's no surprise that we weren't particularly close in our early years. Sharing our stories of spiritual awakening and transformation, however, has closed the gap.

After fifteen years in the pastorate and in spite of a growing congregation, the wicked shimmy of Mike's life could no longer be ignored. By night he would lay awake in bed ruminating on church growth strategies. By day he would demand twenty-plus hours a week from volunteer leaders in exchange for a few measly hours with him. If they didn't produce, he replaced them—leaders revolved through the ministry faster than horses on a carousel. Mike was spinning out of control.

Finally, he broke. He struggled to remember his phone number and address; he found himself repeatedly curled in a corner crying uncontrollably; and he turned suicide over and over in his mind. That's when his wife called an elder brother who didn't shilly-shally in confronting Mike's destructive behavior. Mike was quickly removed from ministry (many rejoiced); placed on a three-month sabbatical to get his life sorted; and forbidden to have contact with anyone at the church.

When he first met Christ, he had dreamed of serving him full time. God had made that dream come true, but now all balanced on the brink of an irreversible collapse— had God put him in the penalty box, or even ejected him from the game? Why had Mike been willing to hurt so many in the pursuit of success? The dark clouds rolling in forced him to find shelter.

The first month of his sabbatical he spent resting under the watchful eyes of his family at a beach house in Nags Head, North Carolina. During that month he oscillated between crushing despair, brought on by guilt and shame, and an all-consuming numbness. It took ten days before he could even sleep through the night, and God still seemed beyond reach.

The second month he spent in a prayer sanctuary in Kansas City, Missouri, where live worship music echoed twenty-four hours a day, seven days a week. (For years unbroken praise had lifted from that room.) Yet even there a shadow remained over his soul.

Most of the time he was critical and angry: Why were the people there oblivious to each other, let alone the worship band? It took time for him to understand that the atmosphere was one of devotional rest. Those who sang were interceding. So there Mike sat, one week turned into two— still no fireworks.

But something was happening: the "great" man of faith, the visionary, the church planter was dying. He came to accept that his ministry was over. Something else also stirred in his soul: a deep hunger, a desire to live, and a desire for Christ. His turmoil continued to burn like an unquenchable torch, and through tears he pleaded for God's presence.

Only after he'd been consumed by grief, only after he truly died, wanting nothing but Christ himself, did it happen: God began to call his attention to scriptures he'd previously blown past. The bridegroom paradigm nearly knocked the wind out of him, as God pressed into his consciousness that the Hound of Heaven was in full cry.

God pursued Mike like a bridegroom pursues his bride. God wasn't mad. Rather, God was waiting and desiring Mike (Song 7:10). The critical question was whether Mike would allow himself to be caught.

For weeks he bloodied his nose against this truth; not until his strength was utterly depleted did he surrender. As he tells it, that was the moment he truly awakened. Love flooded his soul, washing him, setting him free. For the first time he experienced the pleasure of just being in God's presence. Gone was the need to measure himself against others or his own standards. He was free to be a beloved son.

One night when leaving the prayer room, he bumped into a group of young adults. Observing his flushed face, one of them inquired, "Hey man ... you alright?"

"Oh yeah," Mike replied, "I just spent two hours of my life sitting at the feet of Jesus doing nothing, and it felt great! When I meet Mary of Bethany one day, I'll tell her, 'I finally got it!' "

RICHARD FOSTER SAID, "THE HEART OF GOD IS AN OPEN wound of love. He aches over our distance and preoccupation. He mourns that we do not draw near to him.

He grieves that we have forgotten him. He weeps over our obsession with muchness and manyness. He longs for our presence."[15] Mike's drive (no less my own) to be "perfectly" successful transcended his desire for God. His all-or-nothing mentality, coupled with his misplaced focus, had to die. To extract our identity and life from illusions and idols is foolishness. It's like trying to quench your thirst by drinking seawater—it only leads to death. But to a sunbaked, dehydrated castaway afloat on the sea, resisting the urge to drink seawater also feels like death.

The Lord measures out pain precisely to move us into his arms. Too little, and we'd survive by hanging onto flotsam. Too much, and we'd get stuck in Davy Jones's locker. The perfect amount capsizes our ship of safety, so God alone may save drowning sailors.

So while we're so very far from reality's shore, tossing and turning every which way in the open sea, God preempts the climax of our struggling and pulls us under. If you think carefully about that, it's a comforting thought. For it means even in drowning we're already safe in his embrace. When the light of this truth dawns on us, fighting ceases. Thomas Merton understood this; he writes:

> Surrender your poverty and acknowledge your nothingness to the Lord. Whether you understand it or not, God loves you, is present in you, lives in you, dwells in you, calls you, saves you and offers you an understanding and compassion which are like nothing you have ever found in a book or heard in a sermon.[16]

The covenantal God searches the seas of our fantasy for us. He carries us to the beach where he feeds and heals us in the light of his grace. Yet that salvation arrives only through our death that accompanied repentance. In such legitimate pain the cry "Abba! Father!" begins to sound from our souls, and we begin to awaken to the fact that our identity and righteousness are held not in ourselves, but in Christ. The words of the apostle Paul at last make sense: "I have been crucified with Christ. It is no longer I who live, but Christ who lives in me. And the life I now live in the flesh I live by faith in the Son of God, who loved me and gave himself for me" (Gal 2:20).

Centuries after Jeremiah and Ezekiel, Paul wrote of his longing to be found in Christ. He had arrived at the end of himself, where neither his pedigree nor accomplishments amounted to a hill of beans. He could not control himself, let alone others, and he knew it. Therefore, to the church in Philippi he wrote:

> Whatever gain I had, I counted as loss for the sake of Christ. Indeed, I count everything as loss because of the surpassing worth of knowing Christ Jesus my Lord. For his sake I have suffered the loss of all things and count them as rubbish, in order that I may gain Christ and be found in him, not having a righteousness of my own that comes from the law, but that which comes through faith in Christ, the righteousness from God that depends on faith—that I may know him and the power of his resurrec-

tion, and may share his sufferings, becoming
like him in his death, that by any means possible I may attain the resurrection from the dead
(Phil 3:7–11).

Living in reality involves dying to all counterfeit realities, because true life rests in the life and righteousness of
another, like a child who relies on the provisions and protection of a parent. To know spiritual resurrection and transformation of consciousness, being weaned from ourselves
through repentance, is the chasm of death we must cross.

J. C. Ryle once said, "The beginning of all true Christianity is to discover that we are guilty, empty, needy sinners.
Until we know that we are lost, we are not in the way to
be saved. The very first step towards heaven is to be thoroughly convinced that we deserve hell."[17] Such convincing
is the rescuing work of God's Spirit. It is not, however, a solitary event, but a lifelong voyage as the Spirit ushers us ever
further into unknown territory, where we realize how lost
and needy we are. There, our true self emerges with child-
like innocence, unwavering in the awareness of who we
are, refusing to be held captive, terrorized, contaminated
by peers "whose lives are spent not in living but in courting
applause and admiration; not in blissfully being themselves
but in neurotically comparing and competing, striving for
those empty things called success and fame even if they can
be attained only at the expense of defeating, humiliating,
destroying their neighbors" (Anthony De Mello).[18]

The place to which the Spirit leads is indeed a place
where hell on earth, the utter desolation of our unreal fantasies, and the pains of death are encountered. Yet it's also
where resurrection is promised beyond brokenness and real

life waits to be enjoyed in ever-greater fullness. In death we gain the fullness of life.

Suffering blindfolds us, forcing us to walk by faith in nothing but the promise that God is there and has a purpose.

6

peering beyond the depths

THE POET CARL SANDBURG WROTE WHAT HE CLAIMED TO be the shortest poem in English literature: "Born. Troubled. Died."

Can you relate?

Since the Enlightenment, the pursuit of personal happiness has not only become synonymous with "the good life," but has been sought largely through freedom from restraints. Such "freedom" is anchored to the belief that life on our own terms secures gratification and relieves pain.

The thoroughly depressing film *The Hours* depicts the novelist Virginia Woolf convalescing in the English countryside as a remedy for stress in hopes of preserving her sanity. One day she goes for a stroll that ends in her sulking on a train platform bound for London. The sentiments of modern society are reflected in her protests when her husband attempts to bring her home:

"Virginia, we must go home now. Nelly is cooking dinner. She's already had a very difficult day. It's our obligation to eat Nelly's dinner."

"There's no such obligation. No such obligation exists."

"Virginia, you have an obligation to your own sanity."

"I've endured this custody. I have endured this imprisonment."

"Oh, Virginia."

"I am attended by doctors everywhere. I am attended by doctors who informed me of my own interests."

"They know your interests."

"They do not! They do not speak for my interests."

"Virginia, I can see that it must be hard for a woman of your talents to see that she may not be the best judge of her own condition."

"Who, then, is a better judge?"

"You have a history! You have a history of confinement. We brought you to Richmond, because you have a history of fits, moods, blackouts, hearing voices. We brought you here to save you from the irrevocable damage you intended upon yourself. You've tried to kill yourself twice. I live daily with that threat. ... We set up the printing press not just for itself, not just purely for itself, but so you might have a ready source of absorption, and a remedy."

"What, like needlework?"

"It was done for you! It was done for your betterment! It was done out of love! If I didn't know you better I'd call this ingratitude."

"I am ungrateful? You call me ungrateful. My life has been stolen from me. I'm living in a town I have no wish to live in. I'm living a life I have no wish to live. How did this happen? It is time for us to move back to London. I miss London. I miss London life." ...

"If you were thinking, clearly, Virginia, you'd recall that it was London that brought you low. ..."

"If I were thinking clearly, Leonard, I would tell you that I wrestle alone in the dark, in the deep dark, and that only I can know, only I can understand my own condition. You live with the threat, you tell me you live with the threat of my extinction. Leonard, I live with it too. This is my right. It is the right of every human being. I choose not the suffocating antiseptic of the suburbs but the violent jolt of the capital. That is my choice. The meanest patient, yes, even the very lowest is allowed some say in the matter of her own prescription. Thereby she defines her humanity."[1]

There lies the origin of our headlong rush into a happiness that results in misery—we alone feel our woes, and therefore, we reason, we alone must know the remedy. The discovery that our happiness is not happiness at all, however, spurs some to use their freedom to "free" themselves from the debilitating and condemning freedom of such happiness—what existentialist Albert Camus called "the first philosophical question": suicide.

God, you must care, but I don't understand why you don't intervene. Why do you allow terrorism, war, abuse, famine, crime, and selfishness? Why don't you give purpose to my days? Why don't you melt the heart of an offending spouse and bring about reconciliation? Why did my father spend that day working tirelessly in Charleston's sweltering heat to be rewarded with a myocardial infarction? His sore muscles should have relaxed with Anheuser-Busch's finest, not stiffened in rigor mortis at the county morgue. Where were you? Do you *really* care, God?

Pain stirs us to ask questions of meaning and meaninglessness; it awakens us to our humanity; it prods us for answers as to why we make our struggles an end in themselves, drowning the rescuer who swims out to help. Yet we live in a world that lulls us, telling us it's easier to stay asleep. We steel ourselves against the uncomfortable realities behind the door, aiming to remain in perpetual happiness. Happy is advertised as the norm, pain as abnormal. We want normalcy! Where some, like Virginia Woolf, prescribe an overdose of the realities behind the door, others bolt it shut. Recently a dear friend described to me his prescription for pain. He wrote:

> For most of my life, I never associated the word "pain" with anything but physical pain. I put emotional and psychological pain in a different category and chose to avoid it. The effect this had was to limit my emotional experience and even bring me to a point where I didn't treat

my feelings as a reliable source of information about what I was experiencing. Ultimately I became cut off emotionally from other people and even God.

In the eleventh season of the television show *Grey's Anatomy,* Amelia Shepherd, a young neurosurgeon who feels that everyone she's ever loved has died and who has repeatedly hid from pain through addiction to prescription drugs and alcohol, is reeling in grief after the death of her brother Derek Shepherd, the show's star neurosurgeon. Owen Hunt, a former Army trauma surgeon and Amelia's love interest, confronts her as she is on the verge of diving again into prescription drug abuse:

> "All that stuff you're managing, you're not supposed to be managing it. You're supposed to be feeling it. Grief, loss, pain ... it's normal."
>
> "It's not normal," replies Amelia.
>
> "It is normal. It's not normal to you, because you've never done it. Instead of feeling it, feeling the grief and the pain, you shove it all down and do drugs instead of moving through the pain. You run from the pain.
>
> "Instead of being hurt and alone and afraid that this horrible empty feeling is all there is, I run from it too. I am off and sign up for another tour of duty.
>
> "We do these things, we run off, we medicate, we do whatever it takes to cover it up and dull this sensation of pain, but it's not normal. We are supposed to love, and hurt, and grieve,

and break, and be destroyed, and rebuild ourselves to be destroyed again.

"That's humanity, that's being human, that's
being alive, that's the point. That's the entire
point. Don't avoid it. Don't extinguish it."[2]

To not acknowledge and wrestle with pain—our reality
of the present moment—is to define ourselves as either a
cynic, a melancholic, or a suicide.[3] "Ignoring our emotions
is turning our back on reality; listening to our emotions
ushers us into reality. And reality is where we meet God"
(Dan Allender and Tremper Longman).[4]

Did you know that turkeys and eagles react differently
to storms? A turkey runs around, and eventually heads for
cover beneath the barn, wishing the wind away. The eagle
leaves the security of its nest and takes to the wind.
It spreads its wings and rides the air currents of the coming
storm, enjoying the fact that they will take it higher than it
could've soared on its own. When storms come near, which
are you?

PROFESSOR AND AUTHOR HOWARD HENDRICKS ONCE
quipped that there are neither correspondence courses in
swimming nor distance-learning experiences in suffering—
only deeply, inescapably personal ones.[5] Suffering may be
a mark of our existential authenticity, but if we aren't supposed to extinguish it and can't escape it, what are we to do
with it? What's its purpose?

Without an answer, suffering becomes a thing to be
avoided at all costs. But in the darkness, our refrains are
not unlike those of the psalmist. The Psalms of Ascent

(Psalms 120–134) are songs Israelite pilgrims sang as they made their way together to visit the temple for festivals three times a year. The songs helped the pilgrims to think about the heights and depths of life in concert with God's faithfulness. In other words, they sang perspective over their souls. Psalm 130 opens:

> Out of the depths I cried to you, O LORD
>   O LORD, hear my voice!
> Let your ears be attentive
>   to the voice of my pleas for mercy!

When we're most in touch with distress, we're also most in touch with longing for its removal, and thereby open to the one who can remove it. Pain ekes out a plea for the divine. As Eugene Peterson observes, "We accept suffering; we believe in God. The acceptance and the belief both emerge out of those times when 'the bottom has fallen out' of our lives."[6]

God doesn't receive our pain as appeasement for his wrath. Rather, when the bottom falls out of our lives, when we've come face to face with the horror and depth of our sin, when we know the pangs of enduring the sins of others, we are, like no other time, ready to receive the mercy and grace of Christ with gratitude, to even see his movement in the smallest acts of kindness bestowed by others. Our souls are revived, awakened further to God. Joe Church, a missionary revivalist in Uganda in the 1940s, observed, "Revival is not the roof blowing off, but the bottom falling out."[7] For then we are open to being formed and filled with the life of the Lord Jesus. "Revival is just the life of the Lord Jesus poured into human hearts" (Roy Hession).[8]

Famed 1970s songwriter Paul Williams essentially dropped off the edge of the world somewhere around the mid-1980s—some actually thought he had died. He found rock bottom in a high-octane plunge precipitated by alcohol and substance abuse—but rather than shutting it out, his pain ultimately changed him:

> What happened to me is that I wound up finding a place in this world through my recovery that is bigger and more important than anything I ever did as an entertainer. I don't think it is accurate to say that I had so much more and that I was unhappy and I have so much less now. Because I've got more now, to me, you know? I mean, my life is pretty interesting right now. And I've got to tell you, the last couple of years have really [messed] up the end of your movie, and I love that.[9]

He experienced deep personal pain in his life: when his father died in a car crash; when he was separated from his mother; when he was sent to live with his aunt in California due to finances. The pain fueled and gave depth to many of his transparent and touching songs. It was becoming a certified drug rehabilitation counselor and an author after his own recovery, however, that gave him purpose. In one interview he said, "The first thing I did when I got sober at 49, I called my friend Nacho, who is a Methodist minister, and I said, 'Nacho, I have got to get baptized,' and he said, 'Well, sure we can do that someday,' and I said, 'No, I got to get baptized today,' and he said, 'Really, okay, well, get a couple of witnesses and we will do it.' I had my last drink on September of '89. ... I get up in the morning and I say basically two sentences to start my day in the morning. I say, 'Surprise me, God,' which implies complete trust. I am handing the reins of my day to the Big Amigo: 'surprise me, God.' My second sentence is, 'Lead me where you need me,' because if I am someplace where I am needed I'm not in the way. ... My life is a lot easier if I am thinking about other people instead of about myself all of the time."[10]

Pain has a purpose.

It may be growing you, by way of your own story, to a place of greater balance and love. But it's not always about you—perhaps others are awakening as you endure their suffering vicariously. Sometimes suffering is redemptive in that it is personally painful to forgo your rights, to pull back from retaliation, to walk the trail of total forgiveness without asking for anything in return. Willingness to suffer for others continues Christ's redemptive action (Col 1:24). God works out his purpose in and through you and others in the world, and it's impossible to sort out when he's doing what.

British journalist Malcolm Muggeridge spoke well when he said:

> Contrary to what might be expected, I look back on experiences that at the time seemed especially desolating and painful with particular satisfaction. Indeed, I can say with complete truthfulness that everything I have learned in my 75 years in this world, everything that has truly enhanced and enlightened my experience, has been through affliction and not through happiness.[11]

Happiness makes a miserable tutor! It does nothing to unsettle and disrupt the status quo; its puissance insufficiently fosters new questions, deeper searching, or stirring the spirit to richer, more vibrant hues of dependent, creaturely life.

The one who journeys into the depths and learns the contours and crevices of the terrain also learns to have a greater appreciation of the heights. For ironically in their true nature they're the same. What are the heights *or* depths if not places that bring us into greater awareness of God? Pain, therefore, constitutes a potter's wheel on which our soul is formed and reworked to existential authenticity, as well as our essential and eternal humanity.[12] We're self-aware, unlike animals, and such capacity is particularly connected to our awareness of the future, of anxiety, and of death. Animals live in the present. They feel pain, but we alone anticipate the future in terms of anxiety and hope. "Hope," as Thornton Wilder wrote in *Theophilus North*, "is a projection of the imagination; so is despair. Despair all too readily embraces the ills it foresees; hope is an energy and arouses the mind to explore every possibility to combat them."[13] Faith takes hope by the hand and assures it of a future (Heb 11:1).

We, therefore, have the capacity to react counterintuitively to suffering as self-conscious and self-determining creatures. In fact, the scriptures enjoin such thoughts (see 2 Cor 5:7; 4:18; Rom 8:25). "Whether by fighting it or accepting it, whether by surrendering to it or by opening ourselves to its purifying power, whether by protesting against or by integrating it into our lives and making it part of our identity," we have, unlike animals, the dexterity to find meaning and use in pain.[14] Nietzsche's little gibe is insightful: "If we possess our *why* of life, we can put up with almost any *how*. Man does not strive after happiness—only the Englishman does that."[15] Having ruled out the divine, he never discovered the "why" and committed suicide. The cross provides the "why" and encourages us to press into pain without fear—to, in fact, attend to God there.

What longings does pain awaken in you? Are you catching sight of the passions that have the greatest control over you? Maybe it's a passion for being special, doing something significant, having security, being supple and stretchable, being connected and intimately known, being sexually fulfilled, finding self-actualization, or even being spiritually formed. The realization of how such passions drive you—how they, rather than God himself, have become your Mecca of Happiness—points you to God and to whatever is blocking deeper communion with him.

Often I've dwelt on my own disappointments, failures, shortcomings, and unfulfilled expectations. My passion to see transformation in myself and others is at times so intense that I lash out in anger and frustration, or cower in disillusionment and depression. At times I feel that if I had the cash I could easily follow Paul Williams down the rabbit hole. Brennan Manning knew the contours of that hole and all of its rooms well. In his memoir, *All Is Grace*, he confesses:

> At the peak of my speaking ministry I began a game with Roslyn, with myself, and even with God. It was an adult version of my childhood game Ringolevio—hide and come find me. I often over scheduled myself, allowing only a

few days between speaking engagements that were usually on opposite coasts. The rules of my game were these: I would finish the engagement, get a hotel room near the airport, close myself in, and drink. I wouldn't call Roslyn, or any one for that matter, to "check in." The seclusion might last for one to four days. And there you have it: hide and come find me, a child's game played by a grown man.[16]

What is going on here? Doesn't this spiritual giant know Christ? Is this just another example of hypocrisy in the church?

Such thoughts utterly fail to grasp the terrain of the Christian life. They're an affront to grace. The struggle of the Christian life is aiming to see the darkness within ourselves, to truly see where our passions take us, how our goals and values and prescriptions are so titillating and seductive, and yet to find Jesus' grace applied to us in those places—tangibly, not theoretically. We seek to experience his loving presence down the rabbit hole—it's the only thing that brings us out again and into deeper communion. Sometimes I drive myself to such dark places; sometimes I have a chauffeur.

Primo Levi, an Auschwitz survivor, told how on one occasion he huddled in his barracks and, parched, reached through the window for an icicle to provide some moisture for his dry mouth. But before he could wet his cracked lips, a guard snatched the icicle from him, shoving him away from the window. When he asked *why*, the guard responded, "Here, there is no *why*."

Confused, angry, resentful: are you wondering what wrong turn you've made, what peccadilloes you're being punished for? That's how Job felt (Job 19:6–7; 30:19–20). Are you questioning God's love and goodness, asking along with Job, "Does it seem good to you to oppress, to despise the work of your hands and favor the designs of the wicked?" (Job 10:3). John the Baptist felt that way too (Matt 11:2–11). Anne Graham Lotz asks, "Are you interpreting his love by your circumstances, instead of interpreting your circumstances by his love? ... Getting what we want, when we want it is not always the best for us or glorifying to God."[17]

WILLIAM PAUL YOUNG'S NOVEL *THE SHACK* EXPLORES GOD'S work through pain and how he awakens us through it to love beyond our wildest dreams. The novel tells of a man, Mackenzie, who is lost in grief years after his daughter was abducted during a family vacation. One day he receives a mysterious note summoning him to the Oregon wilderness for a weekend hosted by Papa. In the wilderness, Young brings the persons of the Trinity into dialogue with Mack. In one scene, the Holy Spirit, personified as an Asian woman named Sarayu, takes Mack deep into the woods to do some gardening.

> The place where they stood was an open spot surrounded on three sides by peach and cherry trees, and in the middle was a cascade of purple and yellow flowered bushes that almost took his breath away.

"Mackenzie." She pointed directly at the incredible purple and yellow patch. "I would like your help clearing this entire plot of ground. There is something very special that I want to plant here tomorrow, and we need to get it ready." She looked at Mack and reached for the scythe.

"You can't be serious! This is so gorgeous and in such a secluded spot."

But Sarayu didn't seem to notice. Without further explanation, she turned and began destroying the artistic display of flowers. She cut cleanly, seemingly without any effort.

Mack shrugged, donned his gloves, and began raking into piles the havoc she was wreaking. He struggled to keep up. It might not be a strain for her, but for him it was labor. Twenty minutes later the plants were all cut off at the roots, and the plot looked like a wound in the garden. Mack's forearms were etched with cut marks from the branches he had piled in one spot. He was out of breath and sweating, glad to be finished. Sarayu stood over the plot, examining their handiwork.

"Isn't this exhilarating?" she asked.

"I've been exhilarated in better ways," Mack retorted sarcastically.

"Oh, Mackenzie, if you only knew. It's not the work, but the purpose that makes it special. And," she said, smiling at him, "it's the only kind I do."[18]

The cutting down and ripping out of what, by anyone's evaluation, is a lovely patch of purple and yellow flowers is illogical. What we cannot see, however, is what the Lord intends to plant in its place. Faith realizes the necessity of distress and that such arises when we collide into obstructed hopes, dreams, expectations, longings, emotions, and inner drives. Such obstacles can cast us into *passions* of a different sort (from the Latin for "sufferings"): hurts, failures, family tensions, personality struggles, employment troubles, secret temptations, negative emotions, and bitter disappointments. In other words, passion can alert us to our ruling passions—the ways of living and thinking full of self-protective, self-centered relating. It can alert us to the life that is, to the life that is lost, and to the life that is longed for. Hence it can awaken a holy passion to move toward God's perspective, and a passion to have his life manifest in ours that we might become the *imago Dei* (2 Cor 4:8–11). Pain, then, carries us into communion with God in a most counterintuitive manner. It whispers, "You are not alone. In your longing you are united to Christ." The adage is true: You will not actually know Jesus is all you need until Jesus is all you have.

So through pain, God works out his purposes. In his first letter, Peter says: "Now for a little while, if necessary, you have been grieved by various trials, so that the tested genuineness of your faith—more precious than gold that perishes though it is tested by fire—may be found to result in praise and glory and honor at the revelation of Jesus Christ" (1 Pet 1:6–7). The flowering bushes cleared to make space for something, the Spirit's scythe cutting through, the refiner's fire burning, the potter's wheel turning: something glorious and valuable and precious—namely, a child of God who trusts when he doesn't understand and follows when she doesn't know where she's being led—is being reared for the glory of God and an imperishable inheritance (1 Pet 1:4–9).

Transformation includes pain—not always, but often enough. The question is: Will your pain awaken hope—and along with it, a willingness to push into that pain and open, allowing God to bring about his purposes in your life? Or will you harden, and prescribe your own remedy in defense of your dignity?

Twentieth-century German theologian Helmut Thielicke saw that the basis of our dignity is not in what others do to us or what happens to us, but in God's promise. In other words, my dignity is not a quality of my human state, but rather an "alien dignity"—it is held secure in the heart of the one who calls me by my name, and, in fact, gives me my name. Thielicke writes, "The consistency of our identity is the consistency of God's faithfulness."[19]

Audrey Wetherell Johnson's story shows this tangibly. Born in England, raised in an agnostic family, and a student of atheistic philosophy, she became a missionary to China in the 1930s. She became a gifted Bible teacher who instructed many pastors and church leaders at the theological seminary in Beijing; later, she was interned with other missionaries in a Japanese concentration camp in Shanghai as World War II invaded China. For three years she endured intolerable and unmentionable suffering, which robbed her of her health and ministry. At the time of her release she was already in her 50s. Little did she know that her subsequent time of forced rest in California would lead to numerous invitations to speak to students at InterVarsity

Christian Fellowship camps, as well as to others at colleges, seminaries, and conferences.

One day after church she was approached by five ladies who asked her to give them a Bible study. Her simple home study grew and expanded into a nearby church. Within a short period folks in other cities began asking her to start studies in their areas. A few years later Bible Study Fellowship was born, a ministry that today reaches a million internationally. It all stemmed from Johnson's painful and transformative personal journey. In the introduction to her autobiography she writes, "What I would have missed had I not cried out as an agnostic to God and discovered that I was 'created for commitment' to Him and to His purposes for my life."[20]

Suffering blindfolds us, forcing us to walk by faith in nothing but the promise that God is there and has a purpose. Anne Graham Lotz said, "*Why me?* Whenever that question tends to fill my mind, I hear Him whisper to my heart, 'Anne, why *not* you? Just trust Me!' "[21]

WHERE IS GOD? MARY AND MARTHA OF BETHANY HAD THE same question when their brother died. Why didn't Jesus come when they called? Why would God dillydally over something so important?

Pain creates an environment in which we experience God and his glory. This is on display in Jesus' request for the stone to be removed from Lazarus' tomb after he'd been dead for four days, prompting Martha's understatement: "Lord, by this time there will be an odor" (John 11:39). Jesus' retort puts the whole ordeal of suffering into perspective:

"Did I not tell you that if you believed you would see the glory of God?" (John 11:40). Sadly, my pain seems to reveal not my belief, but my unbelief—how about yours?

Belief trusts that God is not oblivious to our woes, that he is not an unmoved spectator. It waits for him like a watchman for the dawn (Ps 130:6). Jesus was not far off from Bethany; he did come, and he did weep. The Divine heart reaches out to his children, "and if he commits the suffering to go on, it is because he sits as a refiner of silver, waiting to purge them from all dross, that his own countenance may be fully manifested in them."[22] His silence isn't deafness, or indifference, or preoccupation, or inability. It is neither a denial of your predicament nor your need. His silence is in service of fixing a greater need in you.

At Bethany, the sisters discovered that Jesus' delay *was* purposeful. It was the very thing that stretched their faith, bringing them to absolute helplessness and hopelessness. It awakened them to the fact that their Lord could be trusted beyond today, beyond the physical, beyond the visible, beyond the emotional, beyond the temporal, and beyond the grave.

God is spiritually present in our suffering when we remember his promise to be with us in the valleys and back alleys. Awakening to this promise affects our experience of pain; for God is in his Word, and his Word recalled surrounds us with his presence, which grants sustaining peace in the midst of pain. Karl Barth puts it this way:

> The free inclination of God to his creatures, denoted in the biblical witness by grace, takes place under the presupposition that the creature is in distress and that God's intention is to

espouse his cause and to grant him assistance in his extremity. Because grace, the gracious love of God, consists in this inclination, it is, and therefore God himself is, merciful; God's very being is mercy. The mercy of God lives in His readiness which springs from His inmost nature and stamps all His being and doing. It lies, therefore, in His will, springing from the depths of His nature and characterizing it, to take the initiative Himself for the removal of this distress. For the fact that God participates in it by sympathy implies that He is really present in its midst, and this means again that He wills that it should not be, that He wills therefore to remove it.[23]

He is not far off; he is in his Word, and his Word is "in your mouth and in your heart" (Rom 10:8).

Corrie ten Boom once spoke to a group facing persecution and the threat of death. While talking to them she became acutely aware that some of those she addressed would die for Christ. She sensed their fear and told them of how when she was a little girl she would go often to the train station with her father. He would put her on the train to go and visit relatives, but he would not give her the money for the ticket until she was already seated on the train. Only then through the window would he pass her the ticket money. Then Corrie told the people that when it came time for them to suffer and even die that their heavenly Father would give them the money for the ticket, that his Spirit would be present to comfort and strengthen them from within.[24]

P. T. Forsyth has said, "Think more of the depth of God than the depth of your cry. The worst thing that can happen to a man is to have no God to cry to out of the depth."[25] In the cry that goes out to him, he is present, drawing us into communion. The psalmist says, "Deep calls to deep at the roar of your waterfalls; all your breakers and your waves have gone over me" (Ps 42:7). The psalmist is drenched and drowning, yet his soul's cry is for the Divine, and in that cry he is quieted and sustained.

Notice how the psalmist in Psalm 130 is immersed both in God and his pain. He cries out to God: "Out of the depths I cry to you, O Lord!" (v. 1). He recounts the mercies of God: "If you, O Lord, should mark iniquities, O Lord, who could stand? But with you there is forgiveness" (vv. 3–4). He tells himself to wait upon the Lord: "My soul waits for the Lord more than watchmen for the morning" (v. 6). He proclaims the Lord's steadfast love to the congregation: "O Israel, hope in the Lord! For with the Lord there is steadfast love, and with him is plentiful redemption" (v. 7). He never indicates that the distressing situation has subsided. The psalmist is simply aware of God's nearness, and he is renewed within— spiritual awakening.

Whatever has sent you into your personal predicament cannot separate you from God. "[Pain] doesn't change the fact that you're able to endure all such struggles only … by abandoning yourself to trust in the character of God, which the gospel proclaims, that you see those struggles, no matter how arduous, as light momentary afflictions."[26] Pain and suffering are not the bottom line; God and his redeeming purposes are. He seeks the hurt and maimed, the lost and wounded; he woos the rebellious and confused.[27]

The LORD is near to the brokenhearted and saves the crushed in spirit (Ps 34:18).

In all their affliction he was afflicted, and the angel of his presence saved them; in his love and in his pity he redeemed them; he lifted them up and carried them all the days of old (Isa 63:9).

Pain is the most misunderstood, yet profound tool to awaken us to God's presence, love, and all-encompassing sufficiency. It is, in fact, "a sign of God's remembrance of us, for it would be much worse if we were left in ghastly isolation."[28] But we aren't left alone; God isn't distant in our anguish and agony. Rather, pain works to make us receptive so the tenderness of God's voice may be heard. God is in (as well as beyond) our painful experiences in life: neediness, fear, vulnerability, death, conflict, loneliness, sorrow, and doubt. He invites us to share in and connect with Christ in them by reproducing the pattern of his death (Phil 3:10) and by peering beyond the depths of pain to the formation of our true selves.

*Grace exists everywhere because
the loving God is everywhere.*

7

surrendering at appomattox

WILMER MCLEAN COULDN'T ESCAPE THE CIVIL WAR. He lived as a wholesale grocer in Manassas, Virginia when cannon shot ripped through his kitchen, turning his farm into the battleground for the first battle of Bull Run. McLean then moved his family from Manassas to find peace away from the war. Ironically, four years later, General Robert E. Lee selected the home of Wilmer McLean in the village of Appomattox as the location to sign the surrender papers, and McLean reluctantly agreed.

Just as McLean could not flee the war, we're caught in our own civil wars, reluctant to surrender. Repeated disappointment, frustration, and embarrassment fuel our artillery until a tiny spark ignites an explosion, firing anger and resentment like grapeshot across the freeway, the classroom, the office, or the kitchen table. Winston Churchill's rousing speech of June 4, 1940, is taken up as a personal mission statement: "We shall defend our island, whatever the cost may be, we shall fight on the beaches, we shall fight on the landing grounds, we shall fight in the fields and in the streets, we shall fight in the hills; we shall never surrender."[1] We're our own islands, or so we think, and for most of us unconditional and immediate surrender is out of the question—peace a mere mirage.

Søren Kierkegaard quipped in 1846 that in the modern era *ressentiment*—the aggressive attitude that arises with feeling situationally or personally inferior—"becomes the constituent principle of want of character."[2] Over 150 years later, inflation—economic and otherwise—has made this an understatement.

We defend ourselves by leveling others, attempting to drag them down—our inner conflict boiling over. In 1994, two Chicago preteens were charged with murder after they dropped a 5-year-old boy from the 14th floor of a housing project because he had refused to steal candy for them.[3] A few years before, *US News & World Report* ran an article titled, "Kids that Kill."[4] It told of teenagers who'd shot one another point blank. When asked why they did it, they answered, "He put me down." Or, "He made fun of me." Or, "I would have looked like a chicken." How hard it is to cap pride and envy and keep the powder of anger dry.

Internal frustration, conflict, and self-abasement aren't always introduced, however, with gunfire. Sometimes cold wars rage between more than just nations. One woman wrote a columnist at *The Washington Post*:

> My husband and I are on "silent treatment" for close to three months now!
>
> It all started when we got into an argument and he made a statement: "The only reason I'm

with you is because my daughter needs a mom."
I was very hurt by the statement and decided to
use the guest bedroom until he feels he needs
a wife. It's been three months, and there are
no signs he's even making an attempt to sort
things out. Is it over?

In the past, he has made similar statements
that hurt me, such as, "You are not a priority for
me." He has said, "I don't miss you" when we
were on silent treatment in the past.

Every single time, even though he is at fault,
he expects me to break the silence and bring us
back to normal. He avoids discussion and likes
to brush things under the carpet.

I am really, really hurt. I want to talk about
it and resolve it; however, I don't want to raise
the white flag and initiate the conversation.
What do you think I should do?

The columnist wrote a wise response: "As long as you see
every issue in your household as being your husband's fault
and responsibility, you will never find resolution. If you see
initiating a conversation as a form of surrender, you will
never find peace."[5]

Sometimes cold conflicts are subtler—and therefore
more agonizing and deadly. Immortalized in his book *Into
Thin Air*, Jon Krakauer tells how, while he and companions
battled for their lives in a storm on Mount Everest's south-
east ridge, three Indian climbers, Tsewang Paljor, Tsewang
Smanla, and Dorje Morup, were stranded in their attempt
to summit from the northeast. Unable to work their way
down, they spent the night on the face of the mountain

without shelter. The following morning, two Japanese climbers ascending by the same route came across the near-dead climbers. In their lust to reach the peak, they offered no assistance, food, water, or bottled oxygen; they didn't even speak to them. They simply stepped aside, resting a few hundred feet beyond. The Japanese climbers made the summit, then left the Indians to die as they passed them on the way down. Nearly all who climb the north side know about "Green Boots" (the color of Paljor's boots), and most have taken rest in view of him.[6] Overcoming the need for self-preservation is more difficult than scaling the Himalayas; it's sacrifice at the cutting edge, and it's what keeps the cold from becoming deadly.

The battle isn't merely alive *between* us, it exists *within* us: "For the desires of the flesh are against the Spirit, and the desires of the Spirit are against the flesh, for these are opposed to each other" (Gal 5:17). That's the origin of all conflict: warring desires (Jas 4:1–2), fueling an inner conflict that sets in motion a race toward immediate relief, instead of intentional rest in the goodness of God.

But don't I have the *right* to personal relief; the *right* to summit and descend unscathed; the *right* to life, liberty, and to whatever will make me happy? Perhaps you do, but—and here's the kicker—insisting on entitlements neither leads to selfless charity nor secures true peace. The only reward reaped from insisting on rights is *conflict*. The insistence on rights to provide peace (ultimately inner peace) breeds conflict; if a whole community isn't put asunder, personal relations are. Peace is unreachable "unless you are detached even from the desire of peace," wrote Merton. "If you give up all those desires and seek one thing only, God's will, he will give you ... peace in the middle of labor and conflict and trial."[7] In other words, the surrender of rights supplies charity and relational peace—yet such surrender is a whole other war.

THE AMERICAN CIVIL WAR DIDN'T BEGIN OVERNIGHT—IT had been brewing for decades. The right to own slaves had always been a contentious issue. Thomas Jefferson is noted for having said that it was only a matter of time before this ticking time bomb under us exploded. In the years leading up to the Civil War, most states above the Mason-Dixon line gradually outlawed slavery, yet by 1861 the United States was still the largest slave-holding nation in the world.

As the country grew, the debate over whether slavery should expand into the Western territories raged. Southern states, who emphasized states' rights (protected by the Constitution), stood in opposition to northern states, who insisted on the right of all persons to life, liberty, and the pursuit of happiness (also protected by the Constitution)—it was a stalemate. So when Abraham Lincoln, an anti-slavery Northerner, was elected, he became the catalyst. Eleven southern states seceded, threatening the experiment of democracy and self-government that had formed America. President Lincoln quickly denied the legality of this secession—war was imminent. Surrender to the "better angels of our nature" through "firm reliance on Him who has never forsaken this favored land" for the preservation of the Union seemed impossible—in spite of Lincoln's pleading in his first inaugural address, spoken two weeks after Jefferson Davis's inauguration as the president of the Confederacy.[8]

In his posthumously published story, "The War Prayer," Mark Twain insightfully—if acrimoniously—wrote of conflict, capturing the inner disparity between said belief and the transformed heart of *true, undefended reliance* in a prayer spoken over young men being sent off to war:

> O Lord our Father, our young patriots, idols of our hearts, go forth to battle—be Thou near them! With them—in spirit—we also go forth from the sweet peace of our beloved firesides to smite the foe. O Lord our God, help us to tear their soldiers to bloody shreds with our shells; help us to cover their smiling fields with the pale forms of their patriot dead; help us to drown the thunder of the guns with the shrieks of their wounded, writhing in pain; help us to lay waste their humble homes with a hurricane of fire; help us to wring the hearts of their unoffending widows with unavailing grief; help us to turn them out roofless with little children to wander unfriended the wastes of their desolated land in rags and hunger and thirst, sports of the sun flames of summer and the icy winds of winter, broken in spirit, worn with travail, imploring Thee for the refuge of the grave and denied it—for our sakes who adore Thee, Lord, blast their hopes, blight their lives, protract their bitter pilgrimage, make heavy their steps, water their way with their tears, stain the white snow with the blood of

their wounded feet! We ask it, in the spirit of love, of Him Who is the Source of Love, and Who is the ever-faithful refuge and friend of all that are sore beset and seek His aid with humble and contrite hearts. Amen.[9]

Civil religion softens the contrast between the church and the world so much that the conflict between the children of light and the children of darkness is often little more than an occasional scrap—they're regularly seen marching with the same uniform, in the same direction, and under the same flag. Politicking, divisions, and strife occur in most churches—not just among leadership, but also within the church body.

A pastor friend of mine felt under attack and called to talk one night. Just hours before, he had finished preaching the gospel at the Sunday service. No sooner had he said "amen" and stepped from the pulpit than he was met by an elder who handed him a defamatory and accusatory letter, blaming him for the church's decline in membership. The letter required a written response delineating the failures he'd made over the preceding seven years and how he planned to fix it—specifics were demanded! The chairman of the board neither took personal responsibility nor was conscious of the environment he was creating, which just so happened to be on full display.

A power, "in order to maintain its position, musters up conflicts with rival powers. ... Thus it is that the most fatal of vicious circles drags the whole society in the wake of its masters in a mad merry-go-round," wrote Simone Weil. "Power, in general, is always essentially vulnerable; and therefore it is bound to defend itself. ... But it is nearly always believed, with or without reason, by all parties, that the only defense is attack."[10] In issue after issue, inside and outside the church, the self-righteous quotient is far higher than the concern quotient.[11]

My friend realized his political disadvantage and tendered a letter of resignation rather than gear up for battle—they probably wanted that anyway.

The false self always treats symptoms rather than root factors (for to do otherwise would call itself into question), assuaging guilt by passing it on to others or comparing righteousness through works. Vulnerable, humble dialogue leading to reconciliation remains incomprehensible. The state of our interior lives makes the world inside and outside the church a battlefield.

> The conflict is variously portrayed—between Babylon and Jerusalem, between Satan and the elect, but always between God and sin. Christian fellowship and discipleship are episodes in the conflict between God and evil. Because the Christian life is thought of in these conflictual terms—as a struggle with forces which seek to undermine and break down life in fellowship with Christ—then one of the key virtues in the letters [to Revelation's seven churches] is that of perseverance or endurance.[12]

Webster calls out perseverance because fellowship is where egos collide, personalities clash, power-brokers contend, and frustration, anger, and resentment surface. On earth, Christian fellowship looks less like a heavenly utopia and more like the refiner's furnace. And yet it's through fire that we become malleable.

Perseverance is also key because fellowship entreats me to exercise total forgiveness, an act requiring me to discover for myself the sufficiency of God. When God is enough I neither need to be right nor exact a pound of flesh. Total forgiveness, then, places me at a deficit, and thus shows me—as I collide with my own inner darkness, which would rather hate than forgive—both that I'm desperately in need of grace and that Jesus himself is my sole satisfaction.

Heinrich Vogel has said:

> In a world hostile to God, the Christian's life is one of conflict. In life and death he is at war with the most powerful enemy, and would certainly be lost had not his Lord long ago won the battle for him, and daily wins it anew in his stead. In our own day, moreover, there has broken out a totalitarian struggle in which the decision for or against Christ has got to be made. All who bear Christ's name are called to the barricades; all who confess the name of Christ ... are called to a path which is no longer one of safety.[13]

Vogel wrote acquainted with the muddy fields of World War I and II and focused on the external world; I write acquainted with the muddy fields of soul and church and focused on the interior world. There's no escaping either conflict and no safety but in the savior, and so we enter the fray befriended: Our soul's Shepherd nearer than when we first believed. The promise that we shall never be separated from the love of Christ is all the security we really need (Rom 8:35–39).

READING THE HISTORICAL BOOKS OF THE OLD TESTAMENT, I'm struck by the prevalence of conflict. David, for example, isn't only a warrior taking the battle to the Philistines, he's also a womanizer, as well as a man with a price on his head. Conflict, conflict, conflict. David battled his inner demons as much as enemy forces; the struggle starts in the soul— the real ground zero. So it's worth repeating: War rages around us because it's rampant in us.

From Shakespeare's *Hamlet* to *Silence of the Lambs'* Hannibal, all well-told stories have conflict (external or internal, often both). But why? Donald Miller, in *Blue Like Jazz*, suggests we identify with and understand conflict because it is intrinsic to the human experience. Miller, on this topic, wrote:

> Without the Christian explanation of original sin, the seemingly silly story about Adam and Eve and the tree of the knowledge of good and evil, there was no explanation of conflict. At all. ... [Therefore], [t]he heart responds to conflict within story ... because there is some great conflict in the universe with which we are interacting, even if it is only in the subconscious. If we were not experiencing some sort of conflict in our lives, our hearts would have no response to conflict in books or film.[14]

Take for example the story of Robert Gould Shaw, the Union Army colonel whose service was depicted in the Academy Award winning film *Glory*.[15] Retelling the story reels us in, resonating with each of us on some level: conflict between armies, races, nature, exhaustion, or simply within the self in the face of certain death.

Shaw, the son of wealthy Boston abolitionists, enlisted in the Army of the Potomac at the age of 23. He tasted the horror of war for the first time at the Battle of Antietam in September 1862, as a captain commanding a company of a hundred men. Within six months he would be promoted to major and then, weeks later, to Colonel as he received command of the 54th Massachusetts, the first all-black regiment in the Northeast.

The 54th Massachusetts experienced discrimination, as they initially were not allowed to participate in the forefront of the action. Shaw fought for the opportunity to fight alongside white regiments. Finally, on the 16th of July, 1863, the 54th received their chance; at the Battle of Grimball's Landing (James Island, South Carolina) they engaged and diverted confederate reinforcements heading to join in the First Battle of Fort Wagner. The 54th was next sent to Charleston to assault the confederate battery in the Second Battle of Fort Wagner, two days later.

The terrain approaching the fort felt like threading a needle: just one regiment at a time could advance on a narrow sliver of land flanked by the ocean on one side and a marsh on the other. Casualties in the lead regiment were expected to be extreme. So, Brigadier General George C. Strong looked for volunteers. With emotion, yet solemnity, Shaw stepped forward:

"General Strong, the 54th Massachusetts requests the honor of leading the attack on Fort Wagner."

"It's Colonel Shaw, isn't it? ... You and your men haven't slept for two days," came Strong's reply.

"That's right, sir."

"Do you think they have the strength to lead this charge?"

"There's more to fighting then rest, sir. There's character. There's strength of heart. You should have seen us in action two days ago. We were a sight to see. We will be ready, sir. When do you want us?"

That night the men of the 54th sang gospel spirituals and prayed. The following morning they marched through the other brigades, as shouts of: "Give 'em hell, 54th!" rang out, to take the lead position.

Colonel Shaw stopped to hand over a few personal letters to a reporter, telling him, "If I should fall, remember what you see here." He gazed out at the ocean and watched a seagull on the wing, then wheeled around and observed Fort Wagner being pounded by naval shells. Drawing up courage with a deep breath, he dismounted his horse, walked from the rear to the front through his men, ordered the fixing of bayonets, and at quickstep led the 54th into the hell of a frontal assault. When the unit hesitated in the face of fierce fire, Shaw mounted an embankment and urged his men on, "Forward, 54th, forward!" as he was shot thrice in the chest.

Just as we identify with conflict, we also identify with *climax* (the point of decision): to shirk in horror and choose the easy way out, or to choose the unthinkable and attempt the daunting. The ultimate choice before us is to love in the midst of conflict, or not. For love is the deciding factor, even at the center of inner conflict.

In the eleventh century, Bernard of Clairvaux laid out stages of spiritual development in terms of four degrees of love: (1) loving yourself for your own sake (*selfish love*); (2) loving God for your own blessing (*dependence on God*); (3) loving God for God's own sake (*intimacy with God*); and (4) loving yourself for God's sake (*union with God's love*).

The first one is easy; it's our default. The next two come by journeying with the Spirit over many hills and valleys. The last, however, taunts us from a distant, unreachable shore. It's so very hard to love myself when, in intimacy with God, I step out from behind the shield of my false self and am blinded by an ineffable and piercing light. What will he do with my hateful thoughts, my cruel fantasies, my bizarre dreams? What is there to love when all I can see is corrosive self-hatred, insecurity, inadequacy, and inferiority? For the honest person, loving self is absurd because we typically look for the basis of love in ourselves. When love is grounded in God, my own unloveliness—which fuels unrest, stubbornness, resentment, and anger—unveils the quality of God's unconditional love. I'm the canvas on which the wondrous colors of divine love are painted. As Brennan Manning notes:

> So often what is notoriously missing from the external, mechanized concept of salvation is *self-acceptance*, an experience that is internally

personalized and rooted in the acceptance of Jesus Christ. It bids good riddance to unhealthy guilt, shame, remorse, and self-hatred. Anything less—self-rejection in any form—is a manifest sign of a lack of trust in the total sufficiency of Jesus' saving work. Has he set me free from fear of the Father and dislike of myself, or has he not?[16]

Without love, we wallow in inner chaos, neither loving ourselves nor really loving others as we descend into subtle and not-so-subtle attempts to garner love—addicted to *selfish love*. The undefended self, however, stops blaming, stops evading guilt, stops trying to prove to itself just how lovely it is. Grace opens us up to honesty. "Redemption does not resolve conflict as much as it provides a safety net that enables us to go farther and do wilder tricks on the high wire than those who do not have the protection of God's grace."[17]

Paul was a man entangled in external conflict, but in the throes of his greatest conflict—that between himself and Christ—he made the decision to confess that he had been kicking against the goads (Acts 26:14). In surrendering, Paul neither blame-shifted, made excuses, or defended his actions. He simply sat in quiet self-reflection—blind, yes, but also waiting on God.

Attending to his deep inner conflict was essential for his spirit to truly encounter God's.

The chief surgeon and protagonist of the Korean War sitcom M*A*S*H, Captain Hawkeye Pierce, discovered something unexpected and sublime after being blinded by a flash explosion. In the aftermath, he became both intro-spective and euphoric:

B. J. Hunnicutt: Look, will you settle down for five minutes. Sit down. I know what you are trying to do, and I know how you feel.

Hawkeye Pierce: No, I don't think you do.

B. J.: You don't want to think about what might happen, so you keep running.

Hawkeye: No, that's not it. That's not it. No. Look. Look. When Doctor Overman comes in here and unwraps my package, I hope to God I'll have my sight back, but—something fasci-nating's been happening to me.

B. J.: What's that, Hawk?

Hawkeye: One part of the world has closed down for me, but another part has opened up. Sure, I keep picturing myself on a corner with a tin cup selling thermometers, but ... I'm going through something here I didn't expect.

This morning I—I spent two incredi-ble hours listening to that—that rainstorm. And I—I didn't just hear it. I was part of it.

I'll bet you have no idea that—that rain hitting the ground ... makes the same sound as steaks when they're barbecuing. Or that—that thunder seems to echo forever. And you wouldn't believe what—how funny it is ... to

hear somebody slip and fall in the mud. I bet—
it had to be [Frank] Burns.

Beej, this is full of trapdoors, but I—I—I
think there may almost be some kind of advan-
tage in this. I've never spent a more conscious
day in my life.[18]

The tension and conflict that we may find ourselves in
are opportunities to see with a *greater* sight. Participating
in conflict with openness and curiosity toward what the
Spirit of the Lord is doing, how the Spirit may be moving to change me and deepen my unity with Christ, takes
courage. It's more challenging than conflict management
or resolution, and it's surely the opposite of conflict avoidance. It's searching for transcendent purpose and becoming
conscious of peace in the midst of conflict that carries us
from dis-integration to integration in the self-giving love of
Jesus—to be only before him, to find life in grace.

The last entry of Georges Bernanos' novel *Diary of a
Country Priest* speaks from a place on the far side of the conflict immanent in doubt and fear and wrestling with sin and
the false self:

It's all over now. The strange mistrust I
had of myself, of my own being, has flown, I
believe forever. That conflict is done. I am reconciled to myself, to the poor, poor shell of me.
How easy it is to hate oneself! True grace is
in forgetting; yet if pride could die in us, the
supreme grace would be to love oneself in all
simplicity—as one would love any member of
the Body of Christ. Does it really matter? Grace
is everywhere.[19]

Grace exists everywhere because the loving God is everywhere. True Christian spirituality depends on getting comfortable under the blanket of this truth. In the embrace of grace there is freedom from the bonds of self-dependency, self-preoccupation, and self-centeredness (ever fortified by fear, inner conflict, and guilt)—i.e., from *selfish love.* The ramifications of this freedom apply to my whole life's journey.

UNDER THE EVENING MOONLIGHT OF MAY 2, 1863, ON A gloomy forested mountain road, Lieutenant General "Stonewall" Jackson stood beyond his own lines with a small scouting party trying to sort out their next move in the Battle of Chancellorsville in Virginia. It was too dark, so the party decided to return to their encampment. As they neared their lines they were fired upon. In spite of Lieutenant Joseph Morrison's command, "Cease firing! You are firing into your own men!" the North Carolinian pickets, thinking it was a lie, let loose another volley. Jackson, who was wearing a long, black, India-rubber raincoat, was hit by two smoothbore balls. He was rushed to safety and into surgery. His left arm was amputated, but he was on the mend. Then, pneumonia developed. It would claim his life eight days later.

When it was confirmed that, indeed, his own men had fired on him, Jackson replied, "They thought I was asleep. It could not be helped. There's no blame in war. We must all forgive."

Speaking to his wife later, he consoled her, "I know you would gladly give your life for me, but I am perfectly resigned. Do not be sad. I hope I may yet recover. Pray for me. But in your prayers, never forget to use the petition, 'Thy will be done,' I'm so glad you're here."

Not long after, she returned to inform him of the inevitable: "My darling, today is Sunday," she said. "Do you know that the doctor says you must very soon be in heaven? Do you not feel willing to acquiesce in God's allotment if he wills you to go today?"

Jackson replied, "I prefer, I prefer it."

"Well, by the time this day closes, you will be with the blessed Savior in his glory."

Moments before dying Jackson cried out, "Order A. P. Hill to prepare for action! Pass the infantry to the front rapidly! Tell Major Hawks—." He smiled, then with a look of quiet relief said, "Let us cross over the river, and rest under the shade of the trees."[20]

Some surrenders are terribly destructive, but self-surrender accompanies spiritual sight. It is neither cowardice nor a loss of freedom. Rather, it's discovering the wellspring of life, exchanging would-be freedom for freedom. Such spiritual freedom provides the capacity to surrender all—even life—without fear.

In this true freedom, Jesus submitted himself, even to errant, sinful man. Raniero Cantalamessa explains that in "doing so he didn't deny obedience to the Father, but rather fulfilled his obedience, for this was exactly what the Father wanted. Without knowing or wanting it, sometimes in good faith and at other times not in good faith, men—such as Caiaphas, Pilate, and the crowds—become instruments so that the will of God, not theirs, might be accomplished."[21] When we look to the Father while everything within us screams, "Run! Fight!"—that's worship, which is the will of God for us.

"You shall have no other gods before me" (Exod 20:3) is a clear purpose statement, echoed by Jesus when he identified the greatest commandment: "You shall love the Lord your God with all your heart and with all your soul and with all your might" (Deut 6:5; see also Matt 22:37). The only problem with living up to this purpose is that it isn't even close to being natural—our affections are so easily lured away by other things. Therefore, the call to worship is also a battle cry to fight the habit of walking by corporeal sight and to walk by the spiritual sight of faith. Faith does the wildest of things: It surrenders to God, takes him at his word, and overthrows the stubborn, intractable heart whose purpose has always been to co-opt God himself into surrendering.

Surrendering to the movement of the Holy Spirit is no cakewalk, for the Spirit often moves in a direction contrary to our independent and unruly will (Gal 5:17). Would God really ask me to do something so hard, something that threatens to rip me apart from the inside, separating my will and spirit? It's unnatural! God forbid! "Jesus alone lived by radical trust, freely floating on the river of life that is God," we might say. True enough; yet that's not an excuse. Look at it closely: it's encouragement and empowerment.

I'm repeatedly in awe of how, in the Gospels, Jesus neither seems to fight for control nor look to people, things, or events as constituents of who he was. His inner self, defined by the Father's still and peaceful heart, worked its way out into the world through his radically undefended life. Therein lies freedom from slavery to other gods and the cessation of conflict between God and the human heart.

Our trust in Jesus grows, not by retreating or sitting out of the war, but by hearing the drums beat out the signal and responding to the call to arms. The first engagement is against our very own disposition to be self-defined. The way of surrender does indeed crush us at times. Yet by moving through this inner conflict it reveals the sufficiency of grace, pushing us into the swiftly running current of the Spirit.

Salvation abides not in socially acceptable graces or good works but in surrendering to love, riding the river, yielding to the wily currents of holy waters. Jesus calls us to follow him, and "to those who hearken to him, whether wise or unwise, he will reveal himself in the peace, the labours, the conflicts and the suffering that they may experience in his fellowship, and as an ineffable mystery they will learn who he is" (Schweitzer).[22]

When we stop seeking immediate escape and instead confront inner conflict, the turbulence can stimulate growth and transformation. C. S. Lewis wrote in *The Problem of Pain*: "God whispers to us in our pleasure, speaks to us in our conscience, but shouts to us in our pains: it is his megaphone to rouse a deaf world."[23] When the pain of conflict commands our attention, the warpath is an invitation to a scared journey. "Unfortunately, however, we usually evaluate these events negatively and, instead of welcoming them, do everything we can to ignore, minimize, or avoid them," says David Benner. "Many people speak of a significant and valued change to the course of their life following such unwelcome events. Sometimes these changes are limited to behavior or lifestyle, but deeper transformations of self are also possible when one moves beyond simply trying to get back to how things were."[24] The path of faith moves us from an illusionary intimacy of initial fascination with Jesus to authentic intimacy characterized by deepening levels of trust and an undefended willingness to enter into even self-sacrificing moments.

On April 3, 1865, Richmond fell to Union troops as General Robert E. Lee retreated to the west with the Army of Northern Virginia, Lieutenant General Ulysses S. Grant on his heels. A race ensued as each army moved farther west in an effort to outflank each other. Eventually, with his army surrounded and his men exhausted, Lee realized there was little choice but to surrender.

General Grant initiated a series of notes on the 7th of April, which gently entertained the idea of surrender; the notes exchanged led to a meeting two days later. Grant did not, however, dictate the time and place of the meeting, but allowed Lee to choose—giving dignity to Lee and his army.

Preparing to meet Grant, Lee told his staff: "I would rather die a thousand deaths than do this ... but it is our duty to live." He arrived at the chosen meeting place, Wilmer McLean's home, at one o'clock in the afternoon, dressed in his finest uniform and armed with a jeweled sword, unsure if he would become a prisoner on that day. In the eyes of many he was a rebel, and a *Chicago Tribune* editorial had even called for his hanging. Grant arrived a half hour later, wearing a muddy private's blouse and without a sword—a noticeable contrast.

Their conversation first turned to light chatter about the old days. Grant spoke of how he remembered Lee from the days of the Mexican-American War when he'd visited

Grant's division. "You were known as one of the greatest soldiers in all of the war," he told Lee.

After a bit more small talk, it was General Lee who moved them on to business. Grant's proposal was amazingly generous. Lee's soldiers would have to sign a parole, promising not to take up arms against the United States, and simply go home. Arms, ammunition, and supplies would be taken as captured property. Those making use of their own horses could keep them, and officers could remain in possession of their mounts and sidearms. The tendered peace effectively granted amnesty.

"This will have a very happy effect on my army," said Lee. He wrote out his acceptance of the terms and mentioned he had a thousand captured prisoners and could neither feed them nor his own men. Instantly Grant ordered 25,000 rations to be sent through the lines. Lee stood, shook Grant's hand, bowed to the other officers in the room, and left. On the porch outside he drew on his gloves, then mounted his horse.

At just that moment, General Grant emerged onto the porch, and, in an unplanned gesture, tipped his hat to General Lee. This tiny act rippled into every corner of the Confederacy and set the tone for the peace necessary to heal a nation.

The entire story pictures the grace found and dignity received when we come to terms with surrender afresh moment by moment. When we sign ourselves over to a contract—a covenant—of true peace, it produces a union which sight can never surmise, which leads on to ever greater levels of trust and surrender—the undefended life, a life of communion and the cessation of conflict.

We need to know we're relentlessly loved, so that we'll focus on that truth and willingly abandon ourselves into God's embrace.

8

bedazzling embrace

R ENOWNED NEW ZEALAND POET JAMES BAXTER TELLS A
parable of a man who lost sight of the truth of
God's embrace:

> This man decided that life was too hard for him
> to bear. He did not commit suicide. Instead
> he bought a large corrugated iron tank, and
> furnished it simply with the necessities of
> life—a bed to sleep on, books to read, food to
> eat, electric light and heating, and even a large
> crucifix hung on the wall to remind him of God
> and help him to pray. There he lived a blame-
> less life without interruption from the world.
> But there was one great hardship.
>
> Morning and evening, without fail, volleys
> of bullets would rip through the walls of his
> tank. He learned to lie on the floor to avoid

being shot. Nevertheless, he did at times sustain wounds, and the iron walls were pierced with many holes that let in the wind and the daylight in good weather and water when the weather was bad. He plugged up the holes. He cursed the unknown marksman. But the police, when he appealed to them, were unhelpful, and there was little he could do about it on his own.

By degrees he began to use the bullet holes for a positive purpose. He would gaze out through one hole or another, and watch the people passing, the children flying kites, the lovers making love, the clouds in the sky, the wind in the trees, and the birds that came to feed on heads of grass. He would forget himself in observing these things.

The day came when the tank rusted and finally fell to pieces. He walked out of it with little regret. There was a man with a gun standing outside.

"I suppose you will kill me now," said the man who had come out of the tank. "But before you do it, I would like to know one thing. Why have you been persecuting me? Why are you my enemy, when I have never done you any harm?"

The other man laid the gun down and smiled at him. "I am not your enemy," he said. And the man who had come out of the tank saw that there were scars on the other man's hands and feet, and these scars were shining like the sun.[1]

The false self leads us to believe we can live a better life in a manufactured holding tank, shielded from hardships and hazards. But that's neither a perfect nor authentic life.

Stasis is artificial life. And we're likely to remain locked up until we realize who's waiting outside to embrace us. Cappadocian father Gregory of Nyssa held that Christian perfection in this life is simply being on the never-ending journey "towards what is better and never placing any limit on perfection;" it is growing and changing—the emergence of the true, authentic self—in the embrace of God's own infinite life.[2]

To be engaged in the human struggle is to be torn into by ricocheting bullets; to have large and bloody wounds; to know our great tendency to find insulation, dodge pain, and manufacture an embrace for ourselves.

Psalm 23 is one of my favorite psalms. It has quieted my soul and given me rest on many occasions; its words embrace me just as God's name bookends David's life in the psalm: "The Lord is my shepherd. ... I shall dwell in the house of the Lord forever" (Ps 23:1, 6). The serenity of his experience, started and finished by God, isn't solely for spiritual giants. The "bookend" language appears elsewhere in Scripture and applies to us all—the Alpha and the Omega, the first and the last, the beginning and the end (Rev 22:13; see also Isa 44:6; 48:12). He holds us.

When God surrounds us, this embrace invariably is communion. It has a bedazzling ability to quell the greatest fear—namely, that of disconnection, separation, or alienation (in whichever form it may come). And that, it just so happens, is the essence of God's plan—to bring everything in heaven and on earth together under Christ's authority (Eph 1:10). In other words, communion is the *telos*, the ultimate aim, of this cosmic crazy train.

Relational peace rests on the same Rock that faith embeds pitons and chockstones into, allowing us to rappel deeper into our souls, into our authentic selves. Apart from this rock there is nothing secure to hold onto, no grounds for hope, and so we live out of the false self—separated from God and each determining for ourselves the nature of our being.[3]

God doesn't respect our insular lives; he disturbs them with new visions and greater longings. And as Jesus was wounded, so will we be—I wish it weren't so, but wounds are necessary. "Those who wear bullet proof vests protecting themselves from failure, shipwreck, and heartbreak will never know what love is."[4]

The freedom to walk undefended from our self-imposed prisons is possible only by walking into the embrace of the struck and wounded one. Jesus is our rock; he is communion, acceptance, and preservation. In his wounds the cosmos find coherence—not by wandering in some pantheistic fog, but by settling in the Father's presence. In the rest and communion found there, hostility toward God and hiding from one another ends. Entering such inner rest is spiritual awakening, the opening of our consciousness to the greatest love. It's there that souls connect, shame weakens, sin surfaces, failure meets grace, irritations soften, and holy desires grow.[5]

WE'D JUST AS SOON RIP THE PAGES OUT OF SOME CHAPTERS of our life stories. But since we can't, we figure amnesia is the best option. "We must forgive ourselves and forget," we say, shoving the pages in a bottom drawer under a stack of paid bills where no one will look. We hide from ourselves, hating ourselves, rejecting ourselves, pretending the short and condensed version is better—and perhaps even defending ourselves for so long we forget our real story, numb to how the unnatural has turned into the natural. I hope you realize how silly and exhausting this game of hide-and-seek is.

Such disassociation threatens not only to bisect our humanity, but also to guillotine the gospel—to cut out the very pages that bring us life.

A father once approached his infant's changing table with boldness, determined to accomplish the formidable task. It wasn't but a few moments before he ran from the room violently gagging—wives know men are really sissies.

But what sets off God's gag reflex probably isn't what you'd think. Neither petty sin nor rank blunders do it. (The cross can handle those.) What is truly putrid is that, by hiding parts of our stories, we hide God's too. Apart from grace, pride and despair are the only options for the false self that is obsessed with religion.

So bisecting ourselves—which is, at its root, self-rejection—greatly grieves God. As Henri Nouwen observes:

> Over the years, I have come to realize that the greatest trap in our life is not success, popularity, or power, but self-rejection. Success, popularity, and power can indeed present a great temptation, but their seductive qual-

ity often comes from the way they are part of the much larger temptation to self-rejection. When we have come to believe in the voices that call us worthless and unlovable, then success, popularity, and power are easily perceived as attractive solutions. The real trap, however, is self-rejection. As soon as someone accuses me or criticizes me, as soon as I am rejected, left alone, or abandoned, I find myself thinking, "Well, that proves once again that I am a nobody." ... [My dark side says,] I am no good, I deserve to be pushed aside, forgotten, rejected, and abandoned. Self-rejection is the greatest enemy of the spiritual life because it contradicts the sacred voice that calls us the "Beloved." Being the Beloved constitutes the core truth of our existence.[6]

Being the Beloved means we each are fully seen and loved—that's the embrace of bedazzling grace.

Our entire lives, not just the lovely parts, are lived out on the field of grace, which is so green that it makes all of our vaunted goodness seem stiff, brown, and dead. The messy, dirty me is the one that God loves. And as Saint John of the Cross said, "God refuses to be known except by love."[7]

Years ago a young woman barged—without knocking—into the study of a friend of mine and announced she'd attended a Bible study the night before and learned something she was sure he would find useful.

He put his book down and asked what she'd learned.

"I learned," she said grinning, "that you can't hug a stiff kid."

He had teenagers at the time and decided she was on to something. When a teenager is sullen, angry, and upset, hugging him or her is like hugging a telephone pole.

"I learned something else," she said. She had gone to babysit a little boy right after the Bible study. "Pastor, he was the dirtiest kid I've ever seen. He had been playing in the mud all day, and I could hardly see his face for the dirt. When I went to his room he lifted up his arms to be hugged ... and I learned it is easier to hug a dirty kid than a stiff kid."

Our dirt isn't the issue. The issue is our stiffness.

Which David do you think was the man after God's own heart, the lad who tended sheep or the king who slept around? Which Peter did Christ love, the robust fisherman who vowed undying loyalty or the simpering coward who turned his back on his friend? Which Paul did God set apart from his birth, the rabid Pharisee or the repentant missionary? The real Christian isn't the clean one, but the awakened, undefended one (John 3:5–8).

As the Skin Horse in Margery Williams's *The Velveteen Rabbit* tells the Rabbit, who is puzzling over what it means to be "REAL":

> "Real isn't how you are made," said the Skin Horse. "It's a thing that happens to you. When a child loves you for a long, long time, not just to play with, but REALLY loves you, then you become Real."
>
> "Does it hurt?" asked the Rabbit.
>
> "Sometimes," said the Skin Horse, for he was always truthful. "When you are Real you don't mind being hurt."

"Does it happen all at once, like being wound up," he asked, "or bit by bit?"

"It doesn't happen all at once," said the Skin Horse. "You become. It takes a long time. That's why it doesn't happen often to people who break easily, or have sharp edges, or who have to be carefully kept. Generally, by the time you are Real, most of your hair has been loved off, and your eyes drop out and you get loose in the joints and very shabby. But these things don't matter at all, because once you are Real you can't be ugly, except to people who don't understand."[8]

The start and finish of our lives, as well as bumps and bruises in between, have one meeting point—Christ. Before we ever knew him, he chose and redeemed us (Eph 1:4-5). In other words, Jesus isn't a means to an end; he *is* the end. He is the very goal of our lives. In him, our past is redeemed; our present is sanctified; and our future is secured. Apart from him the chapters in our life are disconnected. No matter the failure, our self-imposed isolation, bisection, or rejection leaves us with a false self. Our true self lives by the assurance that all of who we are and where we are is entirely embraced in the love of God.

IN THE SNOWY MICHIGAN WINTER OF 1982, I SET OFF FOR school in a new pair of hiking boots. In spite of the warm school building, the blue Smurfs on the side of my boots left me socially out in the cold. The most powerful rules are seldom published or proclaimed; they're just assumed.

Being an outsider not only feels awkward, the rejection fills one with shame.[9]

Cultures are formed by rules erected on shared assumptions and history. So it's no surprise that breaking a cultural taboo would draw fire (rejection, disinheritance, ostracism, shaming) to maintain societal integrity. The unique, unusual, and unexpected threatens to stretch a culture beyond its elasticity and snap the whole thing—an untenable prospect for any culture, especially elementary school cultures, let alone religious ones. The keeping of a culture relies on the binding of one's outward manner of life (as opposed to the inner spirit), which, in the minds of Lucretius and Augustine, is the very nature of religion.[10] Webster's Collegiate Dictionary traces the etymology of the word "religion" back to the Latin word *religio*, meaning "taboo, restraint." A deeper study uncovers that the word comes from the two words "re" and "ligare." "Re" is a prefix meaning "return," and "ligare" means "to bind;" in other words, "religion" means "to return to bondage."

Bonds are instituted for numerous reasons, but beneath them—even beneath the stabilization of societal harmony and alleviating fear—is the threat that boat rocking will capsize the righteousness that depends on remaining socioreligiously kosher. We're shaped by the rules that bind us.

No one is a free-standing entity; we all rely on something for support and safety. We all long for acceptance and inclusion, and desperately fear shame and disconnection. Dan Allender asks, "What gets us in and keeps us inside? Following the rules—approving of those who are impeccable in their performance, viewing with derision those who are not. As long as we align ourselves with the power base of whatever group we wish to enter, we receive the benefits of membership and avoid the liabilities of being a stranger."[11]

Missionaries often experience a similar dynamic. In India, for example, people often eat from a communal bowl with their fingers. I've heard the story of a mission team that had never eaten this way before; as they gathered around the community rice bowl, the first question they asked was, "What are the rules? Do we have our own sections? What happens if we take rice from the far side of the bowl?"

The impulse behind such an innocent question unveils a deep longing for righteousness, a righteousness gained by rule-keeping. That longing controls our fear-laden relating, which is obsessed with avoiding personal shame or bringing shame on our team. A family is ostracized in an Indian village because their newfound faith in Christ is disloyal to the local gods. A man is killed in Nepal because his conversion brings shame on the name of his Muslim family.

The shaping and maintenance of a culture through rules can also be seen in speech control that has broken out with religious fervor. Since World War I college campuses have been inundated with a mode of thinking that using the wrong word, one deemed offensive or insensitive by the powerbase, is evil. Those who do not dare to cross the erected barriers are judged *a priori* to be "correct"—righteous. Such political correctness has, in recent decades, spread across whole societies from North Korea to America, virtually slamming shut dialogue and debate. It's totalitarianism, socio-cultural Marxism under a different name.[12]

The weapons of fear, isolation, rejection, and banishment are also wielded in the church. Our tendency to keep everything kosher is a fever that prevents us from seeing the fences we're building to keep the culture faultless and flawless.

We want to be "right"; we want to avoid shame; we certainly want to avoid bringing any undue punishment down on ourselves by shaming our team. We live and relate to one another often out of fear and religious façades—that is, out of our false selves.

It's possible to go nearly a lifetime without realizing that we've been living out of a false self, a façade confused for faith. An old woman laid deathly ill in the hospital while a dear friend read to her from the Bible. Wanting the comfort of human touch, the sickly woman asked for her friend's hand.

On the other side of the bed, her husband—who considered himself a very religious man and prided himself for the "Honk, if you love Jesus" bumper sticker on his truck—reached out to take her other hand. She withdrew it, and with deep sadness said, "Herbert, you are not a believer. Your cruelty and callousness over four decades of marriage indicates that your faith is an illusion." Genuine faith is marked by love born out of awakening to our great and personal need for grace. That awakening is more than championing Jesus like a political party bumper sticker; it is being revived by the expanse and depth of our iniquity and our neediness, and the realization of how much we are loved. As Brennan Manning has said:

> The tendency in legalistic religion is to mistrust God, to mistrust others, and consequently to mistrust ourselves. Allow me to become personal for a moment. Do you really believe that

the Father of our Lord and Savior Jesus Christ
is gracious, that He cares for you? Do you really
believe that He is always, unfailingly, present
to you as companion and support? Do you really believe that God is love?[13]

Love is costlier than we might realize at the outset of our
journeys, but knowing that you are the beloved enables you
to pay that price. Those to whom the letter of Hebrews was
written had heard the gospel of grace, tasted its sweetness,
and enjoyed a wonderful experience of joy, liberty, and love.
They had followed the Good Shepherd out of their settled
socio-religious ghetto, leaving behind the Jewish rites—the
days and feasts, the wondrous system of priests, mediations,
sprinklings, the temple ritual, and a host of other rules and
regulations—all of which pointed to, and hence had been
fulfilled by, Christ. They joined him in a new exodus. They
walked in the steps of father Abraham, swimming against
the cultural stream, parting from the bonds of country,
class, subculture, and clan.

And they drew hot fire for it. Some of the Christian leaders were imprisoned—their lives in peril. Others lost property. The duration and cost of being an outsider increased
their distress.

Perhaps it would be better to go back; it would certainly be easier. That's a thought that surfaced amongst the
Hebrews who had left Egypt with Moses. And undoubtedly,
it has also passed through your mind a time or two, especially if your faith has made you countercultural.

Entering that kind of distress makes us wonder: Where's
the promised rest? Why is it so difficult? Why do the wicked
prosper? Why do the righteous perish? Is God really to be

trusted with today, let alone tomorrow? If "trust is like climbing a fifty-foot ladder, reaching the top and hearing someone down below yell jump," can I jump? Can you?[14]

Indeed, we are asked to jump, to trust Jesus as we encounter the disappointing reality of walking against the prevailing winter winds with him. Doing so means living undefended in the face of shame, disconnection, and outright rejection. Robbed of rest and exposed to our own neediness, we need grace after balking at God's loving embrace and detaching ourselves from him; we need to know we're relentlessly loved, so we'll focus on that truth and willingly abandon ourselves into God's embrace.

> Behold, the eye of the LORD is on those who fear him,
>   on those who hope in his steadfast love,
> that he may deliver their soul from death
>   and keep them alive in famine.
> Our soul waits for the LORD;
>   he is our help and our shield.
> For our heart is glad in him,
>   because we trust in his holy name.
> Let your steadfast love, O LORD, be upon us,
>   even as we hope in you (Ps 33:18–22).

The writer to the Hebrews points out a helpful truth—that rest is a present reality to be enjoyed. But it's also a future reality to be fulfilled by the ascendancy of Jesus: "In putting everything in subjection to him [Jesus], he [God] left nothing outside his control" (Heb 2:8). He calls us from our thoughts, absorbed in how high we are above the ground, focuses our eyes on Jesus, and once more yells, "Jump!"

REST CAN BE OURS NOW. YET, ADMITTEDLY, REST ELUDES most of us. Perhaps you feel more like a chewed-up core than the apple of God's eye—I know I do. Unrest develops from seeking a loving embrace from our circumstances, rather than looking to the Creator who provides for our every need and embraces us in any and all circumstances.

A few years ago I bought a house. After getting preapproved for the loan, my wife and I went house hunting. We found a house and negotiated the sale price, then the bank went to work finalizing the loan.

As the days marched nearer to the closing date, I received a call from the bank: They were unable to underwrite the loan. Sitting in my study I felt like I'd touched an electric fence; my anxiety was so intense it collapsed in on itself. The closing was ten days away, the mid-December snows were falling, and we had only two weeks to vacate our rental home. I fought the urge to reach through the phone and ring the agent's neck.

After confirming a time the next day to speak, I said goodbye, hung up the phone, and drove home. As I drove I shot a prayer to heaven and turned on the CD player. The words of Michael Card's "Joy in the Journey" filled the car:

> There is a joy in the journey
> There is a light we can love on the way
> There is a wonder and wildness to life
> And freedom for those who obey

He had my attention, though I wondered where the joy was. A few moments passed, then he sang something that nearly made me drive off the road.

To all who've been born of the Spirit
And who share incarnation with Him
Who belong to eternity stranded in time
And weary of struggling with sin

Forget not the hope that's before you
And never stop counting the cost
Remember the hopelessness when you were lost

There it was! There was the rest.

I belonged to eternity; I was merely stranded in time, becoming focused on the present moment. There was no need to fret. There was no deadline before me.

Life is just a journey with flooded valleys and a couple of scenic overlooks. When I get to the bottom of the valley, God will be there, and an answer will come; even if we're living in someone's garage, we'll be fine. Jesus' resurrection guarantees it.

Because of the resurrection I have hope not only in the forgiveness of sin, but in the fact that Jesus cares as much about my today as my tomorrow; that's the whole point of his intercession.

In that very moment future hope invaded my present, and I was embraced with the true reality: who and where I am can be understood only in union with God. The tension in my body released, and warm joy poured into my soul like hot coffee into a mug on a cold day. The loan status hadn't changed, but my status had as the Holy Spirit moved my thoughts to the relevance of Jesus' resurrection. The rest I experienced rejected my false self to live undefendedly in the story of my present risenness in Christ.

There is no room for anger or debilitating fear in the true self of a beloved son.

Rest isn't about a coming day. It is about a person who already came: the One who can be trusted now. Rest is about awakening to his resurrection and faithfulness and to our own present risenness from death. To have angled for my own peace would have yielded nothing, neither securing the loan nor relieving a milliliter of the cortisol that coursed through my veins.

Consider Joshua, who led Israel into the promised land so they could experience rest from their wanderings. Neither he nor the kings following him secured full rest—individual identity as creatures united to the Creator, my knowing the self I was created to be. The way of authenticity and rest is open to those who trust; in fact, they've entered it. This is why the author to the Hebrews exhorts them to strive to enter that rest all the more by believing the gospel and not to fall by failing to trust (see Heb 4:6–13).

Despite all they'd seen in their exodus from Egypt and their experiences of God's day-to-day leadership and preservation, the Israelites nevertheless doubted God's character. Why? Because they had not yet been weaned from living on their own provisions and by their own power. They didn't trust the abundant inheritance that was theirs, already present in the signs of the life-giving waters from the Yam Suph to Meribah to the desert rock. By believing, however, Joshua and Caleb entered the true spiritual rest that the land signified long before they crossed the Jordan into Canaan.

Mary Magdalene was invited to enter this same spiritual rest, the embrace of God's presence. When she arrived

at Jesus' tomb to anoint his body, she thought someone had taken it and stood weeping. The angel inside the
tomb explained:

> Don't be alarmed. You are looking for Jesus
> of Nazareth, who was crucified. He isn't here!
> He is risen from the dead! Look, this is where
> they laid his body. Now go and tell his disciples,
> including Peter, Jesus is going ahead of you to
> Galilee. You will see him there, just as he told
> you before he died (Mark 16:6–7 NLT).

Mary had objective facts laid out before her, telling her,
in essence, to stop her blabbering, for she was an heiress;
the emptiness of the tomb was an invitation to rest in the
Father's bedazzling embrace.

SHORTLY AFTER THE END OF THE KOREAN WAR, A KOREAN
woman had an affair with an American soldier and got
pregnant. He deployed home to the States, and the woman
never saw him again. Months later she gave birth to a girl
who was different from other Korean children. This mixed-
raced child with light and curly hair was ostracized by the
village. The rejection was so bad that some mothers in similar situations would kill their babies.

But this mother didn't. Rather, for several years she tried
to raise her daughter the best she could. Then when the
pressure of the culture was too high, she did the unthinkable: she abandoned her little girl to the streets.

The seven-year-old girl was a homeless orphan, ruth-
lessly taunted by the people. In Korean they called her *tooki*,

which means "alien devil." It didn't take long for her to draw conclusions about herself, and to begin to live out of those false notions. For two years she lived on the streets until she finally found her way to an orphanage.

One day, word spread among the orphans that an American couple was coming to adopt a little boy. All of the children got excited because at least one of them would have hope for a home and a family. The young girls spent the day cleaning up the boys, giving them baths, changing their clothes, combing their hair, and wondering who would be adopted.

The next day the American couple arrived. The little girl telling the story years later remembered, "It was like Goliath had come back to life. I saw the man with his huge hands lift up each and every baby. I know he loved every one of them as if they were his own. I saw tears running down his face, and I knew if he could, he would've taken the whole lot home.

"He saw me out of the corner of his eye. Now, let me tell you: I was nine years old, but I didn't even weigh thirty pounds. I was a scrawny thing. I had worms in my body; I had lice in my hair. I had boils all over me. I was full of scars. I was not a pretty sight. The man came over to me, and began rattling away something in English, and I looked up at him. Then he took his huge hand and laid it on my face. What was he saying? He was saying, 'I want this child. This is the child for me.'"

As the man reached out to her she said later, "The hand on my face felt so good, inside I said, 'Oh, keep that up. Don't let your hand go.' Nobody had ever showed that kind of affection to me before. I didn't know how to respond. So,

I yanked his hand off my face, and I looked up at him and spit on him. Then I turned around and ran away."

The couple returned the next day. They understood the suffering and trauma the little girl had gone through. In spite of her initial rejection, they returned to the little girl with lice in her hair, worms in her body, and boils on her skin. They said, "We've got to have this child. This one we want to adopt." And they did. They got her the medical attention she needed. They loved her just like she was their own biological child. And she grew up, got married, and had children of her own.

The pain of this life is often too deep to fathom, the valleys too dark sometimes to even see your own hand in front of your face. Even so, our hope rests on the Father who takes full responsibility for providing a home, making sure we aren't excluded, and reassuring us that who we are, safe in his embrace, is our real identity.

REST IS ENJOYED IN KNOWING SOMEONE ELSE PUT THE details in order and will get you home. A few years ago I booked a trip with my family on a discount airline. The rate was seductive, but as we'd soon discover, it would cost us our rest.

The airline offered an *à la carte* service: If you'd like to check a bag, you pay for it. If you want to carry one on board, you pay for it. If you want lunch or a cookie, you pay for it. If you want a bottle of water, you pay for it. If you want to use the toilet … you get the idea. Everything was "pay-as-you-go." Yet we rolled the dice anyway, booking a flight from Aberdeen to Kraków, via Dublin. The first leg was fine; it was a short flight. Because it was an international flight, however, we had to go through customs, and we missed the second leg from Dublin to Kraków. It was truly an *à la carte* experience: we even got the opportunity to pay for rebooking the flight—the airline took no responsibility. By the time we reached Kraków, we wondered to which sunny destination our discount had flown.

By contrast, not long ago my wife and I flew from Detroit to Los Angeles via Houston. Our flight was delayed six hours due to snow and ice, but our all-inclusive fare guaranteed that everything was sorted. The airline took our luggage, gave us a meal, rebooked our flight—not just once, but twice—and gave us 25,000 miles in frequent flyer points, enough for a free domestic flight. Of course, the all-inclusive fare cost more, yet we knew rest: We were able to trust the airline to get us to our destination without having to sort out all of the pieces and potential obstacles ourselves.

Rest comes when we awaken to the reality that God has taken full responsibility to get us to the intended destination—which is not merely heaven, but to make us partakers of his divine nature, transforming us into the image of his Son (2 Pet 1:4; 2 Cor 3:18). What is more, the Father has paid the fare himself, and he frequently sends agents to remind us of the fact. Martin Luther has said:

> The chief point of all Scripture is that we should not doubt but hope, trust and believe for a certainty that God is merciful, kind and patient, that He does not lie and deceive but is faithful and true. He keeps his promises, and now accomplished what he had promised, handing over His only Son into death for our sins, so

that everyone who believes in the Son should not perish but have eternal life (John 3:16). Here there can surely be no doubt whether God has been reconciled and is favorably disposed towards us, whether the hate and wrath of God have been removed; for He permits his own Son to die for us sinners. ... Now it is time to turn your eyes away from the Law, from works, and from your own feelings and conscience, to lay hold of the Gospel, and to depend solely on the promise of God. Then there is emitted a little sigh ... the sigh that says: "Abba! Father! However much the Law may accuse me, and sin and death may terrify me, nevertheless Thou, O God, dost promise grace, righteousness, and eternal life through Christ."[15]

In Christ, the Father has unalterably made his promises effective. He has placed his hand on each of our faces and said, "I want this child." Yet so often we don't feel his touch. So we try to replace his embrace ourselves with an impressive résumé, or education, or sex, or shopping, or filling our emptiness with bourbon or a hobby—or even by writing a book and impressing someone with its pages. Yet a lasting embrace isn't achieved through these means.

Maybe you're feeling empty, bedraggled, beat-up, burned-out, naked, poor, weak, inconsistent, and sinful. Maybe you've awakened to the fact that an iron tank can't actually keep you safe, and that this journey of life is riddled with bullet holes that steal your peace as they put you in touch with rejection, alienation, separation, and disconnection.

It's a purgatory of sorts, not in terms of acts of satisfaction which must be performed to reach paradise, but in that we're conformed to the glorified Christ in the manner of the early Jewish notion of "fire purification"—"the transforming power of the Lord who burns open and melts our closed hearts so that they are fit to be living organisms of his body."[16] We become "real" through unwelcome rejection, which throws us back onto our need for grace as we realize that the all-embracing love of God encompasses *even this* purgatory.

The angel in Thornton Wilder's play *The Angel That Troubled the Waters* is perhaps speaking truth when he tells the stricken physician who intermittently visits the healing waters, "Without your wound where would your power be? It is your very remorse that makes your low voice tremble into the hearts of men. The very angels themselves cannot persuade the wretched and blundering children on earth as can one human being broken on the wheels of living. In Love's service only the wounded soldiers can serve."[17]

Rest is found when we awaken to this truth: the crucible of pain is a paradox at play. We're being made tender, being given the gift of understanding, patience, love, and a willingness to remain undefended—the gift of wisdom.[18] Can it be that beneath rejection and disconnection there lies the bedazzling embrace of the Father's strong, tender arms, communicating his warm affection and setting us free to be our true selves, to exist in union with him?[19]

In the dark it may appear that God is nowhere to be found—silent. But be careful not to equate his presence with the experience of his presence.

9

dancing in the desert

IN THE WINTER OF 1988, I LOOKED ACROSS THE COURTYARD that separated the school from the domed cafeteria— a southern Californian design oddly placed in the Winter Wonderland of Pure Michigan—and realized it wasn't a welcoming place. The previous semester I had started making new friends but ended with a slow slide into obscurity, exacerbated by disdain and outright disparagement from other freshmen. Although I lettered in academics, music, and athletics, I fit in nowhere. As the wind blew snow across that courtyard, I lifted my hand off the door, turned to my left, and walked dolefully down the hall and into the library.

I stopped to talk to the spunky, elderly librarian, then headed to the back of the room and situated myself at a lonely table. For the next three years the library would be a refuge. Eventually I retreated even further, taking up residence in the librarian's private workroom.

Powerless to overcome the agony of rejection by turning myself into something more acceptable, I headed it off, rejecting myself first and eluding as many painful encounters as possible. Among those hundreds of books, I discovered a dream world that was safer than life. I read the available military books and memorized weapon systems. I'd go on to earn an officer commission in the Air Force, but in high school I was simply trying to fend off my feelings of rejection and lack of belonging—not too successfully, I might add. "The worst solitude is to be destitute of sincere friendship" (Francis Bacon).[1]

Brenna, a single forty-year-old, was so absorbed in her work from Monday to Thursday that she didn't feel lonely. After a long day of work, she had little time to catch a meal with friends and craved the opportunity to decompress watching TV shows or browsing the Internet before bed. Friday, however, felt entirely different: Before the workday even ended, she could sense the weight of loneliness pressing in and felt powerless to do anything about it. A couple drinks and a movie with friends helped her cope. She diverted her desires by attaching them to the characters on the big screen whose stories were more fascinating than her own. But all of that merely marked time till the busyness of the workweek would launch her into the wild blue yonder, far above the agony of lonely earth.[2]

We might think to ourselves: Perhaps I just need a lover to come home to, then I won't be so lonely.

That's what I once thought. While in high school, and later in college, I prayed my agony would someday terminate in marriage; marriage as an avenue for spiritual formation wasn't on my radar. Evelyn Underhill experienced in prayer what I was hoping for from marriage. On December 4th, 1923, she wrote in her notebook of the great joy of connectedness with God, as well as how that belonging was graciously given and taken away:

> Today, abruptly, in five minutes of prayer I *knew* the Ocean of Love—the "boundless living substance"—through me, and all of us, immersing us, one Love—it's true, "the plural is never found." Incredible joy—one feels in such a moment, one could never allow oneself an act or feeling below this—that anything but love is impossible—because it's *all* and all GOD—but I *shall* incessantly fall into separateness again. How wonderful that weak and rotten little creatures like me can see this even though one can't "sustain one's gaze."[3]

We run to people to make us whole and relieve our loneliness, and it works for a moment—that's why we do it—but it doesn't last. When our dreams shatter, disappointment triggers the dynamics of hate, which—with an emotional disdain that eats at one's insides—moves to remove disappointment. You know you've arrived at such a place when a wall of awkwardness arises, cutting off personal connection, the blame game begins, and feelings of futility, doubt, and shame flood in.

Many who experience loneliness feel they don't measure up; the energy poured into overcoming such self-hatred only makes them feel worse when it doesn't pay off. Contrary to the old adage, time doesn't heal wounds, at least not in and of itself. And you can be assured that mere church attendance and practicing the classic spiritual disciplines won't either. In debilitating loneliness, the suggestion "have faith" is utterly hollow—when nothing gives joy, bewilderment and ire follow.

Wounds bleed into polluted rivers that run, upstream and down, with hate. It's a matter of flowing with the river or against it—and in this sense I'm not talking about the movement of the Holy Spirit. Hate runs upstream when it runs against myself, while downstream hate is stronger, flowing outward at others, leaving myself intact and dry.

The weaker hate of self-hatred runs upstream; born out of a sense of unworthiness, it's the feeling of being powerless in one's isolation. It looks deep within and, concluding itself unworthy, holds that no one else is either. "If I were 'better,' I'd feel different—I must be pretty bad," weak hate tells us. Then, in a bruised moment, such self-reproach attempts to eliminate loneliness by earning or forcing respect and acceptance. I know the contours of this river better than I care to admit. Nothing cures feelings of unworthiness if we're convinced we're insufficient, powerless, and all alone.

Our self-hatred, however, can also flow in a different direction, downstream. It can unknowingly emerge when it doesn't think of itself as unworthy or alone but instead believes it's justified, and so enjoys hating. Such hatred subsists unaware of our own self-hatred, which we project onto others. In college a suitemate of mine announced one afternoon, "I hate those who aren't comfortable in their own skin." I slinked back to my room a few minutes later. The proud hate others' unworthiness but are unaware of their hate and the spiritual self-destruction it yields.

Unworthiness lurks at the root of both kinds of hate. The unworthy don't feel love, because they don't feel worthy of it. Unworthiness, whether consciously realized or not, is nevertheless manifested in things such as caustic, arrogant condescension or bitter, self-despising, neediness. And so hate sucks the oxygen out of the relational space, plunging us into loneliness.

WHO ARE YOU TURNING TOWARD TO EXPERIENCE COMMUNION as a distraction and remedy to the pain of loneliness? For me, it isn't immediately to Jesus. Too often, my gaze initially is set on others, and when communion doesn't come I find myself doused in the waters of upstream (self-directed) hate: "Life stinks. I always feel this way! Why is it so hard?"

It just dawned on me that such backwash is still strangely lulling us into a safe place, the Cynicism and Self-Hatred Pub. When you're good and drunk on hate, a little soul numbing seems like a great idea: a bottle of booze, a risqué film, a tray of brownies, until you're comfortably unconscious—loneliness subdued, at least until you wake up.

Brennan Manning was occasionally asked how it was possible for him to succumb to alcohol *after* he was saved. He explains in *The Ragamuffin Gospel*:

> It is possible because I got battered and bruised by loneliness and failure; because I got discouraged, uncertain, guilt-ridden, and took my eyes off of Jesus. Because the Christ-encounter did not transfigure me into an angel. Because justification by grace through faith means I have been set in right relationship with God, not

made the equivalent of a patient etherized on the table.[4]

Being found by Jesus doesn't mean all of your wounds are healed, all your self-abasing thoughts are corrected, or that you've got the slightest clue as to how to dance in the desert, to be alone with the Alone, as well as how to apply grace as a balm to your blisters and sunburns. That takes a lifetime of walking to sort out. And what's more, as Manning discovered and Saint John of the Cross rightly said, "The devil prevails with ease over those who are alone."[5]

"So, what about marriage?" you say.

What about it?

I guess marriage can, to a degree, insulate against loneliness and temptation. There were after all two in Eden for a reason: They were uniquely equipped to relieve one another's loneliness. Initially, however, there was just Adam.

I usually slide right by the story of Adam's creation, assuming that either the Lord made a divine blunder or he took a lunch break, finally getting back to his *good work* when he announced the wedding reception would be held at Eden Greens: "It is not good that the man should be alone; I will make him a helper fit for him" (Gen 2:18). But to deduce oversight or a *laissez faire* approach to creation is to overlook the Creator's perfection.

Everything was perfect when Adam was first placed in the garden—and I mean everything!

"Oh yeah, well, what about the loneliness?"

Touché. But has it ever occurred to you that connection with God should preempt loneliness, just as Israel wouldn't have needed a king if they'd been cleaving to God? Nonetheless, perfect Adam was also perfectly hardheaded, so it was the woman to the rescue—see ladies, nothing has changed since then. Marriage came to dispel loneliness, but not in the way you think. It was never met to focus our gazes earthward. Rather, by mirroring the Lord's involvement with us, marriage ought to draw our gaze heavenward in thanksgiving.

Now, that doesn't happen all that often, especially after the honeymoon bags have been unpacked. More often than not, because of the poor expectations brought into it, marriage actually incites and intensifies loneliness. Instead of heaven, many discover hell: relational isolation, feelings of futility, even emotional, physical, and sexual abuse ensue in the attempt to drive the other half to change and so to recapture connection. In troubled waters a tragic hardening can occur in which one spouse deprives the other of their "glory" because they feel they've been deprived themselves. It's all right there in Genesis, including the inability to be naked together and enjoy the intimacy and innocence of pure pleasure and communion without shame. The physical nakedness Adam and Eve attempted to cover was indicative of the spiritual rift that had opened between them as they collided into the ugliness of their interior worlds, seized by shame, fear, hatred, and inner loneliness.[6]

So marriage didn't ultimately cure loneliness. Rather, marriage served to point each back to God: Adam became aware of his need for God when he crashed headlong into his need for forgiveness and grace, consolation and comfort, reconciliation and rescue—he needed a helpmate to discover what he hadn't sorted out on his own. When we live to get what we think we need to be happy and content and fulfilled from others, "[t]he results are always the same: inevitable disappointment, temporary fulfillment, and bitter loneliness. When we doubt God and turn away from him to cry to others, 'I need you,' we never stop crying" (Crabb).[7] Therein lies the root of all loneliness, including Adam's.

Do we have *any* resources to ensure we'll ever be anything but lonely? Gathering more people and accolades is obviously useless, yet there's something. We *can* hold on to the truth that no matter what, God is in it, that he desires communion with us as much as we do, and that he is doing something good in our lives. This recollection carries us into his presence—in our alone-ness we discover we're with the Alone (the all-sufficient One).

> The man who fears to be alone will never be anything but lonely, no matter how much he may surround himself with people. But the man who learns, in solitude and recollection, to be at peace with his own loneliness, and to prefer its reality to the illusion of merely natural companionship, comes to know the invisible companionship of God. Such a one is alone with God in all places, and he alone truly enjoys the companionship of other men, because he loves them in God in Whom their presence is not tiresome, and because of Whom his own love for them can never know satiety.[8]

In recollection, then, one finds the root of authentic communion with God and others, as well as with one's self. It's a spiritual path of relentlessness that dares one to press into loneliness and accept the solitude of what seems like an unbearable, underground dungeon, an *oubliette* (literally, "the place of forgetting"). Such is "paschal spirituality"—complete attachment to Jesus Christ alone, "a sharing in the rhythm of his death and resurrection, a participation in his life and sorrow, rejection, loneliness, and suffering."[9] You may be convinced there's no life in "the place of forgetting," but there's more than meets the eye—a surprising new world.

MY MIND RACED TO AND FRO AS I LAY IN BED ONE ORDINARY evening. How much would I give away and to whom; what house would I build; what car would I drive; which coffee shop would I walk to; where would I vacation? The lottery that week was astronomically high, and I was trying to sort out what I'd do if I won. I hadn't actually bought a ticket— but there I was, tossing and turning till five o'clock in the morning making plans for happiness.

Can you guess what didn't come to mind?

The visions of sugarplums dancing in my head were visions of how I could be happy without God. I hadn't had a single thought about God, save to pray for a winning ticket. Then, during my beautiful prayer of self-satisfaction, the Spirit gently asked, "How ridiculous is this?" Immediately I was alerted to a tug-of-war in my soul. I rolled over and sighed, "Help, Lord. I'm so absorbed in me!"

Consider this: The Lord periodically takes away our dreams of "heaven," lest they become our hell. It's a truth communicated in the brief story of the Tower of Babel (Gen 11:1–9). On the plain of Shinar, folks took steps to build a reputation without God. Having had their hollow core whetted by a hint of "heaven" (community, success, glory), they wanted more—looking for life in the finite and earthbound, not the Infinite. So the Lord addressed their hollow core. He made it ache. He plunged them into emptiness, frustration, cynicism, and loneliness so they'd look and long, like Adam, for God. That spiritual longing is at the center of becoming truly human, and it's what we experience as we grow in deeper communion with God.

Only Jesus fills our hollow core and frees us from self-absorption. Saint John of the Cross noted:

> The mind which still clings actually or habitually to any one affection or particular mode of apprehending, cannot taste the sweetness of the spirit of liberty, according to the desire of the will. The reason is this: the affections, feelings, and apprehensions of the perfect spirit, being of so high an order and specifically Divine, are of another and different kind than those which are natural, and in order to be actually and habitually enjoyed, require the annihilation of the latter.[10]

Put differently: To advance spiritually the natural affections of the soul must be eradicated, the hollow core must be emptied of false light and changed to darkness, so it may be filled with divine light, which is incomprehensible to the natural stupor of the mind (Rom 3:1; John 3:3). Without exception, trust grows in the dark, purified in the fires of disappointments, disillusionments, and loneliness. In the dark it may appear that God is nowhere to be found—silent. But be careful not to equate his presence with the experience of his presence. When it seems he is doing the least, he may be doing the most: calling you to dance with him in the desert of your soul.

In August 1954, Cynthia Donnelly wrote to C. S. Lewis about being a Christian writer. Lewis wrote back and included these words on loneliness:

> Loneliness, I am pretty sure, is one of the ways by which we can grow spiritually. Until we are lonely we may easily think we have got further than we really have in Christian love; our (natural and innocent, but merely natural, not heavenly) pleasure in being loved—in being, as you say, an object of interest to someone—can be mistaken for progress in love itself, the outgoing active love, which is concerned with giving, not receiving. It is this latter which is the beginning of sanctity.[11]

In darkness, we can't dream of filling our own hollowness and are forced to wait for our redemption (Rom 8:23). Contentment, oddly enough, comes as longing increases and carries us along with it as it runs towards its *true* fulfillment—this is loneliness transmuted into real solitude.[12] The courageous trust that the shadow of the cross inspires falls across our unrelieved loneliness. Through the cross, we can embrace loneliness because, just maybe, it is an invitation to be alone with the Alone.

Just yesterday I talked to a friend who explained a nagging depression—filled with frustration, sadness, and loneliness—had persisted in her life for the better part of four years. "I want to be happy," my friend said. "I want to love people again, but I feel so suffocated by their smog."

I know how my friend feels. It's disheartening to catch an honest glimpse of the world, as well as one's self. "Is it possible that there is something more beautiful and beneficial to uncover in your loneliness and depression," I asked my friend, "than mere relief?" I doubt Jesus has romantic notions about the spiritual journey. I do believe, however, that he meets us in our loneliness.

Living the undefended life means looking for something greater than immediate relief, trusting in the dark. After years of proclaiming God's Word and being summarily rejected, cast naked into deep wells (the ancient version of an *oubliette*), encountering plots on his life, being shamed by false accusations, and suffering the agony of an intense loneliness into which everything had thrown him, Jeremiah had had enough! He felt deceived: This certainly wasn't what he'd signed up for when he responded to the Lord's call. His friends had turned on him, encouraged him to denounce God, then waited for his downfall so they could exact revenge. Yet all of this awakened Jeremiah to God's stirring in his soul: "If I say, 'I will not mention him, or speak any more in his name,' there is in my heart as it were a burning fire shut up in my bones, and I am weary with holding it in, and I cannot" (Jer 20:9).

As he awoke to the passion burning within him, he found quiet contentment in the face of abuse. That internal fire had come from beyond himself, and it was more powerful than his need to be freed from the suffocating smog of disparaging people. Pain and loneliness put him in touch with the depths of his soul, the place where

God waited to meet and ask him to share in his loneliness and rejection.

Hope resides in that request, "a hope that thrives when dreams shatter, when sickness advances, when poverty worsens, and loneliness deepens and obscurity continues, the same hope that anchors us to God when dreams do come true," says Larry Crabb. "It's hard to discover our desire for God when things go well. We may think we have, but more often all we've found is our desire to *use* God, not to *enjoy* Him. Shattered dreams are the truest blessings; they help us discover our true hope. But it can take a long, dark time to discover it."[13] Shattered dreams drop us into the desert where we discover how alone we truly are in this world. But it's also where we discover how to trust and relinquish control to God; we meet him in the *real* solitude of our souls.

THROUGHOUT HIS MINISTRY JESUS PERIODICALLY RETREATED to pray, his longest retreat being his 40-day jaunt in the wilderness after his baptism. Matthew tells us of another occasion when he got away, this time after feeding the 5,000: "He went up into the hills by himself to pray. Night fell while he was there alone" (Matt 14:23 NLT). The word *opsios* ("night") probably ought to be understood as "evening," sometime between six o'clock and midnight. But if you'll allow for a bit of indulgence, it's possible there's more here than meets the eye.

Jesus had just held a ginormous fish fry; everyone came and got stuffed—it was a massive hit. It doesn't take much imagination to conceive that the temptation he encountered in the wilderness reared its ugly head once more: Could he gain the nations by somehow sidestepping the cross? So off to the hills he goes, not only to pray but to wrestle as a very different sort of night descended: a darkness of the soul.

Demons love to frolic in the twilight, especially when we're alone. And Jesus *was* alone: He alone saw beyond the crowd's grumbling bellies to their real need; he alone knew the temptation battering against his will; he alone knew his grand purpose. He didn't go up to pick daisies and enjoy s'mores. He went up to find safe harbor in quiet prayer, to be delivered from the "dark night" descending that evening.

The wilderness can be a place of safe harbor and salvation. It was certainly that for the Hebrews who walked out of Egypt. Yet safe harbor doesn't come quickly in the spiritual wilderness; it is reached on the far side of the wasteland we discover in our souls—our grasping, manipulating, self-indulgent, broken selves.

In the fourth century, a number of men abandoned the pagan cities and walked off into the desert to find God in solitude—they were on a quest for salvation. These Christian hermits weren't naive, thinking that simply separating from society would bring moral purity. They did hold that the world was shipwrecked and each Christian had to swim for his or her life, but salvation was by no means confused with moralism. The desert separated them from the city, but not themselves.

In the desert a man "could not dare risk attachment to his own ego, or the dangerous ecstasy of self-will. He could not retain the slightest identification with his superficial, transient, self-constructed self. He had to lose himself in the inner, hidden reality of a self that was transcendent, mysterious, half-known, and lost in Christ. He had to die to the values of transient existence as Christ died to them on the cross, and rise from the dead with him in the light of an entirely new wisdom" (Thomas Merton).[14] The loneliness of the desert forced the Desert Fathers to encounter their own interior worlds with all of their affections and attachments. Victory isn't in the removal of temptation or an exertion of the will. It is learning the long, hard lesson of recollection—that is, turning your gaze from the bottomless pit of your earthly self to the grace reaching for you from the cross of Christ.

You don't have to walk literally into the wilderness to experience the desert. The *oubliette* into which loneliness throws us unwillingly has the same effect. It doesn't become a place of *real* solitude, however, unless we attend to the Spirit there. As Merton attests, "This, then, is our desert: to live facing despair, but not to consent. To trample it down under hope in the cross. To wage war against despair unceasingly. That war is our wilderness."[15]

Real solitude isn't the absence of people. Real solitude is coming into contact with my hollow core, my false self; it is not getting, but giving myself and all my emptiness, waywardness, incompleteness, and imperfections consciously back to God; it is facing my brokenness, distortion, darkness, and offering myself to God at those very points—"it is being who we are with God and acknowledging who we are to ourselves and to God."[16] In this self-giving, I begin to "know fully, even as I have been fully known" (1 Cor 13:12); I begin to discover that "I am my beloved's, and his desire is for me" (Song 7:10). This real solitude is where deep calls to deep (Ps 42:7) and the true self emerges. And as "we see how deeply loved we are by God—in our depths, complexity, totality and sinfulness—we dare to allow God more complete access to the dark parts of our soul that most need transformation. And God precedes us on this journey, waiting to meet us in the depths of our self."[17]

After living for several years on the very edge of his village, Saint Anthony withdrew even farther, walking off into the desert to live in solitude for twenty years. In his isolation, Anthony experienced a terrible turmoil of the soul: the shell of his superficial securities cracked as he stared into the abyss of his hollow core. When he finally emerged from the desert, the villagers expected him to have gone mad. But he was surprisingly in his right mind, serene, an authentic man in mind, body, and soul. He had been victorious, not through acetic exploits or demon wrestling acumen, but through surrender. He'd let his defenses fall, stood before God utterly exposed, and allowed God to love all of him.

After a short intermission in the village, Anthony returned to the desert. This time people flocked to him for soul care, spiritual direction, and healing. Real solitude is the furnace from which transformation transpires, and from the transformed soul flows real ministry.[18]

Being alone with the Alone moves us from rational, abstract knowledge about God to relational knowledge of God—which reaches the cracks and crevasses of the soul, where self-hate hides—with the Savior's song:

> Fear not, for I have redeemed you;
> I have called you by name, you are mine.

> When you pass through the waters, I will be with you;
>> and through the rivers, they shall not overwhelm you;
> when you walk through fire you shall not be burned,
>> and the flame shall not consume you.
> For I am the LORD your God,
>> the Holy One of Israel, your Savior (Isa 43:1–3).

Hope rises from inalienable solitude, and hope curbs the mad pursuit of possible solutions, carrying us to a "humble acquiescence that stabilizes us in the presence of one enormous reality which is in one sense already possessed and in another a 'possibility'—an object of hope."[19] Hope: the possession of God actualized today by faith and realized absolutely in tomorrow's heavenly sight.

PRESSING INTO SOLITUDE IS A PAINFUL PROPOSITION, AS many appetites and affections will go unsatisfied. To the culture of this millennium that craves instant fixes, going without just seems unfair and perhaps unloving. Yet Christian spirituality has always included the odd notion of fasting. Fasting is an affront to addictions, appetites, and affections. It denies their control, revealing the possibility of survival without "bread."

Prior to entering the promised land, Moses gave Israel a pep talk. He explained their time in the wilderness had been a time of testing so that what was in their hearts would become known, even to themselves. Then he said: "[The Lord] humbled you and let you hunger and fed you with manna, which you did not know, nor did your fathers know, that he might make you know that man does not live by bread alone, but man lives by every word that comes from the mouth of the LORD" (Deut 8:3).

Recent years have presented me with circumstances that have forced me screaming and kicking into the agonizing loneliness of the *oubliette*. I had actually put off writing this chapter until it alone remained to be tackled because the subject was just too exasperating. I wasn't sure I'd traveled far enough myself to offer much. Grace has, however, slowly brought awakening and rest. It *is* possible to press into "the place of forgetting" and to embrace solitude as an invitation to dance.

There's a story about a village that was overtaken by enemy forces. All the warriors who inhabited the village were gathered together and imprisoned.

Amidst the villagers were four generous patrons who became aware of the prison conditions that their compatriots were enduring. The first patron went to the prison and said to the captors, "I understand that my brothers are without clean water. I want to take all my riches, and use them to purify the water, so my brothers will have clean water and not get sick." The captors agreed and granted the request. He walked away, glad to be able to bestow charity on his brothers.

The second patron went to the prison, and approached the captors, saying, "I understand my brothers are sleeping on rocks. I want to take all my riches, and provide bedding for the men, so they may rest comfortably in prison." The captors agreed, and the man left, feeling that he had fulfilled his purpose in aiding his brothers' plight.

The third patron went to the prison, and spoke to the captors, saying, "I have heard that my brothers have no food.

They have only bread and water. I have a large farm, and want to harvest all my crops to see that the men have good food to eat while they're in prison." The captors agreed, and the patron left, knowing he'd done much good.

The fourth patron, heartened by the acts of the other three, was disturbed that his brothers remained imprisoned. So he found the keys to the prison, and one night slipped in and freed his brothers from their captivity.

God is love. He will meet you in the desert with charity and grace, and provide refreshment and nourishment and rest from his rich stores. And at the right time—he's never late—having first filled you with hope and strengthened your faith, he will accompany you back to the city. The desert has finished its work. It's a place of trial and wrestling, but really is no less a road to knowledge: knowing ourselves, knowing God, and ready to know others in love. "How much better it is to get wisdom than gold! And to get understanding is to be chosen above silver" (Prov 16:16 NASB).

The Chinese philosopher-mystic Chuang Tzŭ once said, "If the eye is unobstructed, the result is sight. If the ear is unobstructed, the result is hearing. If the nose is unobstructed, the result is smell. If the mouth is unobstructed, the result is taste. If the mind is unobstructed the result is wisdom. If wisdom is unobstructed, the result Tê."[20] Tê is difficult to express, but from a Christian perspective it might be understood as the inner and outer energy bestowed by God that enables each of us to come to our true selves and flourish. What other than love can do such a thing?

Loneliness isn't cured with oodles of company and jam-packed schedules, but by connecting to reality. Wisdom discovers love by dropping defenses, and finding our true selves through love is what empowers us to love others unselfishly, compassionately, and playfully, without using them to fill our hollow core. Until you can enjoy others because you don't need them, you've not yet gotten the drug out of your system.[21]

Jesus was a model of detachment. Applause, accolades, and the assemblage of crowds didn't make him whole. Rather, he attended to the Spirit's song over him. And rather than turning him into a madman, solitude freed him to be present for others, to listen, to engage, to give, and even to suffer selflessly.

Years ago I counseled a single missionary who told me how he diligently practiced all of the Dale Carnegie tips but still felt lonely. He would mechanically express curiosity in others, kindly asking about themselves and their story. Good conversations ensued—who doesn't like to talk about themselves?—but to this man's chagrin, those he conversed with never asked of him in return. He felt stranded in the lonely *oubliette*. He believed he'd been present for others, but he hadn't. He'd been present for himself, using others to distract his focus from his pain by relieving his loneliness, seeking to get from them what he'd not yet discovered in Christ. Operating out of his false self the result was frustration and further loneliness.

The personal discovery of the reality of divine love brings you to love yourself, then authentically to love others. The longing to be loved where all boundaries, even that of one's own ego, can be let down and loneliness can be annihilated is universal. It is a longing for deepest communion and is a mark of the Creator's hand.

The Spirit calls you to the desert so you may attend to reality and discover your true self where you "are alone with the Alone. God's tender feelings for you are no longer dry knowledge. You experience the certainty of God's longing for intimacy unlike anything you've felt in hand-clapping worship or anointed Scripture studies."[22] For those who attend to the Spirit, pressing undefended into the invitation to be alone with the Alone, loneliness leads to awakening, communion—dancing.

The soul, when acquainted with sorrow and saving grace, is transformed by the Father's brush, making something beautiful out of hues of blue.

10

digging for potatoes

DURING HIS LIFETIME HIS WORK WAS IGNORED. TODAY, his masterpieces are among the world's most treasured artifacts. Vincent van Gogh was born the second son of an austere country minister and given the name of his elder brother who'd been stillborn a year earlier. His mother never formed an attachment to him, and he carried the pain of this rejection his entire life.

Forced to leave school at 15 when financial difficulties struck the family, he found work at an art dealership run by his uncle, and after a short while he transferred to a gallery in London. There he was moved by Gustave Dore's paintings of the suffering masses in the English poor houses. He also was moved by the beauty of his landlady's daughter. He proposed to her, but when his unrelenting pursuit was rebuffed, he pleaded and bargained until her mother turned him out.

Distraught, angry, and humiliated, he turned to God, renouncing the comforts of the sinful world; and yet out of his pain he argued constantly with fellow employees and customers. After seven years at the gallery he was fired. A Methodist boys' school in Ramsgate gave him a post as an instructor, and he even preached to their parish congregation, speaking in one sermon of life as a pilgrimage in which man sought God along a lonely, difficult path.

Vincent sensed a strong call to ministry and studied to take the entrance exam for the Amsterdam Theological Faculty. Although fluent in four languages, when he refused to take the Latin exams, reasoning that such a dead language wasn't spoken by the poor, he was denied admission. He would soon find his way to the evangelical church of Belgium, applying to the Missionary Training School in Brussels, but they too denied him ordination on account of "neglect in his person"—i.e., stubbornness. So, he begged to go to the Borinage, a despised and impoverished coal-mining region in the south, as a volunteer missionary to the poor. There he preached the gospel, ministered to the sick, and sketched the desolation and torment of the region—it changed him. He gave up his home to a sick widow, moved into a miner's shack, and slept on the floor—his parishioners called him "the Christ of the Coal Mines." His church superiors, however, were appalled: "A man of God should be dignified," they said, refusing to renew his contract.

In 1880, rejected by his mother, the woman he loved, and the church, at the age of 27, van Gogh examined his life and the pictures on his wall, and decided to keep preaching, yet only through art. He wrote to his younger brother, Theo, of his plan. Theo consented to support him as a painter, in exchange for permission to sell his work.

He would fall in love with a series of destitute women whom he felt he could help; they each would reject and leave him. Painting became the easel that held him emotionally and psychologically upright; he worked hard to learn the new French impressionism, and even moved to the town of Arles, in the south of France, in pursuit of the natural light there.

Mindful of his brother's declining health, Theo pleaded with Vincent's friend Paul Gauguin to pay a visit. Gauguin not only visited; after further imploring, this time by Vincent, he agreed to move to Arles and work alongside his friend. Vincent greatly admired him as an artist and friend in spite of his arrogant and domineering persona, and greatly desired to be received by him as an equal in the establishment of an artist guild. The two men quarreled frequently, though, and Vincent feared that Gauguin, too, would abandon him.

One night, after a routine row, Gauguin walked out. Before long he heard footsteps behind him and turned to find Vincent holding a razor. The two gazed at each other for what seemed an eternity. Then Vincent left. Hours later, he appeared at a nearby brothel asking for Rachel, blood pouring from the side of his head. When she appeared he tenderly handed her his ear, telling her, "Keep this object carefully." Overcome by emptiness, rejection, and blood loss, he was nearly dead when he was found in his room the next morning and taken to the hospital.

While he recovered, he painted by day and returned to the hospital at night. He worked feverishly, believing it was the only thing God had left him to do. But when Theo informed him of his own marriage, Vincent plummeted deeper into darkness, assuming his brother would no longer have room for him. His antics grew worse, the townsfolk of Arles grew tired, and they petitioned for his permanent confinement—rejected again.

He'd been treated viciously, and he desperately wanted to leave. He wrote to Theo of an asylum in another city, asking to be sent there. Theo agreed, and he hoped to also cheer up his brother by informing him of the birth of his son, who'd been named after Vincent. In addition, he'd finally sold a painting of Vincent's.

Theo would, however, soon fall into financial distress and be forced to inform Vincent of his need to tighten expenses to care for his wife and son. Vincent was crushed— he'd never wanted to be a burden. It felt to him as though his brother was going back on their long-standing arrangement.

When he next went out to paint, he packed a loaded revolver with his gear. When he didn't return for dinner, his landlord went to find him. Vincent had shot himself, but hadn't succeeded in killing himself. He was rushed to the hospital, but the bullet lodged beneath his heart couldn't be removed. Theo rushed to be with him. They embraced each other and talked through the night, remembering the old times. At 1:30 in the morning Vincent died. Theo would die of syphilis just six months later.

Vincent van Gogh's life was one of unmitigated sorrow. Many of his paintings sought to capture the darkness of life, while shining the light of dignity upon man. He endeavored to stand with those who suffered. His first oil painting, *The Potato Eaters* (1885), captures human dignity amidst a despicableness that could devour the soul. It depicts peasants as Vincent had really seen them—coarse, dirty, eating their potatoes with the same hands with which they'd tilled them from the earth, under the faint glow of their little lamp.[1]

Many potatoes lie in the dirt, left from moments that we wish had never come, or the monotony and seeming purposelessness of life: go to work, feed the dog, pay the bills, watch the news, go to bed, wake up, and do it all again. Our desire is to be stuffed with the satisfaction of life. "There is no sincerer love than the love of food" (George Bernard Shaw). Yet life is hardly sustained on potatoes. The other day I saw a bumper sticker that read: "Life Sucks, Then You Die." Just about sums it up.

In the midst of it all, we sit alone waiting for the phone to ring or an email to chime, and we catch ourselves wondering if we have any *real* relationships. Why do we long to be touched soul-to-soul, yet fear no one can be trusted? Why do we fear that if "they" really knew us, we'd surely be turned out and abandoned? Why do we feel others have more talents and abilities than us? Why do we dislike ourselves and wish to be someone else? Why the self-pity, the self-loathing, the tears?

These aren't your questions? Then perhaps you know the heavy shadow of emptiness, insignificance, or disapproval.

In *The Journey of Desire*, John Eldridge tells of how he was once delayed at Chicago's O'Hare airport. He watched the man who sold popcorn in a terminal corridor. The man sat silently on a stool as thousands of people rushed by. Every 15 minutes or so someone would stop and purchase a bag. He'd scoop the popcorn from the warm bin, take the patron's money, and make change—all without a single word being spoken. The encounter over, the man would return to his perch, his shoulders hunched over, and stare blankly across the concourse once more; he seemed well past 50. How long had that been his profession? Did he really make a living at it? He wore a weary expression of resignation tinged with shame. "Adam," thought Eldridge, "what happened?"[2] The long lament of human history—triggered by a terrible shift in the heart, passed down to each of us—was on full display (see Rom 5:19).

Van Gogh once said, "Your profession is not what brings home your weekly paycheck, your profession is what you're put here on earth to do, with such passion and such intensity that it becomes spiritual in calling." The popcorn man found sorrow, not calling.

We dine on sorrow when our desires go unfulfilled. Van Gogh dug for honest and good soul food, for love and companionship, but unearthed loneliness and rejection. The truth of the matter is:

> Our longings for material joy are almost always partially blocked; our desire for better health and deeper relationships are never entirely possible; and the illusion of world peace seems no more attainable than the gold at the end of the rainbow. ... The world simply does not bend to the desires that roar or whimper inside us. Our desires—from picking up the quickest line at the bank to the overwhelming hope that our children will walk righteously with the Lord— are rarely satisfied in a way that relieves the

ache of incompleteness. ... Our heart seems to
rage against the ache.[3]

We seize hold of the potatoes within our reach, but
they don't relieve our emptiness, they prolong it. Bud-
dhism observes the idea that unmet desires lead to suffering and sorrow. Its answer to the problem: Eliminate all
desire. Paranoiacs keenly study the tragedy of life—nothing
lasts, all is imperfect, and something is very wrong. Their
response is to predict sorrow, then to create it—it will never
surprise them. Fatalists avoid sorrow by accepting it as normal. Heroes avoid sorrow by seizing it as an opportunity
to grow without acknowledging need or weakness. Opti-
mists avoid sorrow by focusing on all the good that may
surround it.[4] Sorrow stems from disappointed desires, and
all of these modes of avoidance fail to hear the invitation
that the voice of sorrow gives: "Come, realign your desires
in awakening."

The pull to subdue sorrow wrenches us away from
touching what's alive within us, like a tractor beam. If we
had listened to life, we would know we're unable to change
what needs changing; we're desperately in need of grace.
Sorrow can hence become a channel flowing into worship.

Desire is not evil in itself, even though it's the culprit
behind sorrow. Rather, it can be plied as a tool for awakening and as a corrective to sorrow. "Our hearts are restless
till they find rest in Thee," wrote Augustine.[5] No sooner do
we conclude we've discovered some joy outside of God than
it turns stale and sour, seasoned with sorrow. "The fulfillment we find in creatures belongs to the reality of the created being," writes Merton, "a reality that is from God and
belongs to God and reflects God. The anguish we find in

them belongs to the disorder of our desire which looks for a greater reality in the object of our desire than is actually there: a greater fulfillment than any created thing is capable of giving."[6] Life gives us one of our most turbulent dilemmas: to yearn for something and not be able to have it. Isn't this the source of our sorrow?

Van Gogh's friend, Paul Gauguin, uprooted potato after potato. A sailor, then a stockbroker, in 1885 he left his wife and five children to take up the life of an artist (he joined van Gogh in Arles three years later), and lived his final years in poverty, disease, and despair in Tahiti. So deep was his sorrow that in 1897 he also attempted suicide and failed. He lived for another five years, during which time he painted his masterpiece, a three-paneled painting set on an island. The first panel shows three women and a child, representing the beginning of life, and is titled, "Where Do We Come From?" The middle panel (titled "What Are We?") depicts the daily existence of young adults. The third panel ("Where Are We Going?") shows an old woman approaching death. Gauguin painted the existential questions themselves into the corner of the painting. They're spades digging for potatoes in the field of sorrow.

JOB WAS A POTATO EATER. HIS STORY PAINTS A PORTRAIT OF the unfair world in all of its glorious torment. Even the deliberate worship of the one true God was neither a defense against hardship nor a guarantor of health and happiness. Lost family, lost possessions, lost health, and lost support, his lament rang out: "I cry to you for help and you do not answer me; I stand, and you only look at me. ...

212

When I hoped for good, evil came, and when I waited for light, darkness came. My inward parts are in turmoil and never still; days of affliction come to meet me" (Job 30:20, 26–27). There's no strain to see the silver lining here; there isn't one, just raw, unabashed sorrow—potatoes dug and eaten with the same hands.

Biblical laments like Psalm 56:8—"You have kept count of my tossings; put my tears in your bottle. Are they not in your book?"—have no interest in absolving God from the terror and tragedy of our tribulations. Perhaps that's why I live so much in the psalms. They aren't tidy or whitewashed. They put into words what I feel yet cannot (or am afraid to) say. I take their very existence in holy writ as an active exhibition of the fact that God understands the sorrow of stymied desires; the sorrow of emptying one's self to make another rich (2 Cor 6:10); the sorrow of stumbling into self-righteousness in the attempt to turn my neighbor into something lovely; the sorrow of abandoning the life I've erected through habits, addictions, memories, and coping mechanisms just to follow Jesus—Peter, when you said, "We have left everything and followed you" (Matt 19:27), did you think it was worth it?

Living only in the here-and-now stunts my soul and saps my strength. Then I stumble into sorrow over my failure to curb that very addiction, and even more sorrow when I realize I need grace once again.

Such sorrow, however, leaves the very vacancy needed for us to know grace. Peter experienced the unconditional love of grace when, after being asked by Jesus if he loved him, Jesus said, "Feed my lambs" (John 21:15)—restoration, resurrection. That's so very good. Yet in spite of its attractiveness, such unconditional love is so desperately resisted because it demands our unconditional vacancy—no parley, just surrender. Only grace vanquishes the dark destructive inkling to don a white robe with a golden sash and proclaim to be my own god. Only grace gives freedom to potato eaters to admit their inner poverty—and then satisfies it.

Flannery O'Connor described her work as variations on the theme of "the action of grace in territory held largely by the devil."[7] In her short story "A Good Man Is Hard to Find," a grandmother takes center stage. Her son planned a vacation to Florida, but she wants to visit relatives in East Tennessee; moreover, an escaped murderer, the Misfit, was last spotted heading toward Florida. On the morning of the trip, grandmother rises early and loads herself into the car, her cat in a basket at her feet, dressed in her best outfit complete with an ostentatious hat—if she should die, folks gazing upon her corpse would know she was a refined lady. Once on the road with her family, she talks incessantly to her grandchildren, trying to gain their attention. Finally she succeeds by telling them of a mysterious house with a secret panel. Enthralled, the children harass their father to make a side trip until he relents. As they turn down a remote dirt road grandmother startles herself—the house she was thinking of was actually in Georgia—and kicks the cat, which jumps onto her son. The car veers into the ditch and flips over.

Waiting for help, grandmother flags down a passing car. Three men carrying guns get out, and grandmother identifies the Misfit; he confirms her suspicion, saying it would have been better for them if she hadn't recognized him. While the Misfit tells grandmother that he was falsely imprisoned for killing his father, his cohorts take her son and grandson for a walk in the woods. Moments later two shots echo. The men return for her daughter-in-law and granddaughter, and grandmother begins to plead for her life.

The conversation between the Misfit and grandmother turns to Jesus, and he becomes agitated, expressing his doubts that Jesus ever raised Lazarus. Thinking he's about to cry, grandmother reaches out and touches him tenderly on the shoulder, and says, "You're one of my own children!" The Misfit jumps back, shooting her three times. Then, cleaning his glasses, he tells the others, "She would have been a good woman if it had been somebody there to shoot her every minute of her life."[8]

O'Connor's abrupt and ironic conclusion vividly portrays the poverty of the human heart. The grandmother experienced transformation, but only under the duress of sorrow.

In her prayer journal, O'Connor herself wrestled with her own inner poverty:

> Dear God, I am so discouraged about my work. I have the feeling of discouragement that is. I realize I don't know what I realize. Please help me dear God to be a good writer and to get something else accepted. That is so far from what I deserve, of course, that I am naturally struck with the nerve of it. Contrition in me is largely imperfect. I don't know if I've ever been sorry for a sin because it hurt You. That kind of contrition is better than none but it is self-ish. To have the other kind, it is necessary to

have knowledge, faith extraordinary. All boils down to grace, I suppose. Again asking God to help us be sorry for having hurt Him. I am afraid of pain and I suppose that is what we have to have to get grace. Give me the courage to stand the pain to get the grace, Oh Lord. Help me with this life that seems so treacherous, so disappointing.[9]

Sometimes I know sorrow for true and right reasons, like Flannery O'Connor's imperfect contrition. Yet I wonder, could there not even exist the smallest hope that surrender and silent waiting will provoke the Lord to swoon in amazement at the show of strength with which I cling to his promises and thus goad him to bring about the cessation of my sorrows? Zero, zilch, zip, nada, nothing! No sustenance is found in the hope that my actions will twist God's arm. Is good withheld so I'll crave something better?[10]

I'm so very addicted to me. I want to be fixed, and I want God to fix things for me; I don't want *just* God. That, Virginia, is the sorrow of the journey—I've bemoaned that grace has barely come; demanded it be shipped express for my own vanity, to lift me over others, to turn it into my own profit; and insisted on such because *I am*, after all, a friend of God.

What could possibly be better than relief and profit? Maybe awakening to the fact that I can't force the grace of God, because it's already present. I do not lack it, I abide in it. Yes, perhaps that.

Habitually resisting this and grasping at grace is a compulsion from a despicable mode of thinking. Job didn't come to his true self until God showed up. And in case you missed it, he didn't show himself in order to soothe Job's wounds, but to confront his demanding and miserly spirit. We're not, therefore, walking too far out on a ledge to say that God pushed Job into sorrow—squint, you'll see it. He did it so Job would release his grip on the material, lower level of reality and thereby fall into deeper awareness of God and the grace that already upheld him. His sorrow was a great gift of love. "Love," as Merton has noted, "is the gift of God's mercy to human sorrow, not the reward of human self-sufficiency. Great sorrow for great evil is a tremendous gift of love, and takes us out of ourselves in ecstasy at the mercy of God."[11] It's out of this reality that Paul said, "We are ... sorrowful, yet always rejoicing" (2 Cor 6:10). So the undefended soul knows its poverty and rests with gratitude in the midst of all things.

This was Henri Nouwen's perspective. He courageously trusted that all that came to him was guided by God's loving hand.

> To be grateful for the good things that happen in our lives is easy, but to be grateful for all of our lives—the good as well as the bad, the moments of joy as well as the moments of sorrow, the successes as well as the failures, the rewards as well as the rejections—that requires hard spiritual work. Still, we are only grateful people when we can say thank you to all that has brought us to the present moment. As long as we keep dividing our lives between events and people we would like to remember and those we would rather forget, we cannot claim

the fullness of our beings as a gift of God to be
grateful for.[12]

MY NATURAL REACTION TO PROLONGED PAIN AND SORROW IS
to duck and cover. Many times I've walked the long way
around, sent a text message rather than meeting face-to-
face, griped to a friend to erect an emotional barrier. If God
cares, then why do storms keep coming when I'm down?
Up goes the barrier, and anger (which is likely unrecognized
and ultimately aimed at God) becomes the ruling passion.

Beneath it, however, lies the false assumption that we
shouldn't be sad, unhappy, or uncomfortable; that we
should be able to eradicate bad feelings and maximize
good ones. But the mind is not something "fixable." I don't
know exactly when our society got the idea that we're to
be our own creations; perhaps the notion stems from the
fact that the behavioral sciences (i.e., psychology, psycho-
biology, cognitive science, etc.) have long been functioning
with a "medical model," which aims to cure disease and correct defects.[13] Such a model leaves no room to embrace the
disruptive sorrows of life as a process whereby something
truly creative might emerge; it simply sees us as victims of
life's stressors who need to be fixed and then deserve a vacation as a reward for our trouble.

A few years ago I attended a week-long seminar at a
beautiful retreat center in the mountains of North Carolina.
The seminar leader was a notable figure I love and respect.
After class one night I shared a personal story, longing for
him to speak directly into my life. His response shocked
me: It was short, blunt, unstudied, and saturated with shal-

low stereotyping—it stung. My desires were dashed; I felt anger, tinged with rejection, stirring within me before I was overcome with deep sorrow.

Eventually I slunk back to my room and wrote a letter to him, tilling the dirt for any potatoes I could find. I contemplated leaving the seminar; could I remain in the same room as this man, could I learn anything from him? Then, something miraculous happened.

After an hour of writing, I found myself dissecting my sorrow, asking: *Why this emotion? What happened? What came alive within me?* Deeper still I cut, question upon answer upon question. Then, a sorrowful epiphany: My hurt wasn't due to what had been said; it was due to my unmet desires. I warred against this discovery. I had too much invested in my anger—I wanted to blame. The truth, however, wouldn't leave the room. Then another question came into my consciousness: "Do you really need to be discovered and touched by this man? What do you hope to find in him? Am I not enough?" "No, Lord, you're not," I confessed. More sorrow—I awoke to the dirt within me and then, slowly, to the grace over me.

I went to bed and slept the sleep of the pure. The next morning I destroyed the letter and showed up an hour late to the seminar—but I showed. I struggled to tear down the barbed wire fences around my heart and set my soul free.

A couple of days later the leader asked me to a private lunch. As we ate we spoke of how I'd journeyed through my sorrow. "I'm glad God used my blunder for something marvelous," the leader said. The relational space between us narrowed and opened to love. Sorrow can tempt us to turn from God's provision, or it can propel us into the Trinity's creative dance.

Do you want to meet God? He frequently moves along unkempt, unpleasant, remote dirt roads. Spiritual awakening lies in the transformation of ruling passions. To say, "My pain and sorrow are not my problem, my determination to relieve it at all costs is," is hard. Yet when alleviating our woes and sorrows becomes our ruling passion, we've moved off the road on which the opportunity for awakening and creative growth is possible.[14] I do desire to be blessed with sunny days and smiles, yet true blessing and joy is to receive my true self by receiving God. "Our lives are in God's hands. All understanding of blessing must be in terms not of what is ours by right, but what is lent by gift," says Gerrit Dawson. "Receiving the blessing means trusting our Father even in sorrow and pain."[15]

WHEN OUR FAÇADE IS TORN DOWN AND TOSSED INTO THE dirt, sorrow gives us a new vision of what could happen. "What is stirring inside you?" it asks. In answering the question are you aware of a self-ward pull—a growing feeling of depletion, desperation, and emotional limpness? The God-ward pull runs across the grain; it leans in reliance on Christ, released from an insistence on tangible progress and improvement, and rests in hope, trusting that grace is sufficient.

A marginal note appears in the King James translation of Zephaniah 3:17, which reads: "He will be silent in His love." It's an interesting suggestion to think about. God does walk so softly at times that he's hardly noticeable. His silence is an invitation to faith. In fact, faith and patience seem to grow best in the soil of uncertainty and sorrow. Why so? Because they slow us down and beckon us to sit and consider, which is when new visions emerge—just think about Elijah's flight to Mount Horeb (1 Kgs 19:1–18). The soul, when acquainted with sorrow and saving grace, is transformed by the Father's brush, making something beautiful out of hues of blue.

Kyle Coble had gone to the fair to ride the Ferris wheel and play at the petting zoo for his birthday with his younger sisters, Emma and Kate, his mother, Lori, and his grandmother. When the fun was done and a nap needed, Kyle and his sisters loaded into the minivan for the ride home. No sooner had they begun their return journey than they hit a traffic jam. Lori turned to tickle little Katie on the foot, when suddenly they were rear-ended by a semitruck traveling at full speed—the minivan was obliterated. The children were rushed to the hospital. A call went out to their father, Chris, who rushed to the hospital too. But it was too late. Emma and Kate had died, and Kyle was on life support with no chance of survival. With heavy hearts Chris and Lori said goodbye before life support was terminated.

The pain was unbearable. Every time Lori and Chris heard the laughter of children outside their home they closed the shades and withdrew deeper inside. When Halloween came they went on vacation to avoid seeing little ones ring doorbells. But despite their sorrow they made a pact with each other: they wouldn't kill themselves, even if it seemed like the only viable option. "At a certain point you just want to break through the grief. You want to take your life because you think you'll be with your kids again," confessed Chris. They chose a different path: to try to have more children. They underwent artificial fertilization, hoping for one child. Then, several eggs fertilized—it was a sign. Almost a year after tragically losing Kyle, Emma, and Katie, into the world entered Ashley, Elie, and Jake. "They will never replace Kyle, Emma, and Katie," Lori said. "But there is joy in our hearts again. They fill our lives with love, happiness, and laughter."

The triplets know three children came before them; they talk about it, see their pictures, and occasionally picnic at the cemetery so the whole family can be together.[16] Sorrow can be a creative brushstroke—what might God be painting?

Fourteenth-century mystic Johannes Tauler prayed for eight years that God would send him a person who would teach him the way of perfection. Then, one day while in prayer he sensed the Lord directing him outside to the steps of the church, where he would meet his mentor. Without hesitation he obeyed. On the steps he found a barefoot man, dirty and caked in blood. "Good morning, dear brother," Tauler announced. "May God give you a good day and grant you a happy life."

"Sir," the man replied, "I do not remember ever having had a bad day."

Tauler was stunned, to say the least. He asked how it was possible, since grief and sorrow are so prevalent in the human experience.

The man explained: "You wished me a good day, and I replied that I cannot recall ever having spent a bad day. You see, whether my stomach is full or I am famished with hunger, I praise God equally, when I am rebuffed and despised, I still thank God. My trust in God's providence and his plan for my life is absolute, so there is no such thing as a bad day."

He continued, "Sir, you also wished me a happy life. I must insist that I am always happy for it would be untruthful to state otherwise. My experience of God has taught me that whatever he does must of necessity be good. Thus, everything that I received from his loving hand or whatever he permits me to receive from the hands of others—be it in prosperity or adversity, sweet or bitter—I accept with joy and see it as a sign of his favor. For many, many years now, my resolution each morning is to attach myself to nothing but the will of God alone. I have learned that the will of God is the love of God. And by the outpouring of his grace, I have so merged my will with his that whatever he wills, I will too. Therefore, I have always been happy."[17]

Gratefulness for everything is an excruciatingly difficult concept to agree with, let alone live up to. My aversion to the idea, however, is grounded solely in my habitual letting go of the cross of Christ. The cross, you see, invites us to find hope where we see pain, and resurrection where we see death. So the call to give thanks in all circumstances (1 Thess 5:18) is simply a call to believe that the cross claims every moment and leads us to new life. Looking at all things—not all things except sorrow (and all that fits within it)—and receiving them from the hand of God, alters their effect. Resting in the reality that all things belong to the Son of God and we are the Son's and the Son is the Father's enables the transcendence of pleasure and pain, joy and sorrow, so every circumstance may be an offering of praise.

I do think there is a place for mourning the fact that we can't remain on the mountaintop but must traverse the valley. It is, however, the gift of grace that testifies with David that "the LORD is my shepherd; I shall not want" (Ps 23:1). Julian of Norwich captures the point:

> It is God's will that we receive three things from him as gifts as we seek. The first is that we seek willingly and diligently without sloth, as that may be with his grace, joyfully and happily, without unreasonable depression and useless sorrow. The second is that we wait for him steadfastly, out of love for him, without grumbling and contending against him, to the end of our lives, for that will last only for a time. The third is that we have great trust in him, out of complete and true faith, for it is his will that we know that he will appear, suddenly and blessedly, to all his lovers.[18]

"The life and soul of all our comforts lie treasured up in the promises of Christ."[19] "His left hand is under my head, and his right hand embraces me!" (Song 2:6). The solace and stillness encountered at the foot of the cross and the blossoming of a new vision that turns Godward in hope is what it means to be apprehended by his Spirit. It's a most penetrating communion, but to our chagrin, it's also most profoundly discovered when we realize that we're sitting in the dirt digging for potatoes rather than for God.

Doubt isn't the opposite or the absence of faith, but an active part of faith's journey.

11

living at tether's end

WEDNESDAY AFTERNOON, AUGUST 10, 1921, FRANKLIN Roosevelt took his wife Eleanor and their sons, James and Elliot, for a long sail on Friars Bay off Campobello Island on the south coast of New Brunswick. They spotted a forest fire on one of the outlying islands, extinguished it, and sailed home again. Franklin then took everyone swimming at the family's favorite pond and even insisted on racing the boys back to their cottage.

Once home he felt a bit feverish, looked at his mail while sitting on the cottage porch, then announced, "I feel so funny that I'm going to go to bed." He went upstairs to bed and never walked again.

"The next morning, when I swung out of bed my left leg flagged," reported Franklin. "I tried to persuade myself the trouble with my leg was muscular, and it would disappear as I used it. It refused to work, and then the other. By the end of the third day, practically all the muscles from the chest down were involved."

He shook with fever and suffered severe pain. Eleanor and his friend and aide, Louis Howe, nursed him and took turns massaging his limbs, despite the pain it caused. Local physicians were mystified; Franklin's fever rose higher still. He became delirious, cried out, and momentarily lost his faith. He couldn't understand why God, who seemed to have favored him for so long, would turn away.

Eventually a specialist from Boston made the correct diagnosis: Infantile Paralysis, Polio—a mysterious virus that attacks the central nervous system, randomly destroying muscles. In those days it was a little-understood, greatly feared illness that killed or crippled tens of thousands every summer, mostly children. Franklin Delano Roosevelt was 39 years old.[1]

Polio didn't merely paralyze the body; it also paralyzed the mind with fear. It held Roosevelt underwater until he gasped for air, while agonizing doubt and darkness taunted from the shore. In that moment his bewildered questioning bypassed earth and drew upward to heaven alone.

NOT LONG AGO A FRIEND RELAYED SOME QUESTIONS THAT had been long weighing on her. She wrote: "I'm still dealing with a lot of big picture issues, like: Why have dreams for the future when they all get shattered? Why have a leading and yearning to act, yet no ability to do so? In this physical and mental state what good am I to my family or even the world?" Such raw questions. Such profound self-doubt.

For years my friend has lived at the end of her rope—at tether's end, suffering from a strange neurological malady, a thyroid condition, the day-to-day stress of raising and schooling three young boys, and on top of it all has been unable to get enough hours at work to provide for her family, despite being a well-educated and highly skilled pharmacist.

When demons yelp at her heels, she's been pulled under, thinking, "I care about nothing! Why get out of bed today?—okay, I've little ones to care for, but still ... All is darkness. And God? ... I don't see him anywhere. The scriptures are a dead letter; my prayers are plain pleading: 'Do you really have my best interest in heart, Lord?—seems you've no heart at all. I do doubt that you care, that you're aware, that you're even there.'"

A spiritual attack is hard to see in the dark. The voice on the wind tells you you're worthless; God doesn't love you; this is all there is to life. It sows seeds of doubt: "If you're truly saved, how could you possibly think this way?" More devilish lies.

My own thoughts have frequently echoed David's:

> How long, O LORD? Will you forget me forever?
>> How long will you hide your face from me?
> How long must I take counsel in my soul
>> and have sorrow in my heart all the day?
> How long shall my enemy be exalted over me?
> Consider and answer me, O LORD my God;
>> light up my eyes, lest I sleep the sleep of death,
> lest my enemy say, "I have prevailed over him,"
>> lest my foes rejoice because I am shaken (Ps 13:1–4).

DOUBTING SELF AND GOD IS PERFECTLY UNDERSTANDABLE when you're clinging to the end of your tether. But if God is really God, he can handle our feeling that his sovereignty doesn't actually make things okay, but makes him seem distant and inaccessible. If God is God, he can handle our disgusted questioning: "Why have I suffered?" If he's God, he can handle us feeling worthless and discarded; after all, we've sought him for perspective, consolation, and deliverance, and slammed into immutable silence. God can handle our dark deduction that he doesn't care, that perhaps he is simply a projection of ourselves onto the cosmos to make a cold reality a bit more bearable.

"It would almost seem better if God did not exist at all. Having no God may be preferable to having a weak or a cruel God," says Jerry Sittser. "Suffering doesn't allow us the luxury of keeping the question at a safe distance. Rather, suffering forces us to think about God's essential nature. Is God sovereign? Is God good? Can we trust him?"[2]

That's the critical question, isn't it? If we're honest enough to scrap our over-spiritualizing for a moment, we might just hear our souls confessing, "Well, no, I don't really trust. I'm confused and lost. Why didn't he keep abuse and violation at bay? Why does my friend no longer like me? Why did my body fail me? Why did my employer turn me out? If you want me to trust you, Lord, why didn't you save me? What will you let harm me next?"

The bleeding hour is as much the hour of awakening as it is the hour most disposed to doubt. In darkness I ponder and pray, moving toward God and then away. I wrestle with doubt, feeling exposed and utterly undefended. But ultimately, wrestling is indispensable to discovering that, in turning back and choosing God again, in the "nevertheless" of faith, God himself was active in choosing and leading me. This is why he doesn't recoil from guiding me down a path that may just include the darkness of profound doubt.

Few have had their confidence shaken by pain and confusion as Horatio Spafford did. A couple of years after losing his fortune when the Chicago Fire of 1871 burned his real estate holdings to the ground, Spafford decided to take a family vacation to England. Detained by business, he sent his wife Anna and their four daughters on ahead. While crossing the Atlantic aboard the steamship *Ville du Havre*, they were struck by an iron sailing vessel and sank. Anna reached England and wired Horatio simply: "Saved alone." Spafford boarded the next ship. When he reached the location where his daughters had perished he penned the words to the hymn "It Is Well with My Soul"; two stanzas read:

> When peace like a river, attendeth my way,
> When sorrows like sea billows roll;
> Whatever my lot, Thou hast taught me to say,
> It is well, it is well, with my soul.

> Though Satan should buffet, though trials
> should come,
> Let this blest assurance control,
> That Christ has regarded my helpless estate,
> And hath shed His own blood for my soul.

He's a modern Job clinging to his God because he knows nothing else will keep him afloat. I have no doubt he wrestled with the critical question: *Are you good, Lord?*

The question of God's goodness in light of daily experience has confused many. The writer of Ecclesiastes alighted on the confusion when he wrote: "There is a vanity that takes place on earth, that there are righteous people to whom it happens according to the deeds of the wicked, and there are wicked people to whom it happens according to the deeds of the righteous" (Eccl 8:14). This practical paradox is so perplexing that in wrestling with its reality, many give up the voyage and maroon themselves on an island of addiction, safekeeping as a consolation prize the small happiness they possess. In this unreality, accolades become more significant than the Lord's acceptance; the loss of friendship hurts more than the loss of the Lord's fellowship; immediate justice becomes more urgent than waiting on the Lord's vindication.

Such is the profile of nine-to-five doubt, a life lived behind the mask of the false self. Yet it's madness to think, says Larry Crabb,

> that we must make up for God's deficient involvement in our lives by taking care of a few things on our own. ... Until we see Christ fully, we will in some measure try to preserve, protect, and develop that fragile thing we call the *self*, that sense of who we are that longs to enjoy love, respect, and meaning. Until our tendency to evaluate God by what we see is exposed and weakened, we will continue looking for ourselves with all our heart and soul. The result is that we never find God.[3]

One thing Ecclesiastes has taught me is that chasing the wind never fills the sails with lasting peace and joy, because true peace and joy are not made; they're received as a gift.

To discover the quiet and secure presence of God—even when difficulties don't change—to be shown new landscapes from life's precipices, to progress in ever-growing consciousness, is a gift, and such a gift has the uncanny ability to subdue doubt.

IF IT FEELS LIKE ABANDONMENT, THEN HAVEN'T I BEEN ABANDONED? "God forbid such unbiblical sentiments!" many would answer.

But God himself says, "Not so fast: 'For I will be like a lion to Ephraim, and like a young lion to the house of Judah. I, even I, will tear and go away; I will carry off, and no one shall rescue. *I will return again to my place*, until they acknowledge their guilt and seek my face, and in their distress earnestly seek me'" (Hos 5:14–15). The prophets tell us that the Lord may indeed hide himself:

> Behold, the LORD's hand is not shortened, that it cannot save, or his ear dull, that it cannot hear; but your iniquities have made a separation between you and your God, and your sins have *hidden his face from you* so that he does not hear (Isa 59:1–2, emphasis mine).

> For any one of the house of Israel, or of the strangers who sojourn in Israel, who separates himself from me, taking his idols into his heart and putting the stumbling block of his iniquity before his face, and yet comes to a prophet to consult me through him, I the LORD will answer him myself. And *I will set my*

> *face against that man; I will make him a sign and*
> *a byword and cut him off from the midst of my*
> *people*, and you shall know that I am the LORD
> (Ezek 14:7–8, emphasis mine).

There's no wiggling free of the unsettling fact that there are obvious situations in which God has hidden himself from those who've claimed to be his. And where he is not, neither are peace and freedom and joy found (Ps 16:11; 2 Cor 3:17)—distress and chaos abound. Yet the purpose in allowing us to "sow the wind" and "reap the whirlwind" (Hos 8:7) is good: To awaken and call them to himself, through their discovery that evil trips over its own shoelaces and is unable to accomplish what it promises (Hos 5:15; 1 Cor 5:5).

Those who have no desire to give the Lord obscene gestures, but desire his active presence and nonetheless experience his relational absence, may at this point be perplexed: "Does God have me on hold until I get it right? But maybe he'll never say, 'Well done,' because I'm lazy, stupid, and selfish—don't I know it!"

Be assured: God isn't mad at those who seek and stumble. If the Lord has a correction for you, you'll know it (Ps 3:12; Heb 12:6). The feeling of abandonment doesn't share an absolutely linear relationship with sin. The adage "if you feel far from God, guess who moved?" implies a one-sided relationship—that intimacy wholly depends on us. Balderdash! The experience of God's distance has been a common complaint of the faithful for millennia:

> O LORD, rebuke me not in your anger,
>   nor discipline me in your wrath.

Be gracious to me, O Lord, for I am languishing;
    heal me, O Lord, for my bones are troubled.
My soul also is greatly troubled.
    But you, O Lord—how long? (Ps 6:1–3)

My God, my God, why have you forsaken me?
    Why are you so far from saving me, from the
words of my groaning?
O my God, I cry by day, but you do not answer,
    and by night, but I find no rest (Ps 22:1–2).

But you have rejected us and disgraced us
    and have not gone out with our armies.
You have made us turn back from the foe,
    and those who hate us have gotten spoil.
You have made us like sheep for slaughter
    and have scattered us among the nations. ...
All this has come upon us,
    though we have not forgotten you,
    and we have not been false to your covenant
(Ps 44:9–11, 17).

Distress, especially when we feel faithful, compounds our doubt. Yet pay special attention to the compulsion of pleading and searching as distance and darkness descend. In a letter dated from 1959, Mother Teresa confided to her spiritual director, Lawrence Picachy, about her experience of abandonment, emptiness, and doubt:

In the darkness ...
    Lord, my God, who am I that You should
forsake me? The child of your love—and now

become as the most hated one—the one You have thrown away as unwanted—unloved. I call, I cling, I want—and there is no One to answer—no One on Whom I can cling—no, No One.—Alone. The darkness is so dark—and I am alone.—Unwanted, forsaken.—The loneliness of the heart that wants love is unbearable.—Where is my faith?—even deep down, right in, there is nothing but emptiness & darkness.—My God—how painful is this unknown pain. It pains without ceasing.—I have no faith.—I dare not utter the words & thoughts that crowd in my heart—& make me suffer untold agony. ... If there be God,—please forgive me.—Trust that all will end in Heaven with Jesus.—When I try to raise my thoughts to Heaven—there is such convicting emptiness that those very thoughts return like sharp knives & hurt my very soul.—Love—the word—it brings nothing.—I am told God loves me—and yet the reality of darkness & coldness & emptiness is so great that nothing touches my soul.[4]

Teresa's longing for God was so very intense.

Doubt isn't the opposite or the absence of faith, but an active part of faith's journey. The loving and caring that lead to longing means, at times, also aching. With the faithful, distance does effectively what it hardly ever does with the godless—namely, draws them closer through intensifying their longing.

With my voice I cry out to the LORD;
    with my voice I plead for mercy to the LORD.
I pour out my complaint before him;
    I tell my trouble before him. ...
Look to the right and see:
    there is none who takes notice of me;
no refuge remains to me;
    no one cares for my soul.
I cry to you, O LORD;
    I say, "You are my refuge,
    my portion in the land of the living"
(Ps 142:1–2, 4–5).

Our infinitely creative God uses our damaged lives, our wounded hearts, and our abject neediness—all that has invaded our peace, wreaking havoc and destruction, plunging us into despair, burying us beneath shame, reducing us to powerlessness and numb ambivalence, entombing us in the *oubliette*, and causing us to reach the out-and-out end of our tether. "The goal of spiritual maturity is seldom at the forefront of our thinking nor much comfort in our pain," says Dan Allender.

> But God knows that joy—real, succulent pleasure—is being like him. And we will not move to become like him and know the sweet joy he desires for us if we are comfortable where we are. When our peace is shattered, the resulting doubt and confusion send us on a deeper personal search that can transform us and lead us to abundant joy.[5]

The removal of our many defenses activates the search for God. A search which leads not so much to finding God—as it is still chock-full of self-serving aims—but to our awakening to the truth that *he* has found *us*. To be found and touched, then to find ourselves cooperating with God in dismantling the false foundation of our being, is freedom. Spiritual *life* is relational—it's about awakening and amity. "Awake, O sleeper, and arise from the dead; and Christ will shine on you," says Paul (Eph 5:14).

Pay attention to the tension in your neck, the pain in your back, the uneasiness in your stomach, the slight elevation of your heart rate and breathing, as the soundtrack in your head replays that stinging comment or hurtful act. These physiological reactions are the default mental sifting process that is intended to reduce stress, eliminate fears, and recapture some semblance of psychological equilibrium. Yet they paralyze instead, reinforcing our fear.[6] Fear looms large when we doubt our employer's or spouse's or friend's sincerity; when we doubt our adequacy to parent a difficult child or earn enough to support the family; when we doubt the school or the government to play their roles well; when we doubt God is good and has a worthwhile purpose for us. Our fear yearns to be anything but undefended, and those physical symptoms alert us to the drama of doubt.

Have you ever wondered why the Lord let Pharaoh's horses get so close to the fleeing Israelites that they could feel the breath of their nostrils? Why incite such doubt and fear? Why the drama? All I can fathom is that in the end drama works: grabbing our attention, arousing our curiosity, shaking our fortifications, knocking us from a safe and predictable, yet false, existence. "It is suspense and drama that bring out the reality of what is in our hearts. ... Drama reveals. It exposes us and allows the work of God to proceed in our lives."[7] Faith in God would remain pedestrian and depthless without it.

The doubt drama elicits isn't a rejection of God. For just as there can be no hope without anxiety, or no trust without worry, there can be no true faith without doubt. For many, faith is that which we fall back on when we lack certainty; it's not knowledge. Such a view, however, forces a false division between faith and knowledge. In his book *Proper Confidence*, Lesslie Newbigin writes:

> One does not learn anything except by believing something, and—conversely—if one doubts everything one learns nothing. On the other hand, believing everything uncritically is the road to disaster. The faculty of doubt is essential. But...rational doubt always rests on faith and not vice versa. The relationship between the two cannot be reversed. Knowing always begins with the opening of our minds and our senses to the great reality which is around us and which sustains us, and it always depends on this from beginning to end. The capacity to doubt, to question what seems obvious, is a necessary element in our effort to know reality as it is, but its role is derivative and secondary. Rational doubt depends on faith; rational faith does not depend on doubt.[8]

In other words, doubt throws us back onto faith, to take stock of it, to test it, to make it our own. Doubt is the struggle that leads to the maturing, the making real, of what is to some degree already present—namely, faith. Merton puts it well:

> If there is no *light* of faith, no interior illumination of the mind by grace by which one accepts the proposed truth *from* God and thereby attains to it, so to speak, in his divine assurance, then inevitably the mind lacks true peace, the supernatural support which is due to it. In that event there is not a real faith. The positive element of light is lacking. There is a forced suppression of doubt rather than the opening of the eye of the heart by deep belief.[9]

The spiritual journey proceeds through dark places, and doubt can be used to remove our defenses and reveal to us our helplessness, the instability of our minds, and, more than anything, our need for mercy. "The seldom-stated truth is that many of us have a longing for God and an aversion to God. Some of us seek him and flee him at the same time. We may scrupulously observe the Ten Commandments and rarely miss church on Sunday morning, but a love affair with Jesus is just not our cup of tea," writes Manning.

But what satisfies our palate doesn't satiate the transcendent God. What God really longs for is intimacy that "is not well served by gauzy sentimentality, schmalz, or naked appeal to emotion, but rather in the boiling bouillabaisse of shock bordering on disbelief, wonder akin to incredulity, and affectionate awe tinged by doubt."[10] Hear Merton again, this time on the rather counterintuitive functioning of maturing and perfecting faith:

> The more perfect faith is, the darker it becomes. The closer we get to God, the less is our faith diluted with the half-life of creative images and concepts. Our certainty increases with this obscurity, yet not without anguish and even material doubt, because we do not find it easy to subsist in a void in which our natural powers have nothing of their own to rely on. And it is in the deepest darkness that we most fully possess God on earth, because it is then that our minds are most truly liberated from the weak, created lights that are darkness in comparison to Him; it is then that we are filled with his infinite Light which seems pure darkness to our reason.
>
> In this greatest perfection of faith the infinite God Himself becomes the Light of the darkened soul and possesses it entirely with His Truth. And at this inexplicable moment the deepest night becomes day and faith turns into understanding.[11]

When Paul said, "In everything by prayer and supplication with thanksgiving let your requests be made known to God. And the peace of God, which surpasses all understanding, will guard your hearts and your minds in Christ Jesus" (Phil 4:6–7), he indicated a relational knowing, a relational certainty that surpasses the outlining of facts. God in his infinite goodness disrupts our fixed thoughts, created lights, and created images—our very mode of existence— to free us that we may know him as he is and thereby *experientially* know the peace of his presence.

I'VE NEVER BEEN PLAGUED BY DOUBT WHEN ATOP THE PRO-verbial mountain. The air is cool and crisp and the view is marvelous—so, up there I naturally *must* be closer to God. In one season of my life I was looking for a job. I'd applied to a few places and waited anxiously for months to receive word back. So much time had passed that I assumed they were uninterested. Then, out of the blue a phone call came to set up an interview—I was bowled over. Tears streamed from my eyes. I fell to my knees with a mouth full of worship. More conversations came, then a couple of flights to visit in person, but the job didn't pan out. Nevertheless, my soul had been strangely warmed. God was there, he'd remembered me—I was sustained, awakened to his presence.

But was I really *closer* to God atop the mountain, warmed by that internal fire? God is no less Emmanuel ("God with us") when I'm lost in the parched valley than when I'm in residence at the mountain lodge.

Feeling his absence, then, is actually a matter of awareness. The Apostle Paul noted this in speaking to a group of Greeks: drawing upon one of their own poets, he proclaimed that "[God] is actually not far from each one of us, for 'In him we live and move and have our being' " (Acts 17:27–28). Growth in the spiritual life is not about reaching ever-higher elevations, placing more and more distance between myself and suffering and sin, but growing in sensitivity and continuing to surrender to the Spirit, who inhabits the relational space between the Father and myself. Surprisingly, the spiritual life grows faster in the valley, where I'm undefended and my need is most acute.

I'd rather have mountain retreats and a snag-free spiritual life, straightforward and sure to alleviate suffering and strife. It would certainly relieve doubt, but it would be a spirituality devoid of the cross. Paul wasn't delusional when he said, "I want to know Christ and experience the mighty power that raised him from the dead. I want to suffer with him, sharing in his death, so that in one way or another I will experience the resurrection from the dead!" (Phil 3:10–11 NLT). Rather, he knew that outside the valley, where one is susceptible to real doubt, faith commonly consists of simple, blind conformity to someone else's prejudged decisions. Faith becomes active in our doubt; it blossoms by wrestling against the temptation to seek solace in something not liable to doubt. True faith, therefore, lives in the "nevertheless," groping in the dark for a handhold, uttering under its breath, "I do doubt, for I'd hoped God's goodness meant peace, not pain. Nevertheless his unfathomable goodness *must* encompass both my pain and pleasure, dependence and disbelief. 'Though he slay me, I will hope in him' (Job 13:15)." Missionary Helen Roseveare reportedly put that "nevertheless" like this: "If I truly believe in Him, I'll trust Him to desire for me that which is my highest good, and to have planned for its fulfillment."

This level of undefended living is anything but comfortable. That's why, like an ancient Israelite traversing the Sinai, we whine and doubt. So what's keeping us from relentless trust? What is it we really doubt? Imagine what it would be like if you were to hold onto God in each valley with deep-seated trust in his goodness. Imagine that everything you encounter throughout your days and nights is encapsulated by his goodness and faithfulness. Imagine knowing peace, discovering the capacity to endure hardship patiently, catching sight of joy welling up from a subterranean stream in the midst of drought and finding hope quietly invading your darkness. In such hope you're awakening to God, for you're beginning to rest, believing in his goodness no matter what happens—no matter if a job loss forces you into poverty; an unfaithful spouse shreds your heart; you're lost in consuming loneliness; a child dies; the memory of abuse haunts your waking hours; or self-hate and personal failure rob you of a reason to live.[12] Intimacy comes with awareness of God's goodness—the antidote to doubt and the silencer of fear.

THERE WERE ONCE IDENTICAL TWINS WHO WERE ALIKE IN every way but one. One was a hope-filled optimist who only ever saw the bright side of life. The other was a dark pessimist, who only ever saw the drawbacks in every situation.

The parents were so worried about the drama of optimism and pessimism in their boys that they took them to the doctor. He suggested a plan. "On their next birthday give the pessimist a shiny new bike, but give the optimist only a pile of manure."

It seemed a fairly extreme thing to do. After all the parents had always treated their boys equally. But in this instance they decided to try the doctor's advice. So when the twins' birthday came around, they gave the pessimist the most expensive, top-of-the-line racing bike a child ever owned. When he saw the bike his first words were, "I'll probably crash and break my leg."

To the optimist they gave a carefully wrapped box of manure. He opened it, looked puzzled for a moment, then ran outside screaming, "You can't fool me! Where there's this much manure, there's just gotta be a pony around here somewhere!"

A nearsighted and pessimistic view of yourself and your circumstances, projected into the future without so much as a wink at the goodness of God, leaves you disparately believing you've been excluded from Garrison Keillor's idyllic town of Lake Wobegon, where "all the women are strong, all the men are good looking, and all the children are above average." Breathing the fumes of doubt, rather than the cool oxygen of divine goodness, not only leaves us with spiritual emphysema, it misses the amazing and unforeseen miracles that are breathed into our lives from above.

Scottish missionary Eric Liddell, who died in a Japanese internment camp in Weihsien, China, just five months before it was liberated in 1945, once said, "Circumstances may appear to wreck our lives and God's plans, but God is not helpless among the ruins. God's love is still working. He comes in and takes the calamity and uses it victoriously, working out his wonderful plan of love."

Joseph also knew the feelings of exclusion, abandonment, and imprisonment. He was sold into slavery by his brothers, taken to Egypt, and spent 13 years in the service of Pharaoh's captain, Potiphar, the last two in prison. Yet in a miraculous turn of events at the age of 30 he went from prison to the pinnacle of Egyptian government. His suffering and servitude had molded him into a humble and wise man, deeply dependent upon the God of his father. The words he spoke to his brothers nine years later displayed his awakening to the goodness of God: "You intended to harm me, but God intended it all for good. He brought me to this position so I could save the lives of many people" (Gen 50:20 NLT). "At the end of the storm, there's a golden sky" (Elvis).[13]

Jesus' crucifixion stands as the quintessential example of God's goodness working through a dark storm of doubt. On the cross, he cried, "My God, my God, why have you forsaken me?" (Matt 27:46). The authentic self is the spiritually awakened self, living in relentless dependence upon the divine lover even when he seems distant and non-existent. Fumbling for life in circumstances and people is desperately limiting; it leaves you trying to piece yourself together out of the rubbish of humanity, rather than receiving the gift of yourself-in-Christ. David Benner writes:

> In all of creation, identity is a challenge only for humans. A tulip is exactly what it is. It is never tempted by ways of being. Nor does it face complicated decisions in the process of becoming. So it is with dogs, rocks, trees, stars, amoebas, electrons and all other things. All give glory to God by being exactly what they are. For in being what God means them to be, they are obeying him. Humans, however, encounter a more challenging existence. We think. We consider options. We decide. We act. We doubt. Simple being is tremendously difficult to achieve and fully authentic being is extremely rare. Body and soul contain

thousands of possibilities out of which you can build many identities. But in only one of these will you find your true self that has been hidden in Christ from all eternity.[14]

After fifteen rounds with doubt, there's no strength remaining to hold the ropes. I've arrived at tether's end; there, God has my attention. I long for a word of hope and in its vocalization become aware of watching his watchfulness over me; listening attentively to his declarations of love; letting them wash over me and not *trying* to believe them.[15] Such knowing beyond doubt just so happened to be the substance of Paul's prayer in Ephesians:

> I pray that from his glorious, unlimited resources he will empower you with inner strength through his Spirit. Then Christ will make his home in your hearts as you trust in him. Your roots will grow down into God's love and keep you strong. And may you have the power to understand, as all God's people should, how wide, how long, how high, and how deep his love is. May you experience the love of Christ, though it is too great to understand fully. Then you will be made complete with all the fullness of life and power that comes from God (Eph 3:16–19 NLT).

*I'm aware of something stirring
deeper within, something I don't
want and yet is drawing me.*

epilogue

simply undefended

Y EARS AGO, MY WIFE AND I SPENT OUR CHRISTMAS IN LON-
don. The ticket prices were cheap, as it was just a few
months after the horror of September 11th. One morning
we rose early and headed for the Thames to take in the
magnificent sights while sipping hot coffee aboard a slow
cruise up the river.

We can live here, on the happy surface of life, enjoying
the cruise and wearing a mask that shields us from the cold
air, providing a measure of self-protection. But if such a brisk
morning cruise is what we expected of this book, then the
preceding chapters have fallen short. For in these chapters,
the beautiful sites have often mingled with an unsettling
exploration of the world beneath the waterline of our hearts.

The discovery of God, the journey toward authentic gospel spirituality and dropping our guard for God, is rarely a
pleasant one for spiritual awakening; transformation never
occurs without a disruption to our complacency. "An inside

look opens the door into the dark room of terror," writes Larry Crabb, "where we try to live as men and women without any guarantee that things will work or that we'll be affirmed as adequate or that we'll enjoy the thrill of acceptance."[1] Why would we ever want to remove the mask, even when life isn't working? Why in the world would we want to plunge into terror by jumping deeper into the river of our lives?

That's a question I have been working to provide an answer to through this book. Tightening the mask of our false self isn't the only means of survival; in fact, it's not surviving at all. Yet most of the Christians I've met, worked with, and worshiped with have been adamant that it's so. But we know differently now.

There is resurrection—life after death. Embracing fear and pain, doubt and conflict and loneliness, pressing into the *oubiellete*, not out of morbid curiosity but because of a grander vision—there we'll meet forgiveness and grace and love face-to-face as we awaken to our deepest longing.

That longing is a prerequisite to receiving the gospel's promise, which releases us into hope and our true selves. It's a longing defined neither by talents or turned heads, nor by aches and demands for self-protection, but solely by our covenant-keeping God through the energy of his Holy Spirit, which fills our life with his own.

The year over which I've written this book has been one of my most difficult, not least because it seems as though hot spears have been inserted into many of my oldest and deepest wounds while writing these chapters. For the most part I've been virtually unemployed, and thereby perhaps afforded too much time to explore the groanings and face the terrors of my own inner world. The sheer duration of silence, coupled with periodic periods of noninterest and declining family finances, produced within me a saturninity from which I often doubted I would reemerge.

The waiting has been excruciating and the episodes of darkness frequent enough that I've personally explored everything in this book. I've caught the angels yawning in boredom at my frequent complaints of, "Why, Lord, why me? Can't I have even a little bit more of what that other guy has?"

On more than one late evening, the descending darkness has awakened a ruling passion to be free of loneliness and worthlessness that is so overwhelming that I doubt the very existence of God, question the credibility of gospel promises, and collide headlong into my inner two-year-old, who insists relief is a right granted in the U. S. Constitution. Then my mind fills with fantastical images: I'm the great, gilded knight defending eternal truth against everyone— my own smugness and condescension betray me. Darker still I descend; the struggle to defend my sense of self-importance, to persuade, and argue, and control, still alive: I want relief; I want my life to work; I want approval, acceptance, and a few more accolades. But I'm aware of something stirring deeper within, something I don't want and yet is drawing me. I don't really want to embrace mystery; I don't really want to connect deeper with the supernatural; I don't really want to be formed—yet I do.

Jonathan Edwards wrote, "How worthy is heaven that your life should be wholly spent as a journey towards it. ... If our lives not be a journey toward heaven, they will be a journey to hell."[2] The tenderness that bids me to come and journey undefended towards heaven is the voice of Jesus, the Spirit brooding over the unformed emptiness and the darkness covering the deep, telling me that I'm not as alone as I feel.

> I was so foolish and ignorant—
> I must have seemed like a senseless animal to you.
> Yet I still belong to you;
> you hold my right hand.
> You guide me with your counsel,
> leading me to a glorious destiny.
> Whom have I in heaven but you?
> I desire you more than anything on earth.
> My health may fail, and my spirit may grow weak,
> but God remains the strength of my heart;
> he is mine forever (Ps 73:22–26 NLT).

I want to play hooky. But you, Lord, you want to show me my illness and weakness, to make me nothing so you might become everything. You want communion and formation. You orchestrate redemptive recollection. You gave me the key to my story, wounds, and darkness in the story of the undefended Nazarene.

Jesus fills the forty-six parables that occur in the Gospels with characters who are the last, lost, and least, yet their lastness, lostness, and leastness aren't portrayed as inconveniences from which they're saved, but strangely as disasters they're saved in.[3] We too, in navigating the difficult channels of our existence, are living parables, joining Jesus in his own death and resurrection (Phil 3:10; 1 Pet 4:13).

Agitated.

Awakened.

Authentic.

Again Larry Crabb: "The path to maturity requires a commitment to replace false certainty, pretend satisfaction, and smug spirituality with disturbing levels of confusion, disappointment, and conviction which in turn create the opportunity to develop faith, hope, and love. *And joy.*"[4] In *The Lord of the Rings,* Bilbo Baggins sings a song as he leaves the Shire and again as he falls asleep after the hobbits have returned from their arduous journey—

> The Road goes ever on and on
>   Down from the door where it began.
> Now far ahead the Road has gone,
>   And I must follow, if I can,
> Pursuing it with eager feet,
>   Until it joins some larger way.
> Where many paths and errands meet.
>   And whither then? I cannot say.
>
> The Road goes ever on and on
>   Out from the door where it began.
> Now far ahead the Road has gone,
>   Let others follow it who can!
> Let them a journey new begin,
>   But I at last with weary feet
> Will turn towards the lighted inn,
>   My evening-rest and sleep to meet.[5]

We might think of the "road" of Bilbo's song as a river: It is meaningful and mighty, and meets a variety of obstacles and obstructions on its way, flowing over waterfalls, through swamps, out into the desert, and home again (Matt 7:14). The paths that spring from each of our doors and the countless chapters of our lives, are currents—channels of knowing—leading us ultimately to Christ. But only if we will attend to them—if we surrender to the direction of the Spirit's current—will we find rest in and communion with him who alone is the Way, the Truth, and the Life (John 14:6). These tributaries and currents come together into the river flowing into the ocean of God's love, but will you resist the current's pull? Or will you gladly flow where it carries you?

The more I awaken to the passions roaring within me; the more I sit in my darkness; the more I journey up the channels of knowing, the more I become aware that I cannot escape the still small voice that tenderly whispers: "You're not in control, you never were. You don't need to be—trust me. I am good; good enough for you to trust entirely." No matter how much I argue back—"Am I not your child? Why do you spurn and afflict me?"—that voice comes back again and again.

It's the Savior's whisper, beckoning me to a banquet beside still waters, welcoming me to trust, asking me to surrender control and self-protection, and simply live undefended.

afterword

JESUS, WHO IS ALWAYS SO FRUSTRATINGLY HIMSELF, FOR-
ever changed our understanding of truth by coming
into the world. Because of the incarnation, any concept, in
order to be seen as truth, must now be reflected somewhere
within the perfect dimensions of his life. If it is not a part of
incarnate truth, it simply is not true.

Undefended is grounded in incarnate truth. It is revealed
in the gospels on almost every page.

Jesus is born undefended. Though a recognized king, he
must flee to Egypt. In the wilderness, when he is tempted
to use his power to fight the hunger of a forty-day fast, he
chooses not to exercise that power, although he will use
it later to feed the multitudes. Jesus never uses power to
protect himself. During the same attack in the wilderness,
Jesus chooses not to defend himself against Satan. His only
defense is of his Father and the word of God.

In Gethsemane Jesus surrenders, much to the shock and confusion of the Twelve, especially Peter. Though he says he has twelve legions of angels (that's roughly 70,000) awaiting his command (Matt 26:53), Jesus chooses "undefendedness," even with such immense power waiting in the wings. (Vespasian took Jerusalem with only six human legions. When you consider the havoc just two angels brought down on Sodom, the power of Jesus' Jerusalem army is inconceivable.)

JESUS' PROVISION FOR OUR DEFENSE, FOR OUR SALVATION, came as a result of his choice of defenselessness. It could have come no other way. It is an incarnate truth. He is not a helpless victim, he is a willing and immensely powerful victim—the point is, he chooses not to use his power in his own defense. It is how he uniquely conquers and establishes the kingdom. After the cross and the blinding victory of the resurrection, he will always be recognized by his scars, the marks of the Undefended One (Rev 5:6).

It all comes down to Jesus ... not simply our faith, but our faith in him. Not simply our trust, but our trusting him. He delivers us from the illusion of self-defense and invites us into the utter security of becoming undefended, to be willingly known by our scars even as he is recognized by his. Those wounds, his and ours, are the source of the healing flow. That defenselessness is the impenetrable fortress. It is trusting Jesus in the dark and thru the pain. The incarnate truth that he is the light, the man of sorrows. It is letting go of the illusion of self-protection in order to stand, defiant, with the immensely powerful, Undefended One. It is transfer of trust, a shift of alliance. It is to recognize that our residency for now is the wilderness, the only place we can hope to find living water and the manna of the Living Bread. It may look like inaction, or giving up, but it is in fact the precise opposite; life thru death, light thru darkness, freedom thru slavery, maturity thru childlikeness, riches thru poverty, security thru undefendedness. These are not clever paradoxes, but a part of the fabric of incarnate truth. They fix nothing. Rather, they illumine.

So, the choice of taking up our cross, of choosing the undefended death that is life, is always a possibility. From that cross, and only from there, can we hope to look across to Jesus and whisper, "Remember me."

The journey, every journey, will always lead back to Jesus. When the walls come down or the door is finally open, it will always be Jesus waiting there waiting with his wounds and with his indestructible life (Heb 7:16). Drop the illusion, the lie of defending yourself. That is only another wall, another door. It is an indescribably inadequate way to spend your life. The truth is we have really been defenseless all along. Now is the time to turn around and behold, to let go and embrace, to close our eyes to see the mystery of the undefended life. It is not a new discipline, another thing to "do," not a new spiritual exercise or technique, not even a new way of interpreting the world around you. It is simply what the word calls coming into the light.

Michael Card
singer-songwriter;
author of *The Hidden Face of God, A Sacred Sorrow,*
and *Scribbling in the Sand*

acknowledgments

U^{*NDEFENDED*} BEGAN IN CONVERSATION WITH MY DEAR friend Noel Due, with whom I've authored two other works. His encouragement to venture out on my own with this book, while startling, turned out to be a great blessing bestowed from a wise elder brother upon a younger. Noel is a true embodiment of many traits that characterize the undefended life put forth in this book.

My publisher and friend, Brannon Ellis, listened with interest and curiosity as I attempted—over long telephone conversations—to communicate what this book was to be all about. His openness and willingness to brainstorm and make early suggestions was immensely encouraging and kept me from grounding the project before it was even in the air. He had the early insight to send this project over to Kirkdale and to bring in Justin Marr, whose interest and excitement in the submission of each chapter has been tremendously supportive in its own right. I hope that both

Brannon and Justin find the finished product worth the risk they took.

From time to time I've shared a chapter with friends, who kindly squinted their eyes, grit their teeth, and stuck with me through those unpolished editions. They not only provided me confidence that I should keep at it, that there was truly something worthwhile in all the spilt ink, but also gracefully pointed out places of confusion that needed work. These willing victims included: Craig Willingham, Gerrit Dawson, and Steve Brown.

Jeff Pipe, my own iron sharpener, heard excerpts read aloud and took delight in turning my own analysis back upon me—asking me to dig deeper still (beware of what you share with a psychologist). Jeff has made sure that I've gotten as much out of writing this book as I hope you will in reading it.

Lastly—and I've purposely saved the best for last—I want to express my deepest appreciation to my editor, Abigail Stocker. She has worked tirelessly to turn poorly put pontifications into elegant prose, run every idea and thought to ground, ask hard questions, call out places that demanded clarification and rewriting, and simply fix what was broken. She has managed this project from beginning to end, shepherding it, as well as myself, through each and every phase of its development. You hold in your hand a book that could not exist without her faithfulness and skill. It is as much her triumph as mine, and for her I am sincerely grateful. Through it all she has become a true friend whom I implicitly trust and pray for regularly. Abigail, you are a blessing from above, a consummate encourager, and a gentle guide extraordinaire—you are my Maxwell Perkins!

notes

prologue: let them see you

1. Brennan Manning, *Abba's Child: The Cry of the Heart for Intimate Belonging* (Colorado Springs, Colo.: NavPress, 2002), 12.

2. Adam Grant, "Unless You're Oprah, 'Be Yourself' Is Terrible Advice," *New York Times*, June 4, 2016.

3. Jose Luis Gonzalez-Balado, *Mother Teresa: In My Own Words* (Liguori, Mo.: Liguori Publications, 1997), 9.

4. Eugene Peterson, *A Long Obedience in the Same Direction: Discipleship in an Instant Society*, 20th anniversary edition (Downers Grove, Ill.: InterVarsity, 2000), 79.

5. David Benner, *Spirituality and the Awakening Self: The Sacred Journey of Transformation* (Grand Rapids, Mich.: Brazos Press, 2012), 7.

6. Martin Luther, "The Heidelberg Disputation," Thesis 26. http://bookofconcord.org/heidelberg.php

chapter 1. crossing all points

1. St. Augustine, "On the Trinity," *A Select Library of the Nicene and Post-Nicene Fathers of the Christian Church*, series 1, vol. 3, ed. Philip Schaff (Buffalo, N.Y.: The Christian Literature Company, 1887), (6.5.7) 3:100.

2. Michael Downey, *Understanding Christian Spirituality* (Mahwah, N.J.: Paulist Press, 1997), 95.

3. Story quoted and amended from Mark Buchanan, *Your God Is too Safe: Rediscovering the Wonder of a God You Can't Control* (Colorado Springs, Colo.: Multnomah Books, 2001), 201.

4. Eugene Peterson, *A Long Obedience in the Same Direction: Discipleship in an Instant Society*, 20th anniversary edition (Downers Grove, Ill.: InterVarsity, 2000), 79.

5. J. W. C. Wand, *The Four Great Heresies* (London, England: A.R. Mowbray, 1955), 129, 136.

6. Corrie ten Boom, *Each New Day: 365 Reflections to Strengthen Your Faith* (Grand Rapids, Mich.: Revell, 2013 [1977]), 107.

7. Adapted from H. A. Ironside, *In the Heavenlies: Practical Expository Addresses on the Epistle to the Ephesians* (Neptune, N.J.: Loizeaux Brothers, 1937), 97–98.

8. N. T. Wright, *Revelation for Everyone*, in New Testament for Everyone Series (Louisville, Ky.: Westminster/John Knox, 2011), 134–35.

9. Louw and Nida, *Greek–English Lexicon of the New Testament*, ad. loc. *parakletos*.

10. Simone Weil, *Waiting for God* (New York, N.Y.: Harper Colophon, 1973 [Putnam, 1951]), 120.

11. Christina Levasheff, "God's Presence Revealed through a Blind and Suffering Boy," *Biloa Magazine*, Winter 2009.

12. Aeschylus quoted by Robert Kennedy, "Remarks on the Assassination of Martin Luther King, Jr.," April 4, 1968; http://www.americanrhetoric.com/speeches/rfkonmlkdeath.html

13. John R. W. Stott, *The Cross of Christ* (Downers Grove, Ill.: InterVarsity, 2006 [1986]), 326.

14. John Webster, *Confronted by Grace: Meditations of a Theologian*, eds. Daniel Bush and Brannon Ellis (Bellingham, Wash.: Lexham Press, 2015), 118.

15. Martin Luther, *Luther's Works: Vol. 36: Word and Sacrament II*, eds. J. J. Pelikan, H. C. Oswald, and H. T. Lehmann (Philadelphia, Penn.: Fortress Press), 340.

16. Brennan Manning, *The Signature of Jesus: The Call to a Life Marked by Holy Passion and Relentless Faith* (Colorado Springs, Colo.: Multnomah Books, 1992 [Chosen Books, 1988]), 23.

chapter 2. leaving eden

1. Cesar Millan with Melissa Jo Peltier, *Cesar's Way: The Natural, Every-day Guide to Understanding and Correcting Common Dog Problems* (New York, N.Y.: Harmony Books, 2006), 2.

2. Carl G. Jung, *The Development of Personality*, in Collected Works of C. G. Jung, vol.17 (New York, NY: Bolligen Foundation; Princeton, N.J.: Princeton University Press:, 1981), 198.

3. Mohandas K. Gandhi, *Gandhi on Non-Violence: Selected Texts from Mohandas K. Gandhi's Non-Violence in Peace and War*, ed. Thomas Merton (New York, N.Y.: New Directions Publishing, 2007 [1965]), 18.

4. Helmut Thielicke, *Being Human ... Becoming Human* (Garden City, N.Y.: Doubleday, 1984), 411–13.

5. Gerald G. May, *Addiction and Grace: Love and Spirituality in the Healing of Addictions* (New York, N.Y.: Harper One, 1988), 14.

6. Thomas Merton, *No Man Is an Island* (Boston, Mass.: Shambhala, 2005 [New York, N.Y.: Harcourt, 1955]), 88.

7. Dan B. Allender, *The Healing Path: How the Hurts in Your Past Can Lead You to a More Abundant Life* (Colorado Springs, Colo.: WaterBrook, 1999), 107.

8. Richard Rohr, *Everything Belongs: The Gift of Contemplative Prayer,* (New York, N.Y.: Crossroad, 1999), 103.

9. Brennan Manning with John Blase, *All Is Grace: A Ragamuffin Memoir* (Colorado Springs, Colo.: David C. Cook, 2011), 56–57.

10. Brennan Manning, *The Ragamuffin Gospel: Good News for the Bedraggled, Beat-Up, and Burnt Out* (Sisters, Oreg.: Multnomah, 2000), 85.

11. Richard Sibbes, *The Bruised Reed* (The Banner of Truth Trust, 1630), 7, 10.

12. Thomas Merton, *No Man Is an Island*, 96–97.

13. Helmut Thielicke, *Being Human ... Becoming Human*, 70–75.

14. Simon P. Walker, *The Undefended Life: Rediscovering God's Freedom to Live Beyond Fear* (Wiltshire, England: Simon Walker, 2011), 32.

15. Martin Luther, *Luther's Explanatory Notes on the Gospels*, ed. E. Mueller, trans. P. Anstadt (York, Penn.: P. Anstadt & Sons, 1899), 375 (notes on John 17:6).

16. Richard Rohr, *Falling Upward: A Spirituality for the Two Halves of Life* (San Francisco, Calf.: Jossey-Bass, 2011), xxvi.

17. Augustine of Hippo, *The Confessions of St. Augustine*, in Philip Schaff (ed.), *The Confessions and Letters of St. Augustine with a Sketch of His Life*

and Work, Nicene and Post-Nicene Fathers, vol. 1.1, trans. J. G. Pilkington (Buffalo, N.Y.: Christian Literature Company, 1886), 45.

18. Gerald G. May, *Addiction and Grace*, 93.

19. Robert Farrar Capon, *Kingdom, Grace, Judgment: Paradox, Outrage, and Vindication in the Parables of Jesus* (Grand Rapids, Mich.: Eerdmans, 2002), 368.

20. Robert Farrar Capon, *Kingdom, Grace, Judgment*, 222–24.

21. Thomas Merton, *No Man Is an Island*, 248, 255.

chapter 3. taming the mississippi

1. Ben Hoyle, "Kalashnikov Wrote of 'Unbearable' Guilt," *The London Times*, January 15, 2014.

2. Martin Luther, *Luther's Works, Vol. 30: The Catholic Epistles*, eds. J. J. Pelikan, H. C. Oswald, and H. T. Lehmann (Saint Louis, Mo.: Concordia, 1999), 293.

3. From Brennan Manning's message, "Live at Woodcrest," *Woodcrest*, Columbia, Mo. (2004); http://youtu.be/pQi_lDV2bgM; accessed on October 27, 2014.

4. Brené C. Brown, *The Gifts of Imperfection: Let Go of Who You Think You're Supposed to Be and Embrace Who You Are* (Center City, Minn.: Hazelden Publishing, 2010), 57.

5. Brennan Manning, *The Ragamuffin Gospel: Good News for the Bedraggled, Beat-Up, and Burnt Out* (Sisters, Oreg.: Multnomah, 1990, 2000), 75.

6. Robert Capon, *Kingdom, Grace, Judgment: Paradox, Outrage, and Vindication in the Parables of Jesus* (Grand Rapids, Mich.: Eerdmans, 2002), 18–19.

7. Anthony De Mello, *The Way of Love: Meditations for Life* (New York, N.Y.: Image, 1992), 132–33.

8. R. T. Kendall, *Total Forgiveness*, revised and updated ed. (Lake Mary, Fla.: Charisma House, 2010), 5.

9. Anne Lamott, *Traveling Mercies: Some Thoughts on Faith* (New York, N.Y.: Anchor Books, 2000), 143.

10. Saint John of the Cross quoted in Thomas Merton, *The Ascent to Truth: A Study of St. John of the Cross* (London, England: Continuum, 1994), 53.

11. T. F. Torrance, *The Mediation of Christ* (Edinburgh, Scotland: T&T Clark, 1992), 33.

12. Adapted from M. Robert Mulholland, Jr., *The Deeper Journey: The Spirituality of Discovering Your True Self* (Downers Grove, Ill.: InterVarsity, 2006), 72–73.

13. David G. Benner, *Spirituality and the Awakening Self: The Sacred Journey of Transformation* (Grand Rapids, Mich.: Brazos Press, 2012), 82.

14. Mark Twain, *Life on the Mississippi*, Wordsworth Classics (Hertfordshire, England: Wordsworth, 2012 [1883]), 82–88 (chapter 9).

chapter 4. shadow boxing

1. James F. Masterson, *Search for the Real Self: Unmasking the Personality Disorders of Our Age* (New York, N.Y.: Simon & Schuster, 1988), 63.

2. Brené C. Brown, *Daring Greatly: How the Courage to Be Vulnerable Transforms the Way We Live, Love, Parent, and Lead* (New York, N.Y.: Avery, 2012), 117; and *The Gifts of Imperfection: Let Go of Who You Think You're Supposed to Be and Embrace Who You Are* (Center City, Minn.: Hazelden, 2010), 70, 81.

3. Brené C. Brown, *Daring Greatly* 40.

4. Larry Crabb, *Connecting: Healing Ourselves and Our Relationships* (Nashville, Tenn.: Thomas Nelson, 1997), 151.

5. Simone Weil, "The Power of Words," in *An Anthology*, ed. Siân Miles (New York, N.Y.: Grove Press, 1986), 236.

6. Austin Cooper, *Julian of Norwich: Reflections on Selected Texts* (New York, N.Y.: Bloomsbury Academic, 2002), 134.

7. Steve Brown, *Born Free: How to Find Radical Freedom and Infectious Joy in an Authentic Faith* (Grand Rapids, Mich.: Baker, 1994), 20.

8. Brennan Manning, *Ruthless Trust: The Ragamuffin's Path to God* (New York, N.Y.: HarperOne, 2000), 16.

9. Kristen A. Culp, *Vulnerability and Glory: A Theological Account* (Louisville, Ky.: Westminster John Knox, 2010), 4.

10. Brené C. Brown, *Rising Strong* (New York, N.Y.: Spiegel & Grau, 2015), 4.

11. Paul Simon and Art Garfunkel, "I Am a Rock," on *Sounds of Silence*, written by Paul Simon (Eclectic Music, Paul Simon Music, 1966). Columbia label.

12. Simone Weil, "Chance," in *An Anthology*, 278.

13. Marianne Williamson, *A Return to Love: Reflections on the Principles of a Course in Miracles* (New York, N.Y.: HaperCollins, 1992), 190–91.

14. Gerald G. May, *Addiction and Grace: Love and Spirituality in the Healing of Addictions* (New York, N.Y.: HarperOne, 1998), 169.

15. *Freedom*, directed by Peter Cousens; screenplay by Timothy A. Chey and John Senczuk; starring Cuba Gooding Jr., William Sadler, and Sharon Leal (Production One, 2014).

16. Stanley Volk, *Personal Revival: Living the Christian Life in the Light of the Cross* (Milton Keynes, U.K.: Authentic, 2004 [CLC, 1964]), 35.

17. Sebastian Moore, *The Crucified Jesus Is No Stranger* (Mahwah, N.J.: Paulist Press, 1977), 100.

18. David Benner, *Surrender to Love: Discovering the Heart of Christian Spirituality* (Downers Grove, Ill.: IVP Books, 2003), 82–83.

19. David Benner, *Spirituality and the Awakening Self: The Sacred Journey of Transformation* (Grand Rapids, Mich.: Brazos Press, 2012), 71.

20. *Cinderella Man*, directed by Ron Howard; screenplay by Cliff Hollingsworth and Akiva Goldsman; starring Russell Crowe, Renée Zellweger, and Paul Giamatti (Universal Pictures, Miramax, Imagine Entertainment, 2005).

21. M. Scott Peck, *The Different Drum: Community Making and Peace* (New York, N.Y.: Simon and Schuster, 2010 [1986]), 233.

22. Steve Brown, A *Scandalous Freedom: The Radical Nature of the Gospel* (New York, N.Y.: Howard Books, 2004), 209.

23. Friedrich von Schiller, *Anmut und Wurde*; cited in Helmut Thielicke, *Being Human ... Becoming Human: An Essay in Christian Anthropology* (Garden City, N.Y.: Doubleday, 1984), 129.

24. David Benner, *Surrender to Love*, 60.

25. Maxwell Evarts Perkins, *Editor to Author: The Letters of Maxwell E. Perkins*, ed. John Hall Wheelock (New York, NY: Charles Scribner & Sons, 1950), 3.

26. Dietrich Bonhoeffer, *Life Together: The Classic Exploration of Christian Community*, trans. John W. Doberstein (New York, NY: HarperOne, 1954), 23.

chapter 5. drowning the victim

1. Charles Colson, *Loving God: An Inspiring Message and a Challenge to All Christians* (Grand Rapids, Mich.: Zondervan, 1993), 120; quoting R. C. Sproul.

2. Frederick Buechner, *Telling Secrets* (San Francisco, Calif.: HarperSanFrancisco, 1991), 45.

3. John Webster, *Confronted by Grace: Meditations of a Theologian*, eds. Daniel Bush and Brannon Ellis (Bellingham, Wash.: Lexham Press, 2014), 5–6.

notes

4. Augustine of Hippo, "The Confessions and Letters of St. Augustine with a Sketch of His Life and Work," in *A Select Library of the Nicene and post-Nicene Fathers of the Christian Church, vol. 1*, ed. Philip Schaff, trans. J. G. Pilkington (Buffalo, N.Y.: Christian Literature Company, 1886), 75 (IV. xiv. 22).

5. Adapted from Charles Colson, *Loving God*, 107–08.

6. Treadwell Walden, *The Great Meaning of Metanoia: An Undeveloped Chapter in the Life and Teaching of Christ* (New York, N.Y.: Thomas Whitaker, 1896), 1–9.

7. Richard C. Trench, *Synonyms of the New Testament*, 9th ed. (London, U.K.: Macmillian, 1880), 255–61.

8. Robert Farrar Capon, *Kingdom, Grace, Judgment: Paradox, Outrage, and Vindication in the Parables of Jesus* (Grand Rapids, Mich.: Eerdmans, 2002), 183–84.

9. C. S. Lewis, *The Weight of Glory: And Other Addresses*, new ed. (New York, N.Y.: HaperOne, 2001), 25–26.

10. Ben Hei, *Ethics of the Fathers*, 5:21.

11. Carl G. Jung, *Psychology and Religion: West and East, vol. 11*, trans. R. F. C. Hull, in Collected Works of C. G. Jung, ed. Gerhard Adler (Princeton, N.J.: Princeton University, 1970), 75.

12. M. Scott Peck, *A Road Less Traveled: A New Psychology of Love, Traditional Values, and Spiritual Growth*, 25th anniversary ed. (New York, N.Y.: Touchstone, 2003; 1978), 17.

13. Curt Thompson, *Anatomy of the Soul: Surprising Connections between Neuroscience and Spiritual Practices That Can Transform Your Life and Relationships* (Carol Stream, Ill.: Salt River, 2010), 94.

14. Larry Crabb, "A Note From Larry—Cancer Update," *NewWay Ministries Prayer Initiative*, 3 July 2015.

15. Richard Foster, *Prayer: Finding the Heart's True Home* (San Francisco, Calif.: Harper, 1992), 1.

16. Thomas Merton, *The Hidden Ground of Love: Letters* (New York, N.Y.: Farrar, Strauss, and Giroux, 1985), 146.

17. J. C. Ryle, *Expository Thoughts on the Gospels*, vol. 3 (Ada, Mich.: Baker Books, 1982), 40.

18. Anthony De Mello, *The Way to Love: Meditations for Life* (New York, N.Y.: Image/Doubleday, 1992), 75.

chapter 6. peering beyond the depths

1. *The Hours*, directed by Stephen Daldry; screenplay by David Hare; novel by Michael Cunningham; starring Meryl Streep, Nicole Kidman, Julianne Moore, and Ed Harris (Scott Rudin Productions; Paramount Pictures and Miramar Films, 2002).

2. *Grey's Anatomy*, "She's Leaving Home," directed by Chris Hayden; written by Stacy McKee; American Broadcasting Company, April 30, 2015 (season 11, episode 23).

3. Eugene Peterson, *A Long Obedience in the Same Direction*, 20th anniversary ed. (Downers Grove, Ill.: IVP Books, 2000), 139.

4. Dan Allender and Tremper Longman III, *The Cry of the Soul: How Our Emotions Reveal Our Deepest Questions About God*, new ed. (Colorado Springs, Colo.: NavPress, 1999), 24.

5. A saying attributed to Professor Howard Hendricks.

6. Eugene Peterson, *A Long Obedience in the Same Direction*, 145.

7. Statement attributed to Joe Church, a missionary mentor to British evangelist Roy Hession; quoted from Roy Hession, *My Calvary Road: Autobiography by the Author of the Modern Classic* The Calvary Road (Fort Washington, Penn.: CLC Publications, 2011 [1978]), 14.

8. Roy Hession, *Calvary Road* (Fort Washington, Penn.: CLC Publications, 2011 [London, 1950]), 21.

9. *Paul Williams: Still Alive*, directed and written by Stephen Kessler; starring Paul Williams (Brainstorm Media, 2011).

10. Josh Belcher, "Paul Williams—Interview With a Legend," *Rockin' God's House*, August 30, 2015; http://rockingodshouse.com/paul-williams-interview-with-a-legend; accessed July 4, 2016.

11. Malcolm Muggeridge, *Homemade*, July 1990.

12. Eugene Peterson, *A Long Obedience in the Same Direction*, 145.

13. Thornton Wilder, *Theophilus North: A Novel* (New York, N.Y.: Harper Perennial, 2003 [1973]), 291.

14. Helmut Thielicke, *Being Human ... Becoming Human*, trans. Geoffrey W. Bromiley (Garden City, N.Y.: Doubleday, 1984), 87–88.

15. Friedrich Nietzsche, "Epigrams and Arrows," in *Twilight of the Idols and the Anti-Christ*, trans. R. J. Hollingdale (Baltimore, Md.: Penguin Books, 1968 [1889]), sec. 12.

16. Brennan Manning with John Blase, *All Is Grace: A Ragamuffin Memoir* (Colorado Springs, Colo.: David C. Cook, 2011), 146.

17. Anne Graham Lotz, *Why? Trusting God When You Don't Understand* (Nashville, Tenn.: W Publishing, 2004), 37, 51.

18. William Paul Young, *The Shack* (Newbury Park, Calif.: Windblown Media, 2007), 132–34.

19. Helmut Thielicke, *Being Human ... Becoming Human*, 89.

20. A. Wetherell Johnson, *Created for Commitment* (Wheaton, Ill.: Tyndale House, 1982), 15.

21. Anne Graham Lotz, *Why? Trusting God When You Don't Understand*, 38.

22. Harry Ironside, "The Warrior Conqueror from Edom" [Isaiah 63:9], *Sermon*, 1952.

23. Karl Barth, *Church Dogmatics: The Doctrine of Creation*, vol. III.1, trans. J. W. Edwards, O. Bussey, and H. Knight, eds. G. W. Bromiley and T. F. Torrance (London, U.K.; New York, N.Y.: T&T Clark, 2004 [1958]), 369.

24. Adapted from Steve Brown, *When Your Rope Breaks* (Grand Rapids, Mich: Baker, 1996), 47–48.

25. P. T. Forsyth, *The Care of Souls* (Grand Rapids, Mich.: Eerdmans, 1971), 128.

26. Daniel Bush and Noel Due, *Embracing God as Father: Christian Identity in the Family of God*, (Bellingham, Wash.: Lexham Press, 2015), 97–98; pronouns changed.

27. Eugene Peterson, *A Long Obedience in the Same Direction*, 144.

28. P. T. Forsyth, *The Care of Souls*, 113.

chapter 7. surrendering at appomattox

1. Winston Churchill, "We Shall Fight on the Beaches," Speech, House of Commons, London, England, June 4, 1940. Archived by *The Churchill Centre*: http://www.winstonchurchill.org/resources/speeches/1940-the-finest-hour/128-we-shall-fight-on-the-beaches; accessed on July 4, 2016.

2. Søren Kierkegaard, *The Present Age: On the Death of Rebellion*, trans. Alexander Dru (New York, N.Y.: Harper Perennial Modern Classics, 2010 [1962]), 23.

3. "Why are so many children committing murder," *Jet Magazine*, June 8, 1998, p. 14.

4. "Kids That Kill," *US News & World Report*, 1991, quoted in John Piper, "I will Sing Praises to You Among the Nations," June 23, 1991; http://www.desiringgod.org/i-will-sing-praises-to-you-among-the-nations; accessed April 6, 2016.

5. Amy Dickinson, "Ask Amy: silent treatment locks family into quiet war," *The Washington Post*, April 9, 2013.

6. Jon Krakauer, *Into Thin Air: A Personal Account of the Mt. Everest Disaster* (New York, N.Y.: Anchor Books, 1999 [Villard, 1997]), 136–39. Since 2014 'Green Boots' has gone missing, presumably removed or buried.

7. Thomas Merton, *New Seeds of Contemplation*, reprint ed. (New York, N.Y.: New Directions, 2007 [1962]), 207–08.

8. Abraham Lincoln, "First Inaugural Address," March 4, 1861; www. bartleby.com/124/pres31.html; accessed July 4, 2016.

9. Mark Twain, "The War Prayer," in *Europe and Elsewhere*, ed. Albert Bigelow Paine (New York, N.Y.: Harper & Brothers, 1923), 394–95.

10. Simone Weil, *Anthology*, ed. Sian Miles (New York, N.Y.: Grove Press, 2000), 138, 236.

11. Steve Brown, *What Was I Thinking?: Things I've Learned Since I Knew It All* (New York, N.Y.: Howard Books, 2006), 138–40.

12. John Webster, *Confronted by Grace: Meditations of a Theologian*, eds. Daniel Bush and Brannon Ellis (Bellingham, Wash.: Lexham Press, 2015), 192.

13. Quoted in John Webster, *Confronted by Grace*, 207.

14. Donald Miller, *Blue Like Jazz: Nonreligious Thoughts on Christian Spirituality*, (Nashville, Tenn.: Thomas Nelson, 2003), 32.

15. *Glory;* directed by Edward Zwick; by Lincoln Kirstein and Peter Burchard; screenplay by Kevin Jarre; starring Matthew Broderick, Denzel Washington, Cary Elwes, and Morgan Freeman (Culver City: TriStar Pictures, 1989; Film).

16. Brennan Manning, *Ruthless Trust: The Ragamuffin's Path to God* (New York, N.Y.: HarperSanFrancisco, 2009), 7–8.

17. Dan Allender, *The Healing Path: How the Hurts in Your Past Can Lead You to a More Abundant Life* (Colorado Springs, Colo.: Waterbrook Press, 1999), 231.

18. *M*A*S*H*, "Out of Sight, Out of Mind"; directed by Gene Reynolds; by Ken Levine and David Isaacs; starring Alan Alda, Mike Farrell, and Harry Morgan; distributed by Columbia Broadcasting System (Los Angeles, Calf.: 20th Century Fox Television, 5 October 1976), season 5, episode 3.

19. Georges Bernanos, *The Diary of a Country Priest*, intro. by Rémy Rougeau (New York, N.Y.: Carrol & Graf, 2002 [Macmillan, 1937, 1965]), 298.

20. *Gods and Generals*, directed by Ronald F. Maxwell; by Jeff Shaara; screenplay by Ronald F. Maxwell; starring Stephen Lang, Robert Duvall, Jeff Daniels, James Lawler; distributed by Warner Bros. (Turner Pictures and Antietam Filmworks, 2003).

21. Raniero Cantalamessa, *Life in Christ: A Spiritual Commentary on the Letter to the Romans* (Collegeville, Minn.: The Liturgical Press, 1990), 189.

22. Albert Schweitzer, *The Quest for the Historical Jesus*, trans. W. Montgomery, J. R. Coates, Susan Cupitt, and John Bowden (Minneapolis, Minn.: Fortress, 2001), ix, 487.

23. C. S. Lewis, *The Problem of Pain* (New York, N.Y.: HarperCollins, 2001), 91.

24. David Benner, *Spirituality and the Awakening Self: The Sacred Journey of Transformation* (Grand Rapids, Mich.: Brazos Press, 2012), 7.

chapter 8. bedazzling embrace

1. James K. Baxter, *Jerusalem Daybook* (Wellington, N.Z.: Price Milburn, 1971), 2–3.

2. Gregory of Nyssa, "On Perfection," in *St. Gregory of Nyssa: Ascetical Works*, Virginia Callahan, trans. *The Fathers of the Church* (Washington, D.C.: Catholic University Press, 1967), 58: 121–22.

3. M. Robert Mulholland, Jr., *The Deeper Journey: The Spirituality of Discovering Your True Self* (Downers Grove, Ill.: IVP Books, 2006), 29.

4. Brennan Manning, *Abba's Child: The Cry of the Heart for Intimate Belonging* (Colorado Springs, Colo.: NavPress, 2002), 158.

5. Larry Crabb, *Real Church* (Nashville, Tenn.: Thomas Nelson, 2009), 152.

6. Henri Nouwen, *Life of the Beloved* (New York, N.Y.: Crossroad, 1992), 21.

7. Quoted in Richard Rohr, *On the Threshold of Transformation: Daily Meditation for Men* (Chicago, Ill.: Loyola Press, 2010), 180; and David Benner, *Surrender to Love: Discovering the Heart of Christian Spirituality* (Downers Grove, Ill.: InterVarsity Press, 2009), 29.

8. Margery Williams, *The Velveteen Rabbit* (New York, N.Y.: St. Martin's Press, 1999), 4–5.

9. Dan Allender, *The Healing Path: How the Hurts in Your Past Can Lead You to a More Abundant Life* (Colorado Springs, Colo.: WaterBrook Press, 2000), 238.

10. Sarah F. Hoyt, "The Etymology of Religion," in *Journal of the American Oriental Society* vol. 32, No. 2 (1912), 126–29.

11. Dan Allender, *The Healing Path*, 238.

12. Bill Lind, "The Origins of Political Correctness," *Accuracy in Academia*, February 5, 2000. http://www.academia.org/the-origins-of-political-correctness/

13. Brennan Manning, *The Ragamuffin Gospel* (Sisters, Oreg.: Multnomah Books, 1990, 2000), 75.

14. Brennan Manning, *The Ragamuffin Gospel*, 77.

15. Martin Luther, *Luther's Works, Vol. 26: Lectures on Galatians, 1535, Chapters 1-4* (St. Louis, Mo.: Concordia Publishing House, 1963), 388–89.

16. Helmut Thielicke, *The Evangelical Faith, vol. III, The Holy Spirit, The Church, Eschatology*, trans. and ed. Geoffrey W. Bromiley (Macon, Ga.: Smyth & Helwys, 1997 [Eerdmans, 1982]), 458.

17. Thornton Wilder, *The Angel that Troubles the Waters and Other Plays*, (London, U.K.: Longmans, Green & Co., 1928), 149.

18. Brennan Manning, *The Wisdom of Tenderness: What Happens When God's Fierce Mercy Transforms Our Lives* (New York, N.Y.: HaperSanFrancisco, 2002), 48–49.

19. Archbishop Demetrios, "Voices from the Past Addressing Our Present," *Harvard Divinity Bulletin* 30, no. 4 (2002): 13.

chapter 9. dancing in the desert

1. Francis Bacon, De Dignitate et Augmentis Scientiarum (The Dignity and Advancement of Science), bk. 1, ch. 7, sect. 81.

2. Adapted from Dan Allender, *The Healing Path: How the Hurts in Your Past Can Lead You to a More Abundant Life* (Colorado Springs, Colo.: WaterBrook, 1999), 82–83.

3. Evelyn Underhill, *Fragments from an Inner Life: The Notebooks of Evelyn Underhill,* ed. Dana Geene (Eugene, Oreg.: Wipf and Stock, 2011 [Morehouse, 1993]), 55.

4. Brennan Manning, *The Ragamuffin Gospel* (Sisters, Oreg.: Multnomah, 1990, 2000), 31–32.

5. Elliot Ritzema, ed., *300 Quotations for Preachers from the Reformation* (Bellingham, Wash.: Lexham, 2013).

6. Dan Allender and Tremper Longman III, *Intimate Allies: Rediscovering God's Design for Marriage and Becoming Soul Mates for Life* (Wheaton, Ill.: Tyndale House, 1995), 279–81, 316.

7. Larry Crabb, *Finding God* (Grand Rapids, Mich.: Zondervan, 1993), 115.

8. Thomas Merton, *No Man Is an Island* (Boston, Mass.: Shambhala, 2005 [Harcourt Brace, 1955]), 241.

9. Brennan Manning, *The Signature of Jesus: On the Pages of Our Lives* (Colorado Springs, Colo.: Multnomah, 1996 [Chosen, 1988]), 124.

10. Saint John of the Cross, *The Dark Night of the Soul*, eds. D. Louis and N. P. Wiseman (London, U.K.: Longman and Green, 1864), 397.

11. C. S. Lewis, *Yours, Jack: Spiritual Direction from C. S. Lewis*, ed. P. F. Ford (New York, N.Y.: HarperOne, 2008), 245–26.

12. Brent Curtis and John Eldridge, *Sacred Romance: Drawing Closer to the Heart of God* (Nashville, Tenn.: Thomas Nelson, 1997), 200.

13. Larry Crabb, *Shattered Dreams: God's Unexpected Path to Joy* (Colorado Springs, Colo.: WaterBrook, 2001), 30.

14. Thomas Merton, trans., *The Wisdom of the Desert: Sayings from the Desert Fathers of the Fourth Century* (New York, N.Y.: New Directions, 1970 [1960]), 7.

15. Thomas Merton, *Thoughts in Solitude* (New York, N.Y.: Farrar, Straus and Giroux, 1999 [1958]), 8.

16. M. Robert Mulholland, Jr., *Invitation to a Journey: A Road Map for Spiritual Formation* (Downers Grove, Ill.: InterVarsity, 1993), 138.

17. David Benner, *The Gift of Being Yourself: The Sacred Call to Self-Discovery* (Downers Grove, Ill.: InterVarsity, 2004), 56.

18. Henri Nouwen, *The Way of the Heart: The Spirituality of the Desert Fathers and Mothers* (New York, N.Y.: HarperOne, 1991 [Seabury Press, 1981]), 20.

19. Thomas Merton, *Thoughts in Solitude*, 78.

20. Herbert A. Giles, *Chuang Tzŭ: Taoist Philosopher and Chinese Mystic*, 2nd ed. (New York, N.Y.: Routledge, 2013 [1926]), 264.

21. Anthony De Mello, *Rediscovering Life: Awaken to Reality* (New York, N.Y.: Image, 2012), 122.

22. Brennan Manning, *The Furious Longing of God* (Colorado Springs: David C. Cook, 2009), 130.

chapter 10. digging for potatoes

1. Some sources include "Vincent van Gogh Biography: Painter (1853–1890)," *Biography,* biography.com/people/vincent-van-gogh-9515695; Kenneth L. Vaux, *The Ministry of Vincent Van Gogh in Religion and Art* (Eugene, Oreg.: Wipf & Stock, 2012).

2. John Eldridge, *The Journey of Desire: Searching for the Life We've Only Dreamed Of* (Nashville, Tenn.: Thomas Nelson, 2000), 154–55.

3. Dan Allender and Tremper Longman III, *Bold Love* (Colorado Springs, Colo.: NavPress, 1992), 73.

4. Dan Allender, *The Healing Path: How the Hurts in Your Past Can Lead You to a More Abundant Life* (Colorado Springs, Colo.: WaterBrook, 1999), 14–15.

5. Augustine of Hippo, "The Confessions of St. Augustine," in *The Confessions and Letters of St. Augustine with a Sketch of His Life and Work*, vol. 1, ed. P. Schaff, trans. J. G. Pilkington (Buffalo, N.Y.: Christian Literature Company, 1886), 45.

6. Thomas Merton, *New Seeds of Contemplation*, reprint ed. (New York, N.Y.: New Directions, 2007 [1961]), 26.

7. Flannery O'Connor, *Mystery and Manners: Occasional Prose*, eds. Sally and Robert Fitzgerald (New York, N.Y.: Farrar, Straus and Giroux, 1970 [1957]), 118.

8. Flannery O'Connor, *A Good Man is Hard to Find* (Orlando, Fla.: Harcourt, 1977 [1955]), 23.

9. Flannery O'Connor, *A Prayer Journal* (New York, N.Y.: Farrar, Straus and Giroux, 2013), 10.

10. Larry Crabb, *Shattered Dreams* (Colorado Springs, Colo.: WaterBrook, 2010), 57.

11. Thomas Merton, *No Man Is an Island* (Boston, Mass.: Shambhala, 2005 [1955]), 221.

12. Henri Nouwen, *Bread for the Journey: A Daybook of Wisdom and Faith* (San Francisco, Calif.: HarperSanFrancisco, 1997), 12.

13. Gerald May, *Will and Spirit: A Contemplative Psychology* (New York, N.Y.: HarperCollins, 1982, 2009), 11–12.

14. Larry Crabb, *Inside Out* (Colorado Springs, Colo.: NavPress, 1988, 2007), 201.

15. Gerrit Dawson, *The Blessing Life: A Journey to Unexpected Joy* (Downers Grove, Ill.: InterVarsity, 2013), 48.

16. "The Coble Family's Tragedy and Miracle," published January 18, 2011: http://www.cnn.com/2011/LIVING/01/18/o.coble.tragedy.miracle/; accessed March 1, 2016.

17. George A. Maloney, *In Jesus We Trust* (Notre Dame, Ind.: Ave Maria Press, 1990), 129.

18. Julian of Norwich, *Julian of Norwich: Showings*, trans. Edmund Colledge and James Walsh (New York, N.Y.: Paulist Press, 1978), 196.

19. John Owen, *Communion with the Triune God*, eds. Kelly M. Kapic and Justin Taylor (Wheaton, Ill: Crossway, 2007 [1637]), 376.

chapter 11. living at tether's end

1. Adapted from *The Roosevelts: An Intimate History*, directed by Ken Burns; written by Ken Burns and Geoffrey C. Ward; starring Meryl Streep, Edward Herrmann, Doris Kearns Goodwin, George Will, and Geoffrey C. Ward (Florentine Films; distributed by Public Broadcasting Service, 2014).

2. Jerry L. Sittser, *A Grace Disguised: How the Soul Grows through Loss* (Grand Rapids, Mich.: Zondervan, 1995), 151–52.

3. Larry Crabb, *Finding God* (Grand Rapids, Mich.: Zondervan, 1993), 89.

4. Mother Teresa with Brian Kolodiejchuk (ed.), *Mother Teresa: Come Be My Light: The Private Writings of the "Saint of Calcutta"* (New York, N.Y.: Doubleday, 2007), 186–87.

5. Dan Allender, *The Healing Path: How the Hurts in Your Past Can Lead You to a More Abundant Life* (Colorado Springs, Colo.: WaterBrook Press, 2000), 123.

6. Curt Thompson, *Anatomy of the Soul: Surprising Connections between Neuroscience and Spiritual Practices that Can Transform Your Life and Relationships* (Carol Stream, Ill.: Salt River, 2010), 208.

7. Dan Allender, *The Healing Path*, 118.

8. Lesslie Newbigin, *Proper Confidence: Faith, Doubt, and Certainty in Christian Discipleship* (Grand Rapids, Mich.: Eerdmans, 1995), 24–25.

9. Thomas Merton, *New Seeds of Contemplation*, reprint ed. (New York, N.Y.: New Directions, 2007 [1961]), 133.

10. Brennan Manning, *The Furious Longing of God* (Colorado Springs, Colo.: David C. Cook, 2009), 24.

11. Thomas Merton, *New Seeds of Contemplation*, reprint ed. (New York, N.Y.: New Directions, 2007 [1961]), 134–35.

12. Larry Crabb, *Finding God*, 103–04.

13. Oscar Hammerstein II and Richard Rodgers, "You'll Never Walk Alone" (published by Image, U.S., 1945); recorded by Elvis Presley on September 11, 1967.

14. David Benner, *The Gift of Being Yourself: The Sacred Call to Self-Discovery* (Downers Grove, Ill.: InterVarsity, 2004), 14.

15. David Benner, *Surrender to Love: Discovering the Heart of Christian Spirituality* (Downers Grove, Ill.: InterVarsity, 2003), 78–79.

Epilogue

1. Larry Crabb, *Inside Out*, expanded 10th anniversary edition (Colorado Springs, Colo.: NavPress, 1998, 2007), 241.

2. Jonathan Edwards, "The Christian Pilgrim," in *The Works of Jonathan Edwards: With an Essay on His Genius and Writings*, vol. 2 (London, U.K.: William Ball, 1839), sect. 4.1, 5, p. 246.

3. Robert Capon, *Kingdom, Grace, Judgment: Paradox, Outrage, and Vindication in the Parables of Jesus* (Grand Rapids, Mich.: Eerdmans, 2002), 513.

4. Larry Crabb, *Inside Out*, 250–51.

5. J. R. R. Tolkien, *The Lord of the Rings*, one volume ed. (Boston, Mass.; New York, N.Y.: Houghton Mufflin, 1994), ("Fellowship of the Ring," I.1), 35; ("Return of the King," VI.6), 965.

scripture index

Old Testament

Genesis

1 70
2:18 188
3 35
11:1–9 191
15 99
15:6 9
22:18 100
27:1–35 71
32:3–32 71
50:20 246

Exodus

4:22 99
20:3 153

Deuteronomy

6:5 153
8:3 200
30:14 9

1 Kings

19:1–18 221

Job

10:3 125
13:15 243
19:6–7 125
30:19–20 125
30:20 213
30:26–27 213

Psalms

3:12 234
6:1–3 234–35
13:1–4 229
16:10 8
16:11 234
22:1–2 235
23 .... 87, 161
23:1 .... 161, 224
23:4 16–17
23:6 161
25 xiv
33:18–22 171
34:8 xxvi
34:18 132–33
42:7 .... 132, 197–98
44:9–11 235
44:17 235
56:8 213
73:22–26 252
120–134 118–19
130 .... 119, 132
130:1–7 132
130:6 130
139:7 17
142:1–2 237
142:4–5 237

Proverbs
16:16......................201

Ecclesiastes
8:14 232

Song of Songs
2:6 224
7:10 ....107, 197

Isaiah
43:1–3 199
44:6 161
59:1–2 233
63:9 ....133, 269n17

Jeremiah
2:13 101
4:27...................... 100
5:30–31.................. 94
17:9.......................95
20:9......................194
31:31–34 99
31:33...................... 100
33 98–99

Lamentations
3:21–26...................98

Ezekiel
14:7–8 234

36–37...................... 99

Daniel
2:31–38 28
3:4–6 28
4:24–25 30

Hosea
5:14–15 233
5:15 234
8:7 234

Zephaniah
3:17 220

New Testament

Matthew
7:14....................... 253
7:24–27 9
10:39......................39
11:2–11 125
11:28 12
14:23 195
14:28–29 38
15:21–28 41
15:26 41
15:27 41–42
16:25 97
18:20 2
18:30...................... 88
19:27...................... 213
22:37 .... 100, 153
26:53......................256
27:46 246
28:18–20 13
28:20 13

Mark
6:48........................38

16:6–7 175
16:7...........................59

Luke
6:45 xxvi
10:27 105
11 40
11:7.........................41
11:8 41
14 79
14:12–24............... 79
15:20......................30
22:42 33

John
1:1–2, 14 5
1:4–5......................101
3:1–8.........................2
3:3 192
3:5–8......................165
3:16 179
4:24 17–18
6:38 33

8:44...................21–22
11:39 129
11:40......................130
12:47...................... 40
13:8........................30
14:6.......................254
14:16–17 18
17:6................. 263n15
17:15.........................59
21:15....................... 213
21:17 59

Acts
17:27–28 242
17:28....................... 9
26:14......................148

Romans
3:1 192
3:11......................... 14
5:19.......................210
8:15 53
8:23 193

scripture index

8:25 122
8:28–30 86
8:35–39 .... 76–77, 143–44
8:38–39 63
10:8 .... 18, 131
12:2 103–04
12:19 58
13:10 100

1 Corinthians
1:25 51
5:5 234
13:12 197

2 Corinthians
3:17 234
3:18 .... 78, 178
4:8–11 127
4:18 122
5:7 122
5:6–7 50
6:10 .... 213, 217
11:14 22
12:9 .... 60, 79

Galatians
2:20 109
5:1 61
5:17 .... 138, 153

Ephesians
1:4 62
1:4–5 166
1:10 162
2 10–11
2:1–3 11
2:4–6 11
2:6 11
3:16–19 247
5:14 238

Philippians
3:7–11 109–10
3:10 .... 133, 252
3:10–11 243
4:6–7 241

Colossians
1:15 5
1:24 121

1 Thessalonians
5:18 223

Hebrews
1:1–3 5
2:8 171
4:6–13 174
4:15 8
5:8 6
7:16 257
11:1 .... 87, 122
11:6 73
12:6 234
13:5 87
13:13 13

James
4:1–2 138

1 Peter
1:4–9 128
1:6–7 127
1:7 16
4:13 252

2 Peter
1:4 178

1 John
4:9–10 47
4:18 .... 46, 61, 73
4:19 100

Revelation
5:6 256
14 13
22:13 161